UNIVERSITIES:
COMMONWEALTH AND AMERICAN

UNIVERSITIES:
Commonwealth and American

A COMPARATIVE STUDY

By Oliver C. Carmichael
Former President, Carnegie Foundation for the Advancement of Teaching

HARPER & BROTHERS PUBLISHERS,
New York

To Ruth Mae and Fredalyn Marjorie Carmichael
Wife and Granddaughter
Companions on visits to Commonwealth countries

CONTENTS

vii

PREFACE

This is perhaps the first attempt to compress into a single volume the composite picture of seven systems of universities around the world, located on four continents in two hemispheres. They embrace Britain, Australia, Canada, India, New Zealand, Pakistan and the Union of South Africa. Though they are seven separate systems, in a real sense they are essentially one. At least they represent variations of a single system.

This essay is not an effort to present a panorama of university systems viewed from a single vantage point; it is rather a cineramic sketch. The effort has been to show something of the depth, as well as of the breadth, something of the inner meaning as well as of the outward appearance, of higher education in the several countries. It is not a still life but a moving picture. The story of the founding and expansion of universities serves to throw light on their present status and on the direction of future change. It is, therefore, not a static presentation of programs as they are but an attempt to sketch the past, review the present and comment on the future outlook of the several systems.

It is not a sketch in black-and-white, but in color. It does not attempt merely to picture brick and mortar, laboratories and libraries, or even the nature of its organizations with their boards of control, administrations, faculties and students. It would be simple enough to give a statistical account of the programs of higher education that provide for four million students a year, outlining their patterns of control, describing their administrations and giving numbers of institutions, students, faculty members and trustees. That can be found in the yearbooks. The aim has been rather to give some idea of the spirit of the higher learning in these countries, and of the quality of teaching, of research and of services which they provide.

Much of what follows is descriptive and expository, but it seeks to be something more. It essays analysis, criticism and constructive suggestions. It is a comparative study: similarities and contrasts, common and uncommon features, encouraging and discouraging aspects, bright spots and problem areas are high-lighted and reviewed.

The factors, issues, trends and characteristics, selected as centers of interest in the survey, are matters of judgment for which the author takes responsibility. However, he is not un-aware of the fact that others might have been chosen. The selection was made on the basis of thirty-five years of ex-perience in the field of education—as a high school and college instructor, as an elementary and high school principal, and as a college, university and foundation executive. This experience has been in the United States and followed the acquiring of a first and second degree in an American university, and the award of a degree and a diploma at Oxford after three years of study there. More recently the author has visited nine of the eleven Australian and New Zealand universities, eight of the nine in South Africa, ten of the thirty in Canada, twelve of the thirty-eight in India and Pakistan and seventeen of the twenty-seven in the United Kingdom and Ireland.

For the opportunity to make this study, entailing visits to the Commonwealth countries, I am deeply indebted to The Fund for the Advancement of Education which financed the study, and to Alvin C. Eurich, its Vice President, for his wise and sympathetic counsel and advice over a period of two years. I am indebted, also, to those with whom I discussed the pro-grams of higher education in the various countries, the vice-chancellors, rectors, presidents, principals, faculty members, students and non-teaching staff members of these universities. They were uniformly hospitable, courteous and generous in answering questions, in furnishing information and explaining programs. I shall always cherish the memory of the warm cordiality, the delightful associations and the stimulating discussions.

I owe a special debt to Barnaby C. Keeney, President of Brown University, Douglas W. Logan, Principal of London University, Humayun Kabir, Minister of Scientific Research and Cultural Affairs in India, C. Kenneth Snyder, Public Affairs Officer (U.S.I.S.) in the American Embassy, Pretoria, South Africa and Mr. J. J. P. Op't'Hof, Secretary for Education (Arts and Science) in the Union of South Africa. All have read the manuscript and have made many valuable suggestions. Their unselfish labors have enabled me to eliminate many errors and to make numerous improvements in the text. For their generous and encouraging help I shall ever be grateful.

I wish also to express my appreciation to many leaders in all the countries visited who have kindly allowed me to use materials from their published and unpublished works. I am indebted, too, to government and education department Officials who gave generously of their time to discussions of educational and related issues.

Space will not permit a listing here of the many individuals interviewed, but a partial list will be found in Appendix I— grouped by countries and arranged alphabetically. To one and all of these my genuine thanks for their help as well as for their friendliness.

Workers in the educational vineyard around the world constitute a great fraternity. In their midst a fellow worker need never feel himself a stranger. Common attitudes, interests, outlooks and ideals make one feel at home in the university community whether he be in the Antipodes or in the Arctic Circle, whether in the sub-zero weather of the north or in the sizzling heat of the tropics, whether in the Northern or Southern Hemisphere.

Educators and scientists, because of the commonality of their

viewpoints and modes of thought, are man's best hope for the
One World of the future. This, at least, was my deep conviction after visiting the Commonwealth countries and on becoming acquainted with the goals and purposes, the hopes and
aspirations and the contributions of their colleges and universities.

INTRODUCTION

Higher education is a major social enterprise. It engages a vast army of workers—trustees, administrators, teachers and other staff—in its operation. In the British Commonwealth and the United States it enrolled in excess of four million youth in 1957–1958. Its agencies are colleges, universities and institutes. Their function is the conservation, dissemination and extension of knowledge. In reporting on higher learning in the Commonweath and the United States, it may be appropriate to give reasons for the incorporation of these countries in a single study and to comment on the aspects of higher education which seem best calculated to present a significant picture of its development.

The fact that, with the exception of the Afrikaans universities in South Africa and the French universities in Canada, practically all the institutions involved have a common language of instruction provides a basis for considering them as a unit. English is the medium in India, Pakistan and the Colonies except for two or three Indian universities and occasional courses that may be given in the native language. Perhaps more important than the common language is the common background, the common ancestry, of the higher education systems found in these lands. The institutions of England and Scotland set the pattern for the various systems included in the study, though these systems now represent marked variations from the original scheme.

A third reason for looking at this group of institutions as a unit is the fact that all now face certain common problems. A critical appraisal of the current situation in higher education is a present need. New approaches will be required in the decade ahead if the issues, already pressing, are to be met successfully. Those who will have the responsibility of wrestling with these problems might find it useful to know what is going on elsewhere.

Perhaps this will suffice to indicate the logic and the broad purpose of this study. Obviously there are many aspects of so varied and complex an enterprise as higher education in the United States and the Commonwealth. The selection of the significant elements and those likely to be most helpful in understanding the meaning of higher education in our time has been difficult. Perhaps no two people would make the same choices.

If one is to understand a system of higher education, he must have some knowledge of its history and backgrounds, and an appreciation of the units that compose it. To facilitate this understanding the early sections of the report will be devoted to a consideration of the historical factors involved in the founding and development of the several systems under review.

Having presented a sketch of the history and present status of the institutions with respect to their facilities, special services and relations with their communities, the report will discuss the nature and aims of the educational program. What is being taught is a basic concern, but the methods employed and the goals sought are perhaps of equal importance. There has not been a time in the history of modern education when colleges and universities were so self-conscious with respect to their aims and purposes or so serious in their efforts to find the most effective way to achieve them. This is not only a marked characteristic of the modern university but an altogether encouraging aspect of university communities in every quarter.

The relation of the university to its community is an asset or a liability. This relation is expressed in part by the nature of the organization under which it operates, and by the wisdom of its controls. To what extent and how a university is influenced by forces from without is of central importance to its well-being and to its ability to carry out its mission. If the state interferes with its autonomy, with what is to be taught or how it's to be taught, as was the case in Hitler's Germany, the true spirit and purpose of the university are destroyed. Other forces besides the state, such as the wishes of donors or of alumni who seek to dominate the institution, may bring about the same result. The internal organization likewise has much to do with the chances of success in a university. If the administration rather than the faculty seeks to determine the content of the curriculum, or if no control is exercised over its expansion, ineffectiveness or chaos may result.

The method of financing and the sources of support may also affect in many ways the success of universities. Great variations in the type and adequacy of support are found in the several areas. Different kinds of institutions in the same country vary in the means and methods employed to finance operations. For example, in the United States a dual system exists. More colleges and universities are supported by voluntary gifts than by taxes. Cities, counties, states, and even the federal government, provide funds for colleges and universities. In India the states and the central government are the chief sources of support. In Pakistan the state universities receive no central government support. In Great Britain all universities are privately controlled but heavily subsidized by the treasury.

Institutions of higher learning are operated primarily for the students. Service to the state through research and other special activities are also functions of modern universities, but their primary purpose is the instruction of youth. The spirit of the institution, as expressed in the tone and quality of its student life, may be as important as the instruction itself. Student interests and activities are perhaps the best index to the character of a university since they are in the main simply expressions of the social and intellectual atmosphere of the community. To appraise the merits of campus life is difficult, but no account of higher education would be complete without it.

The increase in the number of students in postgraduate study and research in the past decade as well as the increase in support of research represent a new faith in advanced studies and research activities. The unprecedented extent to which government, business and industry have resorted since World War II to research as a means of solving their problems is convincing evidence of this fact. This adds to the responsibilities of universities since they must train the research workers needed. In addition they are called upon to conduct much of the research which these agencies require. Thus any complete picture of modern higher education must include this relatively new aspect of university activity.

Another phase of education beyond the first degree is that of professional education. Much of the training of doctors and lawyers was formerly provided by independent schools. Though some of the oldest European universities began as Faculties of Law or Medicine or Theology, the rank and file of professional practitioners in earlier times received their training outside the universities. That is now no longer true. Hospitals for the traning of doctors and schools for the training of lawyers are now, with few exceptions, affiliated with universities. In addition, a variety of new professions have sought university affiliation for their training schools, such as agriculture, commerce and business, nursing, social work and a host of others. The 1956 edition of *American Colleges and Universities* lists twenty-three different professions for which American higher education provides training. The only one of the older professions in America that trains the majority of its practitioners outside the university is theology. In the British Commonwealth most schools of theology are units of universities. The training colleges for the preparation of teachers in Great Britain were independent of universities until within this decade. These institutions are now affiliated with some university in their respective areas. Professional education is a larger and more important segment of the university program today than at any previous period.

This development has strengthened the professions undoubtedly. It has also had an effect on the universities. The character of university education itself has not escaped the influence of this trend toward an ever-increasing specialization in professional fields. Comments on this aspect of the problem will be reserved, however, for the section dealing with the broad subject of professional education.

The overwhelming emphasis on science and technology in higher education in this atomic age suggests the need for devoting a separate section to this topic. Not only in the United States, where scientific and technical subjects have for years been prominent in university offerings, but in Britain, India and other Commonwealth countries, the concern to speed up scientific and technological training is truly startling. The reports of developments in Russia have spurred all nations to multiply their efforts to keep pace. Both the economic and defense aspects of scientific and technological progress have their bearing on university programs. They constitute powerful and convincing incentives to governments to provide the laboratories and other equipment needed for maximum efficiency in these specialized fields. Thus support for this phase of education eclipses that provided in any other area.

No one acquainted with contemporary issues would gainsay the wisdom of emphasizing this phase of education at this particular time. In view of all the circumstances, institutions have really no alternative. But this should not blind us to the effects of present trends on our educational system, nor keep us from sober and constant reflection on the ways and means of preventing them from changing the character and purpose of university education. As a wise man has recently remarked: "The first task of a true university is to keep alive the flame of civilization itself." [1]

A review of developments in the higher education of women merits special attention in a comparative study of higher education. Though the oldest of Anglo-Saxon universities has a history that spans almost eight centuries, the higher education of women is little more than a century old in the United States and less than that in the Commonwealth countries—eight decades instead of eight centuries. The University of London was the pioneer in coeducation when it admitted women first in 1878. The growth since then has been phenomenal.

Discussions of women's education sooner or later revolve around the matter of the programs of study which were admittedly designed originally for men. This leads inevitably to the question whether there should be any differentiation in courses for men and for women. To what extent has the content of higher education changed since the admission of women to the universities? These and other aspects of the subject will be dealt with in the chapter on Women and Higher Education.

A comparatively recent development in both the United States and the British Commonwealth is the university's acceptance of responsibility for extending educational opportunities to the adult community. Though this program developed before World War II, its expansion since 1945 as a university function has resulted in doubling or trebling the numbers served. In the United States university extension activities, though of considerable magnitude before 1940, have kept pace with those in Commonwealth countries. In some of the private universities this has not been true, but the development in state institutions more than counterbalances.

Both technical and general education programs for adults are attracting vast numbers in America and Britain. In some of the Commonwealth countries the interest is not so marked, but a beginning has been made, and an expansion of adult education is in prospect.

In Britain the technical colleges provide systematic courses of study of one or more years' duration for workers in industry. In many cases industry provides released time for attending classes without loss of pay. In America the universities are offering a variety of technical courses to suit the needs of workers at all levels, from the auto mechanic to the graduate engineer. But courses in the humanities and social sciences are attracting even larger numbers than those which are technical in character. A junior college in California reported that it reached in one year one-third of the adult population in its community.

The extra-mural programs of universities have expanded more rapidly during the past decade than those provided for the full-time students. The interest of adults in understanding their heritage and the forces at work in their society seems to be the motivation for this phenomenon. As long as that motivation continues, universities are likely to continue to render noteworthy service through their extra-mural activities.

Reference was made earlier to the fact that higher education in the countries under review face common problems. An examination of these problems and their variations will throw considerable light on the stages of development of higher education in the different areas and likewise on their prospects for the future. What are the questions raised by educators in Britain, India, South Africa or the United States when they forgather to consider the state of higher education and the ways of improving it?

The author spent seven months in India, Pakistan, South Africa, Britain, Australia, New Zealand and Canada in 1957–1958, where he attended many gatherings of educators. It is difficult to sum up impressions gained through listening in for hours and days on educational discussions in each of the countries visited. Yet certain issues stand out fairly clearly as one reviews the notes collected over a period of several months. The chapter dealing with the Problems and Prospects of Higher Education is an attempt to summarize the issues which have concerned educators in all parts of the English-speaking world in recent years.

"Summary and Conclusions," the final chapter, represents an

effort to take a detached view of higher education as it affects social progress, to suggest the changes in the relation of the university to the community which have taken place during the past half century, to trace these developments and their implications, and to indicate what may be expected before the end of the present century on the basis of the concerns which have been manifested in recent years in the English-speaking countries. Despite the fact that all agree to the need for the current emphasis on science and technology in both the United States and the Commonwealth, there is an undertone of deep concern over the situation. This is expressed in a variety of ways. In England it has been termed "a moral crisis in the universities," "a social crisis," "a crisis in study of values," and "a threat to university integrity." [2]

While there is diversity of view with respect to the state of the universities, educational leaders in all the countries visited have one thing in common. They are engaged in much soul-searching over the adjustments they are called upon to make in view of expanding enrollments and changing emphasis in instruction and research. These matters will be considered in the final chapter.

UNIVERSITIES:
COMMONWEALTH AND AMERICAN

I

The University in Transition

✦✦✦✦✦✦✦✦✦✦✦✦✦✦✦✦✦✦✦✦✦✦✦✦✦✦✦✦✦✦✦✦✦✦✦

The most profound change in the English-speaking university picture in its seven-hundred-year history has taken place since the Second World War. Higher education in this period passed from private to predominantly public support. Student fees, endowment income, gifts and grants were the sole sources of its operating funds for centuries. The first government grant to universities in England was made in 1889. Thirty years later the University Grants Committee was established, marking the beginning of systematic support of universities by the treasury. At the beginning of the war in 1939 the treasury grants approximated 30 per cent of the total university income, and by 1959 more than 75 per cent. The proportion is scheduled to increase each year of the 1957–1962 quinquennium.

The nature of the changes occurring in Britain since 1945 is suggested by a few historical facts. Four centuries elapsed before Parliament recognized the ancient universities of England by confirming their charters; religious tests were required until 1871; the original grant for university education was made only seventy years ago; and systematic support began in 1919.

In South Africa some 65 per cent of the university income is derived from tax sources through the central government. In Australia there are no privately-supported universities; all are supported by the state and central governments. In India and Pakistan universities are either federal or state government institutions, deriving their income chiefly from either state or federal sources, or from both.

Canada in 1954–1955 was the only Commonwealth country in which less than half (42 per cent) of the funds for the operation of its higher education system came from tax monies, and in 1958 the Dominion recurrent grant for higher education was increased from $1.00 per capita to $1.50. There a system of private colleges and universities developed largely under the sponsorship of church groups and many are still partially supported by them.

The United States likewise developed a dual system. It was more than 150 years after Harvard was founded before the first tax-supported university opened its doors. Even so, America was the first of the English-speaking countries to attempt the experiment of state support of university education. Until within recent years it was the leading exponent of tax-supported higher education. Though in 1957–1958 somewhat less than one-half of the operating budgets were met by tax funds, 58 per cent of the students were enrolled in public institutions, and, beginning in 1959, state, federal and municipal grants will bear the major burden of college and university costs. Judged on the basis of its sources of support, university education in the English-speaking world is now a public enterprise. This was not true in any of the countries under review before World War II. In the United States the majority of college and university students were enrolled in private institutions before the war.

While the emergence of tax support for colleges and universities came earlier in the New World than in Britain, the latter has now outdistanced Canada and the United States in the proportion of its support for university education derived from taxes. This emphasizes the rapidity of the growth of public interest in higher education in Britain. The transition from private to public support is so recent that it is impossible to determine as yet the attitude that the British public may develop toward its universities as public institutions. So far the University Grants Committee has served admirably as a shield against public pressures on the universities, but the experience has not been of sufficient length to insure that it will always be able to perform successfully this function.

The implications of this transfer from private to public support of universities are manifold. First, the universities must be more alert than ever to social needs, responsive to governments' requests and more concerned about maximum efficiency in all aspects of their operation. At the same time they must not forget their basic function as preservers, disseminators and discoverers of knowledge. The quest for truth that makes men free is still an essential goal of university education. It is not inconsistent with technological instruction and research, for, after all, technology affects profoundly the life of man and his society, even though its humane aspects are seldom stressed.

Adaptation of university education to the teaching of science and technology as humane subjects will require a major adjustment. If universities fail in this, it will be difficult to distinguish them from scientific or technological institutes. In Europe it is the *Technische Hochschulen* or the *Ecoles Polytechniques* that conduct most of the technological research. In Russia today only about 10 per cent of the higher education is provided by universities; the balance is supplied by scientific and professional institutes. In the countries under review science and technology are included in the university curricula, which imposes the obligation of teaching them as university subjects.

The *laissez-faire* attitude of merely admitting qualified applicants who seek entrance to universities will no longer suffice. Institutions must seek out the gifted, provide guidance for them to the end that talent will not be wasted, and stimulate the development of their full potentialities. Inefficient procedures, whether sanctioned by ancient tradition or not, must be reexamined in the light of current needs and modified to produce maximum results. Among those items that need re-examination are class size, teaching loads, administrative procedures, teaching methods, the use of modern aids to learning and the length of annual sessions. The efficient use of buildings and equipment, of student and faculty time and of all the resources such as libraries and laboratories will be of increasing concern to the public as tax support expands.

Objectives of university education need not only to be clarified but must be made explicit. The public has a right to know what its investment is designed to achieve and the success of the efforts to achieve it. In other words, the public relations of universities will be more important than ever. The traditional attitude of indifference to public criticism on the part of institutions of higher learning is no longer appropriate, indeed could be hazardous. While mindful of public opinion, the universities must not be dominated by it. The lay public may not readily understand the deeper purposes of university education, such as the spirit of learning, the pursuit of truth in its more profound aspects, and the need for objectivity in scientific research. Publication of research findings have been known to collide with traditional thinking or vested interests. In such cases it is not easy for the public to view the result with equanimity and to accept it as a proper university function.

In the United States and in other countries which have had long experience with tax support of colleges and universities, many instances of conflict with accepted modes of thought and special interests could be cited. These will occur more frequently in the future than in the past in these countries, which have more recently come to depend upon the treasury for the maintenance of institutions. It is important that universities be prepared to cope with such conflicts. Universities as pioneers of thought are bound to encounter criticism increasingly as they expand their research activities and depend more on public funds.

A strange dichotomy of purpose in university education has emerged with the advent of predominant treasury support. The traditional aim of *education* has been the development of the mind and spirit of the individual. As Ruskin once said:

And the entire object of true education is to make people not merely *do* the right things, but *enjoy* the right things—not merely industrious, but to love industry—not merely learned, but to love knowledge—not merely pure, but to love purity—not merely just, but to hunger and thirst after justice.[1]

The goal is individual development as an end in itself. The education subsidized by government to produce scientists and technologists has as its primary purpose serving the economic and defense needs of society. In other words, the goal sometimes appears to be chiefly to produce units of specialized man-power. Obviously university education must be concerned about both individual growth and social needs; neither can be neglected. Curricula and methods must reflect this twofold purpose. In the absence of either, the program is incomplete.

The justification for expenditure of public funds on universities is their contribution to society. Society needs doctors, lawyers, engineers and teachers. Preparation for these professions requires training. Hospitals, Inns of Court, technological institutes and training colleges provide such training. But society has not been content to leave it entirely to those institutions. Universities have been called upon to serve this function on the ground that they provide more thorough and adequate education for these professions. Unless they do, in fact, give a broader and more effective preparation the public has a right to be concerned. This would suggest the wisdom of constant reexamination of professional education with a view to insuring that it is of true university quality. In some cases at least the curriculum fails to reflect a real difference between the university and non-university programs. For example, in medicine the curriculum in some of the universities studied contains only scientific, technical and professional courses; and in science and technology, only specialized scientific and technological offerings.

The Arts Faculty programs in some of the countries under review, though designed presumably to educate wise and understanding leaders, provide no insight into the role of science and technology in the modern world. Likewise, the science student has little or no opportunity to become acquainted with the humanities or social studies, which should help him to understand his heritage and social environment. The gaps in the undergraduate programs of both arts and science students are difficult to justify. Educators should be giving serious consideration to this problem.

Every university graduate should certainly have some knowledge of science and of its technological applications. It is an indispensable part of his orientation to the world in which he lives. Viewed objectively, it appears strange that in this atomic age vast numbers of university graduates with B.A. degrees should have had no university assistance in understanding science and technology, their role in the modern world and their influence on social change. By the same token it is equally difficult to rationalize leaving out of the educational menu of science students those courses of study that would help them understand the background of their society and its structure. This is not only a scientific and technological, but also an ideological, age. New social and economic theories have flourished in this century as in few other periods of history. The ideals of democracy and freedom, of human dignity and inalienable rights, and of respect for religion and social justice have been challenged more vigorously in the past few decades than ever before in modern times. In such a situation it is difficult to justify an educational system that produces university graduates who have no real acquaintance with the social, economic and political philosophies upon which Western culture rests.

In short, undergraduate programs of the future must somehow provide a balanced educational diet if they are to succeed in producing wise and intelligent leadership. In English universities, and in their offspring in the Commonwealth countries, basic reforms in curricula will be required. In Scottish, Canadian and American universities, which have recognized the principle in their arts and science college curricula, much more realistic efforts will be required before a really satisfactory program is developed. Neither the Arts Faculties in Commonwealth countries nor the Arts and Science Colleges in Canada and the United States appear to have conceived clearly the basic function of the humanistic-social studies, much less devised an adequate curriculum.

The confusion as to the purpose of liberal education has been responsible, in part at least, for its present unhappy plight. The notion that it is a cultural course in the narrow sense, designed to adorn its possessor with polish, refinement and distinction, has maligned its purpose and distorted the impression of its values. Unless it assists in giving one a realistic understanding of his heritage and of his social, physical and biological environment, it has failed to achieve its objectives. Such an understanding is essential to intelligent citizenship. While this is the broad purpose of arts and science colleges, neither the curriculum nor the focus of instruction are realistically designed to achieve it in many instances. The objectives of the undergraduate programs in all the universities under review need clarification followed by curriculum revisions. This is the task of universities. New courses, new methods of instruction, and adaptations to technological and professional programs will be required.

However difficult these revisions may be, it is important that they be undertaken by the university staffs rather than risk non-university interference, since the public is not likely to be content indefinitely with inadequate curricula and ineffective methods when it foots the bill. The success of these efforts will require educational statesmanship of a high order and will involve both the faculties and administrations. Universities have sometimes prided themselves on their conservatism. One of their functions is the conservation of knowledge, but they must also be progressive, for another of their functions is to discover new facts, new concepts, new principles and their applications. That is the goal of research in all areas, including science and technology. Indeed it is research and the development of research scientists that have attracted the generous support of governments to universities. The public will expect the same creativity and efficiency in university organization, management, curricula and teaching methods as those prevailing in the laboratories. This will require imaginative planning, bold experimentation and courageous action on the findings, if the highest expectations are to be met. It is this kind of educational statesmanship that will be required in the decade ahead.

In the acceptance of funds from the government for the expansion of science and technology the universities acknowledge the obligation to serve national needs. This places upon them the responsibility of determining what the priority of needs is unless they are to become merely instruments of the state. They must be guardians of the less obvious but deeper needs of society if they fulfill their mission. In an age when conflicting ideologies and interests prevail, when confusion and frustration characterize the social scene, and when every other hospital bed is occupied by a mental patient, it may be that emphasis upon moral and spiritual values, upon understanding the nature of individual and social conflict, and upon assisting the individual in the formulation of a satisfying philosophy of life is as important to national stability and progress as scientific knowledge and technological skill.

In short, the health, welfare and progress of a society may depend as much upon the basic studies which assist the understanding of our heritage and social environment as upon scientific-technological education, even though the latter may strengthen national security and produce economic prosperity. The current tide of public opinion is flowing in the opposite direction, and no one is inclined to say that it is misguided. I am convinced, however, that too little attention is being paid to these fundamental considerations in university circles in the countries under review.

Some impressions gained in this study may be worth reporting in summary form in this prologue to the story of Commonwealth and American systems of higher education.

The change in the base of support in the long run will involve changes in the role of the university and in its relationship to society. They are already recognizable, though their full impact is not yet felt. The spirit of higher learning in the traditional sense will be affected by them.

Pursuit of knowledge is tending to displace pursuit of truth and of moral and spiritual understanding as the primary purpose of university education.

The integration of the science and arts faculties in the Commonwealth countries will require a major adjustment for "there is a kind of intellectual curtain separating faculties of science and faculties of arts"[2] in British universities, as Sir Eric Ashby suggested.

Closer collaboration of the arts and science faculties with those of professional schools is also a pressing need in university organization.

Finally, clarification of goals and realistic efforts to modify curricula and methods to achieve them are essential steps in the process of adjustment in both undergraduate and professional areas.

The author is not unaware of the tremendous difficulties involved in effecting the changes here suggested. University faculties move slowly in formulating and adopting new plans. They are already overburdened with day-to-day tasks of teaching, research and service due to rapidly expanding enrollments, and revisions of curricula and methods require much time and effort. Nevertheless, despite the obstacles in the way of achieving needed reforms, it is of central importance that they be undertaken without undue delay.

These facts should be borne in mind as we review the backgrounds, the nature and aims, the organization and control, and other aspects of the systems of higher education in the Commonwealth and American universities in the chapters that follow.

II

Backgrounds: British Commonwealth

❖❖❖❖❖❖❖❖❖❖❖❖❖❖❖❖❖❖❖❖❖❖❖❖❖❖❖❖❖❖❖❖❖

Oxford and Cambridge

For two hundred years Oxford and Cambridge were the only universities in the English-speaking world; for more than six hundred years the only ones in England. Four universities in Scotland and one in Ireland were founded in the fifteenth and sixteenth centuries. They, along with the ancient universities, a total of seven, constituted the higher education system of Anglo-Saxon peoples until Harvard, bearing the name of a Cambridge graduate, was established in 1636. They were the only universities in the British Empire until well into the second quarter of the nineteenth century.

Oxford (1167) was founded a hundred years after the invasion of England by William the Conqueror, and Cambridge a few years later. Both were religious foundations and retained the connection for many centuries. Though Parliament confirmed the charters of both institutions in 1571, religious tests for admission were continued for three more centuries, until 1871. The deeply spiritual tone and atmosphere of these ancient foundations is still a marked characteristic.

A migration of students from Paris in 1167–1168 marked the foundation date of Oxford. A similar exodus of students from Oxford, resulting from trouble with the townspeople, was responsible for the founding of Cambridge. The fortunes of both institutions fluctuated continuously in their early history. Cambridge, in 1261 and 1381, suffered from emigrations of students. The introduction of colleges as a new feature of universities brought a degree of stability, though later in the seventeenth and eighteenth centuries enrollments dropped sharply. While Oxford had some three thousand students during the thirteenth century, Trevelyan reported that in 1750 Oxford enrolled only 190 new students and Cambridge only 127.

In the early years students were admitted at eleven to thirteen years of age. This is reflected in the statutes of the university, which are still included in the book of statutes given to undergraduates at matriculation: "Young gentlemen may not play marbles in front of St. Mary's" . . . "Young gentlemen may not roll hoops down High Street." Fines for being on the streets after dark without an academic gown, for coming into college after nine in the evening, and for a variety of other "offenses" hardly compatible with a mature student body are still the practice. Raising admission requirements and the age of entering students influenced enrollment trends.

Social, political and economic changes constantly occurring in England also affected the life at the universities. However, despite the vicissitudes of more than seven centuries, these institutions have continued to serve British youth without serious interruption. A civil war, the Reformation, the Industrial Revolution, the metamorphosis of the monarchy and the development of the democratic ideal, all have taken place in the lifetime of these universities. Changes in method of instruction, in curriculum, in control, in the maturity of its students and in the size of student bodies did not deflect them from pursuit of their basic objectives.

Forms of government, economic systems, political and social philosophies may change, but life in the university somehow goes on, sustained perhaps by the perpetual youth of its charges. It meets with equanimity changing modes and patterns and continues to minister to the deeper needs of society. The ancient universities of England have adjusted their sails, sometimes too slowly, perhaps, but nevertheless surely, to the shifting winds of social, economic and political doctrine, and have pursued their courses toward distant goals with no basic change in direction.

They established the pattern of university education, the ideals of scholarship, the meaning of higher learning and the conception of the university which have served as the foundation for all colleges and universities subsequently established in the English-speaking world. Their organization, their methods of instruction, their curricula and their provisions for students have served as models for Canada, Australia, New Zealand, South Africa and India, as well as for the civic universities of the British Isles. The pattern which they have set in university organization and operation has been followed by most of the Commonwealth universities to the present day.

Their influence on the American system of higher education has been continuous throughout its history. Harvard originally was modeled on a Cambridge college. The Arts and Science College, the core of American higher education, is but a modification of the program of the Arts Faculties found at Oxford and Cambridge. Swarthmore College, about thirty years ago, established a program of education modeled directly on the Oxford system. Within fifteen years some 150 other colleges in the United States set up honors programs in imitation of the Swarthmore plan. In the nineteen thirties Harvard and Yale established housing systems seeking to divide their large student bodies into manageable groups. The Oxford and Cambridge college plan and idea were the inspiration for setting up these houses.

Thus the contribution of the ancient universities to higher education at home and abroad has been profound, unequalled by any other universities of the world. They are not the oldest, but among the oldest universities; they are by no means the largest nor the wealthiest institutions, but they are the most renowned.

Each institution is a federation of colleges. The college system was not known in Europe or elsewhere when the British conceived and developed it. It has been perhaps the most important single element of strength in their organization.

Table 1 lists the colleges of each of these universities, giving their founding dates.[1]

Cambridge has twenty colleges, eighteen for men and two for women; Oxford has thirty-one colleges, twenty-six for men and five for women. In addition to those shown in the table, Cambridge has two recognized halls for women and one for men, while Oxford has three for men.

Cambridge colleges are, on the average, larger than those at Oxford. Women students are fewer. In 1946–1947 the average size of Cambridge colleges was 270, while that of Oxford was 170. In 1955–1956 the enrollment at Oxford was 7,346, and at Cambridge, 8,128 students.

Traditionally Oxford emphasized the humanities, while Cambridge devoted more attention to the sciences. The differences in program have been less marked in recent years. Oxford has strengthened its science program and admitted more science students. Oxford granted full privileges to women in 1920; Cambridge, in 1948.

Scottish Universities

Three of the four Scottish universities, St. Andrews (1411), Glasgow (1451), Aberdeen (1494), were religious foundations, and the fourth, Edinburgh (1583), was established by the town council. All of these institutions now receive treasury grants on an equal basis with other institutions in the United Kingdom.

For 375 years Scotland has established no new universities, while England in that period has added fourteen, and one degree-granting university college. Nevertheless, in 1957 Scot-

TABLE 1[1]

PERIOD	OXFORD	CAMBRIDGE
Thirteenth century	University (1249) Balliol (1263) Merton (1264) St. Edmund Hall (1278)	Peterhouse (1284)
Fourteenth century	Exeter (1314) Oriel (1326) Queen's (1340) New (1379)	Clare (1326) Pembroke (1347) Trinity Hall (1350) Gonville and Caius (1348) Corpus Christi (1352)
Fifteenth century	Lincoln (1427) All Soul's (1438) Magdalen (1458)	King's (1441) Queen's (1448) St. Catherine's (1473) Jesus (1496)
Sixteenth century	Brasenose (1509) Corpus Christi (1516) Christ Church (1546) St. John's (1555) Trinity (1555) Jesus (1571)	Christ's (1506) St. John's (1511) Magdalene (1542) Trinity (1546) Emmanuel (1584) Sidney Sussex (1596)
Seventeenth century	Wadham (1612) Pembroke (1624)	(None)
Eighteenth century	Worcester (1714)	(None)
Nineteenth century	Keble (1870) Hertford (1874) Lady Margaret Hall (1878) Somerville (1879) St. Hugh's (1886) St. Hilda's (1893)	Downing (1800) Girton (1869) Newnham (1871) Selwyn (1882)
Twentieth century	Nuffield (1937) St. Peter's Hall (1947) St. Antony's (1950) St. Anne's (1952) Mansfield (1955)	(None)

land had one student in its universities per 385 in the total
population, whereas England had one per 625. The enthusiasm
for education which has characterized England since 1945 is
changing the situation.

The Scottish institutions adopted the continental rather than
the English model. In organization and structure they followed
Paris and Bologna, and in their development and practice, the
Universities of Orleans and Angers. Their progressive outlook
and their provision for student participation in the university
government appealed to the Scots.

Due to their poverty these institutions did not develop a
system of colleges like that of Oxford and Cambridge. The
funds required to pay their teachers imposed such a burden
on the community that nothing was left with which to provide
residence halls.

The Scottish universities differed in still other respects from
the older universities in England. They awarded a Master's
rather than the Bachelor's degree; their honors degrees required four years instead of three; the ordinary degree, awarded
for three years' work, has been more common than the honors
M.A., whereas in Oxford and Cambridge the honors courses
have been more popular. Since the Act of 1858 there has been
great progress in the universities of Scotland. All four have
been aided from time to time by grants from the government,
and in 1905 they received a substantial addition to their resources by the donation to the nation of two million pounds
from Andrew Carnegie.

The Scottish institutions are in some respects like the provincial universities of England. They are unitary. They are located
generally in the centers of industry and population. In the case
of Edinburgh the university was founded by the city in which
it is located. Except for St. Andrews, as already noted, there
is little provision for housing students, though Edinburgh has
made a beginning on property given to the university as a site
for residential halls.

The University of Dublin

Though the Republic of Ireland is not a part of the British Commonwealth, it is appropriate to make brief mention of its only university, established during the early period of British history. It was founded by Queen Elizabeth I in 1592. It followed the Oxford-Cambridge pattern. It was expected that a number of colleges would develop as at the ancient universities, and that Trinity College, established in 1592 as the *mater universitatis*, would set the pattern. As a matter of fact, it was the only one to develop. The university does recognize two institutions, McGee University College, Londonderry, for approved courses of instruction in agriculture and forestry, and the Veterinary College of Ireland, for approved courses of instruction in veterinary medicine.

The University of Dublin was designed as a seat of learning for Anglicans. For two centuries its members had to undergo religious tests. These varied according to the requirements of the times. It did, however, open its doors to men of all religious faiths in 1793, more than fifty years in advance of Oxford and Cambridge. It was also the first of the older universities to admit women to its degrees. This occurred in 1904. The university has traditionally been represented in Parliament. It now has three members in the Senate of the Republic, all of whom are elected by the graduates of the institution.

The University of Dublin was the last university to be established in Britain for 240 years. Though university growth had been gradual it had been continuous in Great Britain from the founding of Oxford in 1167, as noted in the development of colleges at Oxford and Cambridge and in the establishment of other universities in Scotland and Ireland. In the seventeenth and eighteenth centuries, however, not only were there no new universities established, but no colleges were added at Cambridge, and only three were added at Oxford. This was a period of the great migration to North America; Europe was

in the throes of the Thirty Years' War between the Catholics
and the Protestants (1618–1648); Charles I was beheaded in
1649, leaving England to be ruled by the Commons and
Councils of State with Cromwell at the head; Britain seized
Manhattan in 1664, incorporating it into the Empire; Gibraltar
was captured by the British in 1704; the Seven Years' War
between the French, English and Indians broke out in 1756,
followed a few years later by the American Revolution; and,
finally, the French Revolution of 1789 and the subsequent
Napoleonic wars disturbed Europe well into the first quarter
of the nineteenth century.

Another reason for this hiatus in university expansion was
the basic adjustment required following the Reformation and
the somnolence of the existing institutions. As the church
lost control of the universities, it no longer gave them support.
Though there was a demand for education of the more secular
type, the Acts of Uniformity, 1559 and 1662, and other such
measures stamped the universities as Anglican institutions. This
resulted in instruction becoming traditional and formal, and
life at the universities more social than academic. Dissenters
were excluded from the universities, and teaching posts were
reserved chiefly for the clergy. The Scottish universities were
more vital than Oxford and Cambridge during this period, but
they, too, had low standards.

Civic Universities

The University of London occupies a place of unique importance. Its forerunners were University and King's Colleges.
The former was originated in 1825 by a Group of Dissenters.
Their aim was to set up an institution with university status
for students excluded from Oxford and Cambridge for religious
beliefs or for lack of funds. It was officially opened in 1828. A
rival group established King's College in 1829. Its curriculum
was similar to that of other institutions, but included "doctrines
and duties of Christianity as the same are inculcated by the

united church of England and Ireland."[2] Neither of these colleges was authorized to grant degrees. In 1836 a non-teaching body called the University of London was established and empowered to grant degrees. It served University and King's Colleges as the degree-granting body.

The University of London was the first of the modern universities of Great Britain. Before 1858 it examined the graduates of University and King's Colleges and such other institutions as the Privy Council approved. A change in the constitution after the Charter of 1858 permitted the University to admit to its examinations those who desired to take them, regardless of the institutions previously attended. From 1858 to 1900 external examinations were held for students, not only in London and the provincial centers, but in other parts of the Commonwealth. Examinations are now given in theology, arts, law, economics and commerce, in more than one hundred overseas centers. Special arrangements for practical science examinations have been made in fourteen localities. While originally the overseas centers were confined to the British Commonwealth countries, they have spread to other areas, notably to the United States and Egypt. In 1900 the University was reconstituted as a teaching institution and, by Parliamentary Acts of 1903 and 1908, authorized to incorporate University and King's Colleges, except the theological department, as "schools of the university."

The teaching units of the University fall into three groups: (a) institutes developed by the Senate, consisting of seven purely postgraduate units and three that also give undergraduate courses; (b) schools of the University, which, with the exception of the Lister Institute of Preventive Medicine and two theological schools, receive grants from the Court (one school, the British Postgraduate Medical School, has fifteen postgraduate institutes); and (c) institutions with "recognized teachers" for whom the University has no financial responsibility.

There are more than seventy units that comprise the teaching resources of the University of London. This does not include thirty-odd training colleges which are affiliated to the University's Institute of Education.

In 1956–1957 when 89,866 full-time students were enrolled in the universities of the United Kingdom, 19,762, or 22 per cent were enrolled in the University of London. If both full and part-time students are counted, London in that year enrolled 27,554 or 26 per cent of the 106,074 university students in Britain. This does not include the enrollment in the affiliated training colleges, or those seeking external diplomas or degrees.

The aggregate of those registered for preliminary degree, diploma or higher degree examinations, under the external examination scheme, and those in university colleges overseas "in special relation" was 23,087 in 1957–1958.

The other civic universities differ from the University of London in two important respects: they are unitary-teaching institutions and they do not provide for external students. In some cases they have been formed through the merging of two or more colleges or institutes. However, when this has happened the merged units became integral and not federated parts of the organization. At Oxford and Cambridge the universities were established first and the colleges of which they are composed came later. In the civic universities the colleges antedate the universities.

Table 2 is a list of the civic universities, dates of founding as university colleges and as degree-granting institutions, including enrollments in 1938–1939 and the autumn term 1956.

Durham, established in 1832, was the first of the civic universities and the only one with affiliated institutions outside Britain. It has three affiliated colleges in which students may matriculate, keep terms, take examinations and qualify for degrees without attending the university. They are Coddrington College, Barbados, British West Indies, affiliated in 1875; Fourah Bay College, Freetown, Sierra Leone, West Africa, affiliated in 1876 in the Schools of Mechanical, Marine, Civil

TABLE 2   CIVIC UNIVERSITIES[3]

Name of University	Original University College	Date of Founding As A University College	Date of Founding As A University	Student Numbers 1938–1939	Student Numbers Autumn Term 1956
Durham	——		1832	1,709	4,300
London	——		1836	13,191	19,403
Victoria, Manchester	Owens	1851	1880	2,108	4,313
Leeds	Yorkshire	1874	1904	1,757	3,793
Bristol	Bristol	1876	1909	1,005	2,871
Sheffield	Firth	1879	1905	767	2,280
Birmingham	Mason	1880	1900	1,433	3,428
Liverpool	Liverpool	1881	1903	2,055	3,164
Nottingham	Nottingham	1881	1948	582	2,345
Reading	Reading	1892	1926	584	1,283
Exeter	Royal Albert Memorial	1895	1955	422	1,051
Southampton	Hartley	1902	1952	268	1,301
Hull	Hull	1927	1954	162	1,058
North Staffordshire University College		1949	1949	——	611
Leicester	Leicester	1950	1957	82	811
TOTAL, England				26,125	52,012
TOTAL, Wales				2,779	5,005
Aberdeen				1,211	1,703
Edinburgh				3,205	4,562
Glasgow				4,175	4,861
St. Andrews				928	2,114
TOTAL, Scotland				9,519	13,240
GRAND TOTAL, Great Britain				38,423	70,257

and Electrical Engineering; and Sunderland College, Durham, affiliated in 1930.

The University College of North Staffordshire, founded in 1949, is significant for several phases of its program. Courses in each of the three broad fields of knowledge, the humanities, social sciences and the natural sciences, are compulsory. Though not a university it is authorized to grant the first degree after four instead of three years. It provides professional education courses enabling students who complete the four-year degree course to begin teaching immediately without the necessity of attending one of the training colleges. The first year of its four-year course is the same for all students. In its provisions and requirements it resembles in many respects an American college of liberal arts.

In most cases the civic universities are located in large centers, have developed in response to local needs, and are therefore close to the people, who have pride in them since they are the outgrowth of community efforts. Gifts from the community have been major factors in their development.

Another feature of these institutions is the freedom they have to experiment. They are not bound by tradition; hence they can more readily adopt new ideas which seem promising. As they are smaller than the older universities, they can focus more directly on limited objectives and thus proceed more effectively toward desirable goals. On more than one occasion men who had formerly been connected with one of the ancient institutions spoke with enthusiasm about the opportunity which they have in the newer institutions to test ideas and try new methods. One of the encouraging characteristics of these institutions is their discontent with things as they are, and their efforts to improve the quality of education. A healthy ferment is characteristic of them.

The provincial universities are chiefly a development of the twentieth century. Only three of them, including London, were founded in the nineteenth. Indeed, in their present form all of them are products of this century. Most of them, however, grew out of the institutions that were founded before 1900. Five of them were raised to university rank before 1910 and five others in the past decade. Between these two spurts of growth only one institution was elevated to university status, Reading in 1926. Hull University College was established in 1927.

Plans for the current quinquennium call for increasing the total number of university students in Great Britain to 124,000, a 40 per cent increase over the figure for 1957. This includes all United Kingdom universities. Thus the present decade will stand out as one of the most remarkable periods in the history of British higher education. Not only has the number of institutions increased, but the expansion in aggregate enrollments is without precedent in modern times.

One vice-chancellor, commenting on developments since World War II—on the increase in number of institutions and in enrollments—remarked that an even more significant fact was the new attitude toward higher education which is evidenced throughout Britain, and particularly in England. Another striking fact is the enthusiasm of the university staffs for the prospects ahead. But this is not uniform. Some divisions of the university have misgivings about the change of emphasis in the curriculum, although the majority approve the course which is being pursued and are enthusiastic about the future. Registrars in these institutions reported five to six applicants for each vacancy every year. On the other hand, more than one expressed the view that very few, if any, really well qualified students are denied admission, since many students apply for admission to several institutions.

Service to their communities is characteristic of the provincial universities. In research and extra-mural activities they assist local industries and provide educational opportunities to youth and adults. This is a proper function, and one which is highly appreciated, yet certain dangers inhere in it. Too great an emphasis on current problems and needs could distort the university ideal. The major objective of the university, the pursuit of truth, is not in conflict with service to the community, but it is important that the primary purpose not be subordinated to the secondary. A seat of learning must be more than a service station. The conflict between the ideal and the practical must often be in sharp focus in the provincial universities because of their historical emphasis upon local needs. Their potentialities are great, both as leaders of thought and as service institutions, but to realize them fully the universal purpose of higher learning must not become subordinate, despite the pressure of contemporary needs.

Welsh and Irish Universities

To complete the sketch of the backgrounds of higher education in the United Kingdom it remains to refer briefly to the institutions in Wales and Ireland.

The University of Wales, founded in 1893, has four constituent colleges: Aberystwyth, 1872; University College of North Wales, Bangor, 1884; University College of South Wales and Monmouthshire, Cardiff, 1882; and University College of Swansea, 1920. The Welsh National School of Medicine, Cardiff, 1931, developed from departments of anatomy and physiology at the University College of South Wales and Monmouthshire. In addition to these integral units, five theological colleges are affiliated to the University.

This institution was established after a long struggle. The chief motivation seems to have been national sentiment, a feeling that it was not proper for a principality such as Wales to be without its university. The present organization, including the four colleges, the School of Medicine and the associated theological colleges, was the result of a compromise after a variety of attempts had failed.

St. David's College, Lampeter, Wales, founded in 1822, would logically be affiliated to the University, but its unwillingness to accept the conditions prescribed by the University is the stumbling-block. It is an independent institution, granting arts and theology degrees. In 1954–1955 it enrolled only 135 students.

Queen's University of Belfast was established by Royal Charter as Queen's College in 1845. It was linked with the Colleges of Cork and Galway as Queen's University of Ireland in 1850. In 1879 it became a constituent college of the Royal University of Ireland, which was purely an examining body. In 1908 it became Queen's University of Belfast. When the Republic of Ireland was formed in 1920 the University was incorporated in the university system of the United Kingdom. It does not, however, share in the funds at the disposal of the University Grants Committee. It receives grants from the government of Northern Ireland on the advice of the University Grants Committee. Since 1920 there has been a great expansion in program, in buildings and equipment and in enrollment.

National University, Ireland, 1908, is a privately-controlled institution, though supported by central government funds. It is frequently called the Catholic University of Ireland. It has three constituent units, the University Colleges of Dublin, Cork and Galway. It also recognizes St. Patrick's College, Maynooth, founded in 1795. Under the provisions of the University Education Act of 1926 the Royal College of Science and Albert Agricultural College were transferred to University College, Dublin, which was empowered to continue the functions formerly performed by these institutions.

Canadian Colleges and Universities

The Canadian system of higher education, composed of thirty degree-granting institutions, represents a variety of influences. It has developed a pattern of its own, but it has been influenced to a marked degree by the British, Scottish and American models. The distinctive characteristics of the

Canadian pattern are its system of French-language universities, such as Laval and Montreal, and their affiliated classical colleges; its various federation plans, which bring together private and public institutions into a coordinated system, such as are found in Toronto, Manitoba and Western Ontario; the number of its institutions that have maintained denominational ties more or less closely, such as Acadia, Mount Allison, Bishop's, McMaster, Trinity and Victoria; and the variation in the number of degree-granting authorities in the different areas. For example, there are fourteen such authorities in the maritime provinces, while in the western section only one degree-granting institution is located in a province.

The British influence is to be observed in the plan of setting up colleges within a university, in the titles, principal, provost, warden, and in the honors course program. Some Canadian institutions have imitated individual universities in Britain. For example, the University of Manitoba, established in 1877, was modeled on the University of London, and Queen's University, established in 1841, was definitely patterned after the University of Edinburgh.

The American precedents are reflected in the titles, president, dean, associate professor; in the establishment of faculties and schools; in the history of private and quasi-private institutions; and in the development of graduate schools, which provide Master's and Doctor's degree programs.

Doctors' degrees were for many years offered only at Toronto and McGill. By 1957 they had been established by Alberta, British Columbia, McMaster, Manitoba, New Brunswick, Queen's, Saskatchewan and Western Ontario. In several cases these degrees are offered in a limited range of subjects, mainly in scientific fields.

The requirements for admission to universities in Canada vary. For example, the provincial universities normally accept the secondary school certificate in their respective provinces, while private and quasi-private institutions use other means of appraising preparation for admission. Some admit on junior matriculation, that is, after eleven years of work (twelve in Ontario and British Columbia), and others require senior matriculation. Usually those admitted on junior matriculation have a four-year program, while those admitted on senior matriculation require only three years. Normally, the honors degree in Canada requires an extra year.

Education is considered chiefly a provincial responsibility. While seven provinces have provincial universities, three have only private institutions. Since 1951 most Canadian institutions receive some Dominion support, though the institutions in the Province of Quebec refuse to accept it.

Table 3 indicates the varieties of institutions which make up the Canadian system.

TABLE 3   CLASSIFICATION OF CANADIAN UNIVERSITIES
ON BASIS OF SUPPORT[4]

Acadia University (c)	University of New Brunswick (P)
University of Alberta (P)	Nova Scotia Agricultural
Assumption University of	College (P)
Windsor (c)	Nova Scotia Technical College (P)
University of Bishop's College (c)	University of Ottawa (c)
University of British Columbia (P)	Queen's University (I)
Carleton University (I)	Royal Military College of
Dalhousie University (I)	Canada (D)
University of King's College (c)	Saint Dunstan's University (c)
Laval University (c)	University of St. Francis Xavier (c)
McGill University (I)	Saint Joseph's University (c)
McMaster University (c)	Saint Mary's University (c)
University of Manitoba (P)	University of Saskatchewan (P)
Memorial University of	Sir George Williams College (I)
Newfoundland (P)	University of Toronto (P)
University of Montreal (c)	University of Trinity College
Mount Allison University (c)	Victoria University
Mount Saint Vincent College (c)	University of Western Ontario (I)

Designations:
   (c)—Church related
   (P)—Provincial
   (I) —Independent
   (D)—Dominion government

In the number of private institutions as well as those with church connections, the Canadian system resembles more the American than the Commonwealth pattern.

Australian Universities

The Australian system of higher education is entirely public. The University of Sydney was established in 1850. The last to be established was New England University, 1954. Monash University, Melbourne, was projected in 1958. Each state in Australia has a university located in its capital city. In addition to these six institutions there are the Australian National University at Canberra, the University of Technology at Sydney, New England University at Armidale (N.S.W.), Canberra University College and Newcastle University College.

Though these institutions are widely separated geographically, they have much the same program of education. Degree courses in arts, science, law and engineering are offered at all state universities; and professional education courses are given at all universities except Sydney, where a government training college for teachers is located on the university's grounds. Social science is offered in all institutions except Western Australia; medicine, dentistry, agriculture, commerce and architecture, in all except Tasmania.

The Australian National University is unique among British Commonwealth institutions. It has no undergraduates; its staff is devoted exclusively to research and postgraduate education; and it serves as a kind of research center for the other universities of the Commonwealth of Australia. It has four schools, representing the medical sciences, social sciences, physical sciences and Pacific studies.

The New South Wales University of Technology is unique among Australian universities in a number of its features. It provides humanistic social studies for engineering students;

it has the power to create constituent colleges; and it provides experience in industry under university supervision. It has specialized programs of training in science and technology and in their application to industry and commerce, and assists through research the development and application of science to industry. Some of its earlier innovations have been dropped. For example, the sandwich courses are disappearing. In 1958 a degree course in industrial arts was inaugurated, as well as Master of Technology and Master of Commerce degrees.

Private gifts were chiefly responsible for the founding and development of three state universities, Sydney, Adelaide and Western Australia. Gifts and grants from private sources have been important to all Australian universities. However, the proportion of funds from this source is now very small, 5½ per cent in 1956, including income from endowment and donations that can be used for general purposes.

The federal government, since 1951, has made annual grants to all Australian universities. In 1958 it approved a greatly expanded program in response to the report of a committee, headed by Sir Keith Murray, that was appointed to look into the needs of the universities.

New Zealand

The University of New Zealand, established in 1870, is the only degree-granting institution in the country. It has four constituent units, Auckland, Canterbury, Victoria and Otago Universities.

There are two conspicuous aspects of New Zealand's higher education program, the proportion of its part-time students and the number of external students. In a university enrollment of 10,608 in 1956, 4,877 were part-time. Not counted in this number were 841 external students.

New Zealand has honors work in the Master's degree but not in the Bachelor's degree program. In 1957 Canterbury

University was considering the establishment of an honors degree at the Bachelor's level, and the plan was being widely discussed at other universities. The requirements for the advanced degrees are much the same as in the United States. One year is the minimum for the Master's and two years beyond the Master's for the Doctorate.

There is a body called the University Grants Committee over which the vice-chancellor of the university presides. It does not have funds at its disposal as does its counterpart in Britain, but serves in an advisory capacity.

South African Universities

The South African system of higher education consists of nine universities. One of these is a non-teaching, examining body, the University of South Africa, located at Pretoria. Of the eight teaching universities, four use English as the medium of instruction and four, Afrikaans. Three of these are located in the Cape Province, the University of Cape Town (1918), the University of Stellenbosch (1916), and Rhodes University (1951); four in the Transvaal, Pretoria (1930), Potchefstroom (1951), Witwatersrand (1922), and South Africa (1873); one in Natal (1949), with branches at Durban and Pietermaritzburg; and one in the Orange Free State (1950), at Bloemfontein.

All South African universities are autonomous. The federal government provides the support. In this respect the Union of South Africa differs from Canada and Australia, where support of the universities is a provincial or state responsibility. The provincial governments provide funds only when they contract for university services.

The university program of studies in South Africa is much like that found in Australia. The pattern of organization is likewise similar. Their councils have traditionally been free to choose their staffs and students and to guide their own development. This right is involved in the Apartheid issue in certain of the universities, which have admitted non-white students in the past, but under the government's policy must refuse them in the future.

The rift developing between the English- and Afrikaans-speaking universities is unfortunate. It affects administrations, staffs and students. In a small country, in which a European population of only three million is served by these institutions, such a rift can have tragic consequences.

The country has great natural resources, a variety of budding industries, growing cities and a virile and forward-looking community. At this stage it is in need of a strong cohesive university system if its potentialities are to be realized. Not only the emerging culture but the economy of the community require it. Some excellent universities already exist and are expanding steadily. The percentage of youth to the total European population in the universities is greater than that in Australia, New Zealand or Canada. The foundations are already laid for a splendid system of higher education, but there is danger that the developing conflict between the institutions may retard progress and dim the bright prospects which existed before the Apartheid issue arose to divide them.

India and Pakistan

While there are still higher educational institutions that deal with the study of ancient Indian or Islamic thought brought into the country during the middle ages, the overwhelming emphasis today is on modern Western education which began with the establishment, under British sponsorship in 1857, of the three Universities of Calcutta, Bombay and Madras. These were modeled on the University of London and set the pattern for the universities subsequently developed there. For the first forty-odd years they were affiliating and examining bodies only. They did no teaching. As such they performed a useful function. The plan enabled schools, whether government or missionary, to be brought into the same system; it provided a method of testing the qualifications of students and of evaluating the work of the institutions; it gave the government a chance to assist mission schools in the secular side of their work; it stimulated the established colleges by providing new targets for their efforts, and, finally, it encouraged the creation of new colleges.

Early in the twentieth century these three universities were authorized to add the teaching function. For approximately twenty-five years the teaching of both the central universities and their affiliated units was on the undergraduate level. In 1927 postgraduate programs were authorized. Since that time an elaborate list of postgraduate offerings has been developed. In 1951 provision was made for postgraduate teaching in affiliated units as well as in the university colleges. In 1957 the University of Calcutta offered postgraduate courses in thirty-two subjects in addition to those in arts, commerce, law, science and technology given by the relevant university councils.

In addition to the three original universities, two others—Panjab (1882), now in Pakistan, and Allahabad (1887)—were founded before the end of the nineteenth century. Fourteen additional universities were established in India before independence, and fourteen since. Pakistan had three universities before partition and had added three by 1957. Table 4 indicates these developments.

The undergraduate programs provide two years of instruction before admission to the intermediate examination and another two years before the final examination for the degree. Examinations are set by a university examining board for all affiliated units and are the sole means of determining who shall be granted the degree. The estimates of the teachers have no weight. In short, the examinations are set and graded by external examiners. As a result students frequently focus

TABLE 4   UNIVERSITIES IN INDIA AND PAKISTAN—1956[5]
(Including founding dates)

Nineteenth Century	Pre-Independence	Post-Independence
	INDIA	
University of Calcutta (1857)	Banaras Hindu University (1916)	University of Rajasthan (1947)
University of Bombay (1857)	University of Mysore (1916)	Panjab University (1947)
University of Madras (1857)	Patna University (1917)	University of Gauhati (1948)
University of Allahabad (1887)	Osmania University (1918)	University of Poona (1948)
	Aligarh Muslim University (1920)	University of Jammu and Kashmir (1948)
	University of Lucknow (1921)	Maharaja Sayajirao University of Baroda (1949)
	University of Delhi (1922)	University of Roorkee (1949)
	Nagpur University (1923)	Shreemati Nathibai Damodar Thackersey Women's University (1949)
	Andhra University (1926)	
	Agra University (1927)	Karnatak University (1949)
	Annamalai University (1928)	Gujarat University (1950)
	University of Kerala (formerly Travancore) (1937)	Bihar University (1952)
	Utkal University (1943)	Sri Venkateswara University (1954)
	University of Saugar (1946)	Jadavpur University (1955)
		Visva-Bharati (1951)
	PAKISTAN	
University of the Panjab (1882)	University of Dacca (1921)	University of Peshawar (1950)
	University of Sind (1947)	University of Karachi (1950)
		University of Rajshahi (1953)

attention on outguessing examiners rather than on education. Throughout the subcontinent the system is deplored. Students, faculty and the general public alike join in excoriating it and in pleading for a more effective method of judging scholarly achievement. It would be difficult to devise a more vicious system, one better suited to distort educational values, and yet no one has so far submitted an acceptable alternative plan. The newness of the universities, their lack of scholarly traditions, the weakness of the faculties in many institutions and the general lack of standards make necessary some form of central control if complete chaos is to be avoided. For that reason it is difficult to find a satisfactory substitute.

Higher education in India and Pakistan is beset with a variety of problems due to its truly remarkable growth. If fewer institutions had been established until standards of scholarship had been more thoroughly crystallized, the situation might have been different, but that was all but impossible in view of the enthusiasm for university education on the part of the Indian and Pakistani youth. The greatest single need is for one or more universities of first rank to set the pace which others might strive to emulate. Such an institution, or institutions, should emphasize the education of teachers for the various faculties, including the professional fields. Graduates of such institutions with well established criteria of quality could be a powerful factor in raising the level of the entire system.

The universities of the subcontinent have the organization, the terminology, the degrees, the curricula, the forms of examinations and research plans common to British institutions, but they sometimes lack the spirit of learning, the quality of scholarship and the vitality of research which are the essence of a university. In short, they have the form but not the substance of higher learning in some cases. This does not mean that there are no bright spots. Some excellent work is found at the three oldest institutions at all levels. The scientific research at Bangalore and Poona, as well as at Calcutta, Madras and Bombay, is of high quality. Substantial work is carried on at Delhi, Aligarh, Roorkee, Peshawar, Panjab and other older universities, but some of the institutions, particularly among the newer ones, are definitely substandard.

The system of affiliation among large numbers of colleges and institutes under the supervision of a single university, whose faculty is often weak, produces a situation in which there is bound to be an excess of failures. Even a stronger university, such as Calcutta, which has 111 affiliated units and an enrollment of more than 100,000 students, has little chance of exercising a really helpful supervision. There is merit in the affiliation arrangement which provides some central control and enables the small colleges to get advice and help in their development from stronger faculties, but when the number of units is so large that only a small fraction of their needs can be met, it becomes ineffective.

Though it is understandable, it is unfortunate, at this stage of development in these two countries, that the government feels it necessary to stress science and technology. If the universities had another decade or two in which to focus attention on the basic areas of higher learning before they undertake the expenditures required for high-level work in science and the technologies, they would have a better chance to advance the cause of higher education. A promising feature of the situation is the concern of university faculties over basic education. Two teams of Indian professors visited Britain and the United States in 1956 and 1957 to study the general education movement, in search of help in building broad and worthy programs.

In conclusion it should be said that despite the low standard of university work now prevailing on the subcontinent, there are many encouraging signs. The enthusiasm for higher education, the interest of government as expressed by its appropriations to the University Grants Commission, the percentage of youth seeking university education, the excellence of research in a few places, the numbers seeking education abroad and the marked spirit of devotion to their country displayed by administrations, faculties and students are never-to-be-forgotten impressions of a two-month visit to the universities of India and Pakistan.

Summary

This brief sketch of higher education in the British Commonwealth as it has developed through the centuries is chiefly the story of the influence of the ancient universities of England and Scotland and, in the modern period, of the University of London. While London arose partly as a protest against the exclusiveness of Oxford and Cambridge, it borrowed from them the form of its organization and sought to emulate them in its program of studies and in the spirit of scholarship which it fostered. Thus the university systems of Canada, Australia, New Zealand, South Africa, India and Pakistan are in a sense largely the projections of the two ancient English institutions. The Scottish universities' influence is in evidence in many places, but it has been of secondary importance.

The changes of fortune in the higher education enterprise have characterized its history. Flourishing periods in the early centuries were followed by waning interest. Fluctuations were characteristic of the thirteenth through the sixteenth centuries, then followed the great depression in the seventeenth and eighteenth, when expansion ceased and the universities reached their lowest ebb. This in turn was followed by great progress in the last half of the nineteenth and early part of the twentieth centuries. Unprecedented developments in all countries under review marked this period. Civic university colleges arose and later became universities. Many Canadian, Australian, South African and Indian universities sprang up

TABLE 5   GROWTH OF COMMONWEALTH UNIVERSITIES BETWEEN 1939 AND 1958[6]

	Universities and university colleges		Teaching and research staff named		Number of full-time students	
	1939	1958	1939	1958	1939	1958
Australia	6	10	800	2,300	9,000	19,000
Canada	20	30	2,800	7,900	38,000	78,000
Ceylon	1	1	30	290	600	2,500
Ghana	—	1	—	120	—	320
Hongkong	1	1	70	180	420	830
India	{18	32	{2,100	{5,700	130,000	{653,000
Pakistan		6		750		57,000
Malta	1	1	50	50	150	300
New Zealand	6	6	300	750	1,700	5,600
Nigeria	—	1	—	140	—	560
Rhodesia and Nyasaland	—	1	—	30	—	70
Singapore: Malaya	{5	1	{800	190	{8,000	1,570
Union of South Africa		10		1,800		21,000
Uganda	—	1	—	110	—	620
United Kingdom	21	25	3,800	10,500	50,000	97,000
West Indies	1	2	20	170	50	600

(Source: *The Times Weekly Review*, London, England, April 24, 1958.)
By courtesy of the Author, R. S. Aitken, and *The Times Weekly Review*.

and enrollments expanded rapidly. Higher education became popular and prosperous as never before in British history.

The growth of the past twenty years has exceeded that of any other period, as Table 5 demonstrates.

Despite this formidable record of growth since 1938, present indications are that the next twenty years will record even greater expansion in all English-speaking countries, including the United States.

III

Backgrounds: The United States of America

❖❰❬❖

Thirty per cent of the college-age population enter college in the United States. They may enter a junior (community) college, a teachers college, a liberal arts college or a university. The total number enrolled in 1957–1958 was 3,068,000, in some 1900 colleges and universities. In Britain technical and teacher-training colleges are not incorporated in its higher education system, hence comparative statistics on the two countries would be misleading.

Types of Institutions

The oldest and most typical of American institutions is the arts college. The minimum requirement for admission is graduation from a standard secondary school. It has a four-year program, awards a Bachelor's degree, and prepares for admission to a graduate school. Its curriculum has undergone great changes in the past few decades. Classical languages, moral philosophy, natural philosophy, mathematics and logic, which formerly made up the core of the curriculum, are now replaced by modern languages, social sciences and natural sciences. Mathematics is still required for courses in science and technology, but it is not universally prescribed. Logic is almost as obsolete as Latin. Arts colleges also frequently provide some technical or vocational courses, but limit the number of credit hours allowed to count toward graduation.

The arts college appears under various designations, such as: the College of Arts and Sciences; the Liberal Arts College; the College of Literature, Science and the Arts, etc. Though the titles may differ, the programs and purposes are essentially the same. They aim at providing a foundation of understanding that will aid in developing a successful and satisfying career and in meeting the responsibilities of citizenship. The college may be one of the organic divisions of a university, or an independent institution with its own board of control and authorized to grant its own degrees.

The Office of Education in 1955 reported 732 independent degree-granting liberal arts colleges. The older universities began as arts colleges and developed their professional programs around them. All except a few technological universities include a College of Arts and Science as the central division. These colleges provide basic studies for undergraduate professional schools, such as engineering and commerce, and pre-professional preparation for a variety of graduate professional schools, such as medicine, law and theology. All junior college programs include basic arts as well as technical courses.

The first teachers college was established in 1839. In 1953–1954 there were 105 teachers colleges and 76 state colleges in which the chief emphasis was teacher education. Most of the latter began as teachers colleges and changed their titles, partly because they broadened their curricula to include more liberal arts content and partly because the term "teachers college" had become unpopular. In the beginning these institutions provided a two-year college program. All of them now have a four-year course beyond high school; many have added the Master's degree, and a few the Doctorate. Many arts colleges and a few junior colleges provide recognized teacher-education programs. Altogether some 1,200 institutions are approved by state departments for courses which qualify for a teacher's certificate.

Universities in the modern sense are less than a century old.

Harvard did not organize a graduate school until 1872, though it gave some advanced courses as early as 1825. Johns Hopkins (1876) established the pattern for the "modern" university. Research, graduate and professional education were its chief objects. It was influenced by the German universities, which emphasized research rather than teaching—the development of knowledge rather than simply the imparting of it. In line with that conception of the function of the university, Hopkins established the first research professorship in America in 1878. The president of Chicago (1891), Rainey Harper, was the first to declare "the work of investigation" to be the primary purpose of his institution. As demands for advanced study and research increased, the older institutions followed the lead of Hopkins and Chicago.

The Office of Education includes in its reports in the university category "institutions in which there is considerable stress on graduate instruction, which confer advanced degrees in a variety of Liberal Arts fields, and which have at least two professional schools that are not exclusively technological." This is the criterion used in classifying the newer institutions. It is not applicable to some of the famous older universities, such as Brown and Princeton. The Commonwealth universities would generally conform to this definition, though research and graduate work are less prominent and less well organized than in the United States.

Most American universities are single campus, unitary-teaching and research institutions. A few have more than one branch. The most notable of these are the University of California, with eight branches, and the State University of New York with forty-two units. None is an affiliating institution in the British sense. A few institutions called universities are only liberal arts colleges, having neither graduate nor research programs.

In 1954–1955 Masters' degrees were granted by 415 institutions, and the Doctorate by 180. Graduate school enrollments

TABLE 6   GRADUATE SCHOOL ENROLLMENT
SINCE 1890[1]

Year	Men	Women	Total
1890	1,973	409	2,382
1900	4,112	1,179	5,831
1910	6,504	2,866	9,370
1920	9,837	5,775	15,612
1926	20,159	12,341	32,500
1928	26,540	17,625	44,165
1930	29,070	18,185	47,255
1932	50,379	26,574	76,953
1934	43,170	26,101	69,271
1936	47,410	31,501	78,911
1938	55,854	34,947	90,801
1940	67,628	38,491	106,119
1942	53,220	32,161	85,381
1944	31,060	28,171	59,231
1946	75,006	46,246	121,252
1948	120,177	54,255	174,432
1950	172,161	65,047	237,208
1952	171,363	61,964	233,327
1954	195,462	84,693	280,155

Source: *American Universities and Colleges,*
seventh edition, 1956.

have expanded rapidly as shown in Table 6.

While this expansion was taking place in the universities,
another development was occurring at the other end of the
spectrum of higher education. There were only eight junior
colleges in 1900, all privately supported. In 1953–1954 there
were 598 enrolling 622,864, according to the handbook on
The American Junior Colleges. Eighty per cent of the junior
college students enrolled that year were in publicly-controlled
institutions.

In each of the four types of institutions just described, arts
colleges, teachers colleges, universities and junior colleges,
there are both private and public institutions. This dual system
based on control and main source of support is a notable

feature of American higher education. Originally all colleges and universities were private. The first public institution was the University of North Carolina, authorized in 1789 and opened in 1795. The University of Georgia was authorized earlier, but opened later. Despite this early beginning, tax funds were a small fraction of the total income of higher education until the second or third decade of the twentieth century. In 1958 approximately two-thirds of the four-year colleges and universities were private, but state institutions, including the junior colleges, enrolled 58 per cent of the students. Though college and university endowments aggregated approximately $3.4 billion in 1957, the proportion of the total burden of higher education borne by the income from this sum was less than 6 per cent.

Many private universities receive tax funds for research, and many public ones have accumulated endowments. For example, the University of Virginia had an endowment of $16 million in 1954–1955; the University of California $70 million, and the University of Texas, $232 million. The nature of the control is the hallmark of private institutions. Acceptance of public funds on the part of private institutions does not involve loss of control when public funds are but a minor fraction of the total income.

Professional Education

American Universities and Colleges, seventh edition, defines the professional curriculum as one which "includes instruction in, (1) the techniques and knowledge employed directly in rendering professional service, and (2) the basic sciences and other subjects whose mastery is essential to understanding and learning the techniques in professional subjects." The definition also includes instruction in the liberal arts and sciences, either in the curriculum itself or as a requirement for admission.

For some years after its founding almost one-half of the

graduates of Harvard entered the ministry, though its curriculum was not professional in character. Rutgers University established the first professional school of theology in 1784, the New Brunswick Theological Seminary. The Academy and Charitable School of Philadelphia (predecessor of the University of Pennsylvania) inaugurated instruction in medicine in 1765, the first professional training to be given in a college or university in the United States. King's College (Columbia) followed suit in 1776, and Harvard in 1782. The first instruction in law in the United States was conducted at Litchfield, Connecticut, from 1784 to 1833, but the first permanent program of instruction in the subject in the universities came with the establishment of the law faculty at the University of Maryland in 1816. The Law School at Harvard was opened in 1817. The first institution for the training of teachers, established in 1839 at Lexington, Massachusetts, was the forerunner of teachers colleges and schools of education in the universities.

While institutions of higher education began early to take an interest in professional instruction, it was many years before it became the general pattern. Before 1900 a large proportion of the schools of law and medicine in the United States were proprietary institutions, operating chiefly on the fees received from their students. While there are still some separately-organized professional schools, the majority are now organic parts of universities. For example, only 9 of the 82 medical schools have no university affiliation, and 6 of the 125 law schools. Practically all teacher education is given by degree-granting colleges or universities. Theology is the only profession for which most of the training is provided outside the university. Only 16 of the 73 schools have university affiliation.

Historical Sketch

This sprawling, mammoth system of higher education, accommodating more than three million students in 1958, is chiefly the product of the twentieth century, but its roots reach back to the seventeenth, when the first two degree-granting American colleges were founded, Harvard (1636) and William and Mary (1693). A total of nine permanent colleges were established in the Colonial period, as indicated in Table 7.

TABLE 7   UNIVERSITIES FOUNDED IN COLONIAL PERIOD[2]

Harvard University	1636
College of William and Mary	1693
Yale University	1701
Princeton University	1746
Columbia University	1754
University of Pennsylvania	1755
Brown University	1764
Rutgers University	1766
Dartmouth College	1769

There were 116 colleges by 1850, 182 by 1860, and more than 400 by 1900. The population of the Republic trebled in the period 1850–1900 from approximately 24,000,000 to 75,000,000, while the college enrollments increased twenty-fold, from 11,900 to 238,000. The proportion of college students has continued to increase every decade since 1900. At the turn of the century the ratio of college students to the total population was 1 to 320; in 1958 it was 1 to 57. Table 8 pictures the growth of enrollments.

The high ratio of college population to the total is a tribute to American zeal for higher education, but it must be admitted that not all college programs are of standard quality. In the stronger colleges and universities standards are equal to the best and superior to those of many universities in Commonwealth countries. The growth of the system has been so rapid and the numbers served so large that many weak institutions appear on the American college and university roster. In time some will develop strong programs, others will be merged with nearby institutions or be discontinued. To judge from the past, few will fail to survive altogether. A paramount need in

American higher education is an emphasis upon quality. The quantitative measures used in assessing achievement, sixteen units for the high school certificate and 120 semester

TABLE 8   POPULATION AND RESIDENT STUDENT ENROLLMENT IN HIGHER EDUCATION, CONTINENTAL UNITED STATES, 1870 TO 1958[3]

Year	Total Population	Enrollment in Higher Education*	Ratio of Enrollment to Population
1869–1870	38,558,371	52,286	1—713
1879–1880	50,155,783	115,817	1—433
1889–1890	62,622,250	156,756	1—399
1899–1900	75,994,575	237,592	1—320
1909–1910	91,972,266	355,213	1—259
1919–1920	105,710,620	597,880	1—177
1929–1930	123,076,685	1,100,737	1—112
1939–1940	131,669,275	1,494,203	1—88
1946	140,054,000	2,078,095	1—67
1947	143,446,000	2,338,226	1—61
1948	146,093,000	2,408,249	1—60
1949	148,665,000	2,456,841	1—61
1950	150,697,361	2,296,592	1—66
1951	153,384,000	2,116,440	1—72
1952	156,891,000	2,148,284	1—73
1953	158,320,000	2,250,701	1—70
1954	161,183,000	2,499,750	1—64
1955	164,024,000	2,720,929	1—60
1957–1958	175,000,000	3,068,000	1—57

* The figures prior to 1946 are the cumulative total for the school year. The figures for 1946 and later are the fall enrollment figures (usually considered approximately 10% less than the cumulative figure). (Source: *American Universities and Colleges*, seventh edition, 1956.)

The 1957–1958 figures are based on population estimates and actual enrollment figures.

credits for the degree, has distorted educational values. A more adequate means of assessing educational achievement is a primary need. Units and credits were invented and used as an arbitrary means of defining a college. They were not meant to be used in measuring educational achievement. The story of their origin, purpose and use is a part of educational history worth relating because of their subsequent influence on American higher education.

In 1906 Andrew Carnegie established the Foundation for the Advancement of Teaching, the income of which was to be used to provide pensions for *college* teachers. The president of the Foundation, in view of the confusion prevailing at that time, had great difficulty determining which institutions were really colleges, and therefore eligible under the Charter to participate in the Foundation's program. The result was that he found it necessary to define a college and get his trustees' approval of the definition before he could proceed. Since admission requirements were involved in the definition, he had to go further and define a secondary school.

The secondary school, he concluded, was an institution based on seven or eight years of elementary work which for graduation required the pursuit of a four-year course of study comprising four academic subjects each year. A subject that was pursued for a year he called a unit. Thus a school that required sixteen units beyond the elementary grades he classified as a secondary school. The institution that required four full years of academic work (fifteen hours of class work a week) beyond the secondary school he classified as a college.

These definitions were accepted by the accrediting associations and used by them in determining the eligibility of institutions applying for accreditation. One hour of class work a week for nine months in college constitutes one year, or two semester hour credits. Graduation from the better colleges of that day required four academic years of fifteen class hours per week (with two hours in the laboratory counting as one year hour), a minimum of 120 semester hours or credits.

Thus the quantitative terms units and credits arose and have been used as a yardstick in determining the status of educational institutions. From this the impression emerged that by the accumulation of credits one earned a degree, and that one's knowledge of a subject was scarcely as important as one's credits. A comprehensive examination at the end of the college course, which would require some synthesis of the knowledge acquired on the British pattern, would do much to correct a basic weakness in the American undergraduate program. A few institutions have, indeed, already adopted such a plan.

The most important single factor in promoting standards in American higher education in the past has been the accrediting association. In the Commonwealth countries no similar organization exists. Greater care is exercised in the chartering of degree-granting institutions. The affiliating universities exercise a general supervision over the affiliated units, and conduct the examinations for the degree. Hence the organization of the university system provides safeguards as to the quality of degrees granted which are absent in the American system. It is the accrediting associations that perform this function. The validity of their ratings has been seriously questioned in recent years, but they still remain the only agencies authorized to set collegiate standards. These associations are voluntary organizations of colleges and universities which formulate standards of work and admit other institutions to membership on the basis of these standards. They conduct periodic checks on the work being performed by member institutions. Those falling behind may be placed on probation or dropped from membership. Through this means the association serves as a stimulus to higher standards. Graduates of an unaccredited college are handicapped in being admitted to graduate or professional schools, hence membership in a regional accrediting association is essential to an institution's stability and progress. All qualified institutions belong to one of the five regional accrediting associations in the United States. The Southern and North Central Associations began the last decade of the nineteenth century. The others developed later.

Significant Developments 1850–1950

Five major developments affecting American higher education originated between 1850 and 1950. These were: the passage of the Land-Grant College Act in 1862; the adoption of the elective system beginning in the last quarter of the nineteenth century; the emergence of the conception of the modern university; the rise of the general education movement; and the growth of the junior (community) college. An analysis of these movements will assist in understanding the backgrounds of American higher education.

THE LAND-GRANT COLLEGE

The Morrill Act of 1862 provided land grants to each state for the endowment, support and maintenance of at least one college where the leading object shall be, without excluding other scientific and classical studies, and including military tactics, to teach such branches of learning as are related to agriculture and the mechanic arts, in such manner as the legislatures of the states may respectively prescribe, in order to promote the liberal and practical education of the industrial classes in the several pursuits and professions in life.

This program was revolutionary in three respects. It added subjects to the curriculum never before recognized as worthy of university education; it was designed to provide higher education and training for the "industrial classes"; and it involved a new conception of the function of higher education in society. To the classical scholar of that time the inclusion of agricultural studies and the mechanic arts in the university program appeared not only fantastic but disruptive. The classical curriculum of 1862 was designed for the few who were to adorn the learned professions; the new program was to serve men who worked with their hands. The mission of the university was to educate the upper class for public and professional leadership; the land-grant college purpose was to educate technologists, leaders in agriculture and engineering.

This new philosophy of higher education represented not only a step toward democratization of higher education, but toward the democratization of America. It made available the advantages of higher education to workers who had hitherto been denied them. Previous attempts to gain acceptance for the subjects of agriculture and engineering had not been successful. A few institutions had introduced some agricultural courses, and six engineering schools had been established, but none was affiliated with a university.

The change in attitude resulting from the Morrill Act was influenced by the availability of federal funds, the expressed interest of the Congress, and the organization of more than one-half the new programs within state universities, which gave them prestige. Their development was also facilitated by the adoption of the elective system, which permitted the expansion of the curriculum. Though confidence in the new institutions grew slowly, they made steady gains each decade. By 1954 sixty-nine land-grant institutions were in operation, enrolling 456,015, or approximately 18 per cent of the total college and university population of that year. Their expenditures for the year ending June 30, 1954, aggregated $749,042,587.[4]

The land-grant program stimulated developments in other universities. Engineering schools grew from six non-university schools in 1862 to 221 in 1957, of which most were university schools. The first school of architecture was established in 1865; there are now sixty. Other professional schools, such as commerce and business administration, social work and journalism, found it less difficult to gain recognition as a result of the pattern set by the land-grant colleges. There is little doubt that the precedent set by these institutions paved the way for the large number of professional schools which are now incorporated in American universities. In the area of professional education they exercised the greatest influence on the structure and program of American higher education.

THE ELECTIVE SYSTEM

The adoption of the elective system, which affected the course of American higher education in so many ways, is usually associated with the name of Charles W. Eliot, President of Harvard from 1869–1909. Eliot, who was in his middle thirties when elected President of Harvard, began his attack early on the curriculum, making a plea for the addition of subjects such as history, economics, political science, and for the rights of students to choose, within limits, their subjects of study.* The battle waged by Eliot and others was long and bitter. It had no precedent. British higher education, from which the American system had largely stemmed, was based upon a fixed curriculum. Thus the new principle advocated was not only a radical departure from previous American practice, but a break with European tradition. Success in gaining acceptance for so revolutionary a plan would scarcely have been possible in any other country. A new nation, with relatively few vested interests and motivated by the democratic ideal, provided the climate for its success.

When the battle was won, the flood gates were opened. The demands for new courses were legion, and no criteria of selection had been established. The result was chaos. An unbelievable variety of courses filled college catalogs. All tastes were to be served. Thus the success of the advocates of a more

---

* President Eliot did not originate the idea of expanding the curriculum and of the elective system, though his name is usually associated with it. Professor Wayland of Brown University, after spending a year abroad, wrote a "Report to the Corporation of Brown University on changes in Collegiate Education"[5] in 1850. In this report he advocated: (1) the adoption of the elective system; (2) instruction in the useful arts and sciences, and (3) a residential college.

This report was widely distributed and made a deep impression on the thought of his day. After reading it one is convinced that it influenced Eliot's thinking to a marked extent. It appears likely, too, that Morrill, living in a nearby state, Vermont, may have been stimulated, in part at least, to introduce the Land Grant Act of 1862 by the Wayland report, which advocated the incorporation of instruction in the "Useful Arts and Sciences." Thus Brown University played a significant part in the development of education in the last half of the nineteenth century.

flexible curriculum was by no means an unmixed blessing. Much inappropriate and trivial subject matter found its way into the curriculum. Since the adoption of the free elective system, permitting an expansion of the curriculum, there has been a persistent struggle to establish criteria for the selection of subject matter, to insure a place for basic studies and to reestablish order in the curriculum. Various devices have been used to achieve the purpose. Limitation was placed on the number of technical and vocational subjects permitted for admission to college and for satisfaction of the requirements for the Bachelor of Arts degree. General requirements in the humanities, social sciences and natural sciences were prescribed for the first two years of college, while major and minor requirements were stipulated for the upper two years. One of the objectives of the general education movement, to be discussed later, was to find a way to construct a curriculum with basic and worthwhile subject matter.

The adoption of the elective system led to excesses that retarded educational progress, and yet without this fundamental innovation the present system of higher education in the United States would not have been possible. It is difficult to conceive the state of development in this country in 1950 had the medieval curriculum of 1850 been continued. The educational and economic progress of the past century has, in large measure, derived from the scientific, technological and technical training provided the great mass of American youth. Therefore, as one reviews the history of these developments, the advantages appear to have outweighed the disadvantages. Whether or not one agrees with this view there can be no doubt that it had a major effect upon the course of higher education in the United States.

CONCEPTION OF THE MODERN UNIVERSITY

The university in the modern sense had its beginning with the opening of Johns Hopkins University in 1876. As already noted, its chief characteristic was its emphasis upon graduate and professional education, and particularly on research. The growth of graduate and professional schools and the unprecedented expenditures on research since 1945 represent the flowering of this new conception of the university's function.

Since 1900 the stronger universities of the country have been influenced by this pattern, accounting for the vast increase in graduate school enrollments, which rose from 5,831 in 1900 to 280,155 in 1954. While the overall figures for higher education showed a tenfold expansion in this period, graduate school numbers increased almost fiftyfold. Expenditures for research in American universities in 1953–1954 reached a total of $372 million.

The dependence of government, business and industry on universities for research and for supplying research workers is an indication of the way in which the modern university has identified itself with the interests of the larger community and has been able to minister to its needs. The scholar in the modern university has come down from his ivory tower into the market place, and is thereby making spectacular contributions to the economic and social progress of his community, state and nation.

Concern has been expressed over the demands made on the university by government, business and industry for solving applied science problems. A primary responsibility of the university is basic rather than applied research. It is an obvious fact that when scientists devote an undue amount of their time to project research it is done at the expense of basic investigation. A few industries conscious of this danger support fundamental research in the areas of their interests. The nutrition and pharmaceutical foundations provide funds for basic research in their respective fields. The insurance companies have established a similar foundation for research on degenerative diseases. Both government and industry are beginning to realize that such research provides the essential reserves which must be constantly replenished if science and technology are to prosper.

In each of the British Commonwealth countries a non-university organization conducts applied research for government and industry. In Great Britain it is known as the Department of Scientific and Industrial Research and promotes research institutes associated with specific industries. In India and South Africa it is the Council for Scientific and Industrial Research, and in Australia it is the Commonwealth Scientific and Industrial Research Organization. These agencies, in some instances, relieve the universities of much technological research and permit them to devote a greater proportion of their time to fundamental problems. In the United States non-university research institutes perform a similar purpose, but they bear a relatively small share of the burden of technological research as compared with the Commonwealth research institutes.

THE RISE OF THE GENERAL EDUCATION MOVEMENT

From 1920 to 1930 student enrollments in colleges and universities in the United States almost doubled, increasing in round figures from 598,000 to 1,100,000. This brought with it problems of many kinds. Basic education became diluted as the elective system reached its peak. The fragmentary nature of the knowledge gained by students under the system became evident. The need for depth as well as breadth began to be emphasized early in the decade. To supply this need, major and minor requirements for the Bachelor's degree developed in the colleges. Elective courses of the widest variety still made up most of the first two years. Gradually the need for a core curriculum in the first two years which would acquaint students with the three broad fields of knowledge in humanities, social sciences, and natural sciences—came to be recognized. This gave rise to survey courses.

There was general recognition of the inadequacy of programs, such as the one-year course in a single science as a means of enabling the student to understand the meaning of science and its relation to the other fields of knowledge. But substituting survey courses did not prove satisfactory. They were superficial, covering many subjects but making no vital connection with any. These were largely abandoned after a few years and replaced by inter-departmental courses. Gradually the term *general education* came to be used to describe the kind of program that should be provided all students—the essentials of a well-rounded education.

General education is not simply another name for *liberal education* and it is more than a re-interpretation of liberal education in the framework of the twentieth century. General education seeks to provide a more thorough knowledge and a deeper understanding of man and his society than was comprehended in the traditional college program. The general education movement has not yet realized its full potential. It will require decades to achieve it, for its goals represent revolutionary changes in content and method in undergraduate instruction.

The developments of the twentieth century require a more realistic consideration of the facts of modern life, including the social changes imposed by an advancing science and technology. The reasons for its particular relevance in these times, as the Harvard report suggested, is "the staggering expansion of knowledge produced largely by specialism and certainly conducing to it; the concurrent and hardly less staggering growth of our educational system, with its maze of stages, functions and kinds of instruction; and not the least, the ever-growing complexity of society itself."[6]

The team of educators from India who spent some months in the United States in 1956, investigating programs in several institutions, stated the purposes of general education in slightly different terms: "It is education of the student for life in his times and as such an essential supplement of education for earning a living. General education," according to their report,

seeks to jettison the ballast of inert ideas or knowledge as urged by Whitehead, or views education as an aspect of human activity thus endeavoring to link it with life as suggested by Dewey or seeks to restore transmission of culture as an essential function of the university, thus helping it to escape the consequences of producing "civilised barbarians" against whom Ortega protested.[7]

Such considerations as these have never been prominent in the conventional liberal education program. Perhaps the distinguishing characteristic of "general" education lies in its realistic, objective and conscious approach to the problem of relating education to life. Its major purposes may be summarized as follows:

1. To remedy the lack of balance resulting from specialization, which fails to provide the science student with an understanding of the broad issues underlying the social, economic and cultural life of his time.

2. To insure that the specialist has sufficient social understanding to make him willing to face the responsibilities of decision-making and effective in discharging them.

3. To provide the student with an understanding and appreciation of his heritage and with a sense of values that will fit him for meeting the obligations of common citizenship.

What place this new program of education will ultimately be accorded in the history of higher education cannot be predicted. However, in view of the goals that it seeks and the considerable progress that has been made toward realizing them, it seems safe to list it as one of the significant movements of the twentieth century, and as one likely to play an increasingly important role in educational thinking and planning in the second half of this century.

THE ESTABLISHMENT AND GROWTH OF THE JUNIOR COLLEGE

Two junior colleges were established in Illinois before the end of the nineteenth century, Lewis Institute in Chicago, now the Illinois Institute of Technology, and Bradley Polytechnic Institute in Peoria, now Bradley University. Both of these owed their founding largely to the interest of President Rainey

Harper of the University of Chicago. His encouragement of the school board at Joliet, Illinois, to establish a junior college in connection with its public school system was another of his contributions to the junior college movement. The Joliet Junior College (1902) was the first permanent public junior college to be established in the United States. From these small beginnings sprang one of the remarkable developments in American higher education. About 600 junior colleges enrolled more than 600,000 students in 1956.

There are two types of two-year colleges: (1) the community college, which serves primarily the community in which it is located, and (2) the special junior college, which provides instruction in a limited number of fields. The earlier junior colleges were in many cases the first two years of a four-year program. They now tend more toward courses that are terminal in character, with emphasis upon community needs. A listing of their functions will indicate the variety of objectives which they serve.

1. They lift the economic barriers to college education for vast numbers of youth who otherwise would be deprived of the opportunity. The major cost of higher education is living away from home. A college in the community obviates that cost.

2. In the next decade the demands on higher education will be overwhelming. The community colleges will have a special service to render in helping to absorb many that cannot be accommodated by the older institutions. Among these will be many who can profit more from the two-year than from the four-year college program. Likewise students who are late "bloomers," or for other reasons have poor secondary school records, will have a chance to retrieve lost opportunities by satisfactory achievement in the local college.

3. The community college, through training young people for service in local industries, can provide a better community understanding of science and technology and the role which they play in modern society.

4. Adult education is one of the significant functions of the modern community college. An instructive illustration is found in Modesto, California. Its Junior College reported in one year an enrollment of a third of the adult population of that community.

5. Changes resulting from the growing responsibility of America and Americans in the international community require a new emphasis on international understanding. The adult comuity leaders, in particular, need an opportunity to keep abreast of what is taking place in other lands that affect their lives. The university extension programs can assist in this task, but the community college also has an important role to play in this special phase of adult education.

The scope of service of the junior, or community, college is tremendous. It is illustrated by the example of Long Beach City College in California. In 1954–1955 it enrolled 39,915 students, 15,960 of whom were taking traditional freshman and sophomore courses, while 23,955 were taking special courses designed to meet the widest variety of needs. Among these were some who were doing part-time work while studying, and others who were taking courses while carrying full-time jobs.

In the realization of its several purposes the junior college is making notable contributions to social progress. The fact that its growth has been more rapid in this century than any other phase of higher education is evidence that it is meeting essential needs. There is little doubt that history will rank the rise of the junior college among the significant developments in American higher education.

Conclusion

This sketch of American developments is designed to provide some understanding of the backgrounds of the largest and most complex system of higher education in the world. In 1956 it comprised 1,855 institutions, each a center of initiative relatively unhampered by outside controls. American colleges and universities are free to experiment, to adopt their own goals, curricula and methods. This accounts for the vitality of the system and for the variety of its offerings. It is both an element of its strength and the source of its weakness. In allowing freedom, it permits trivial and inappropriate subject matter and thus contributes to the chaos which prevails. On the other hand, through the historic use of the trial and error method, some of the most important contributions to the philosophy and practice of higher education have been made. The land-grant college program, the general education movement, the modern university development and the junior college system are examples.

The demands of the next decade or two will require still further experimentation. Enrollments aggregating more than three million in 1958 will climb to six million by 1975, according to current estimates. New curricula and new methods will be required to meet new needs as the ratio of college students to the total population continues to rise. The flexibility of the American system, the traditional use of the experimental method and the experience of American educators in developing new programs will be assets of first importance in meeting the crisis that lies ahead.

IV

The Nature and Aims of Higher Education

✦❮❰

The roots of higher education in the British Commonwealth and the United States may be traced to the ancient English universities. In Scotland the influence of Bologna and other continental universities is also apparent in university organization, but the ideals of scholarship and of the higher learning of Oxford and Cambridge have prevailed. The patterns that developed outside Great Britain in some cases bear little resemblance to their original models, but to understand them it is important to remember their common ancestry.

This chapter is concerned with the nature and purposes of the programs that are now found in the several parts of the Commonwealth and in the United States, and with their interactions in the course of their development. More important than these interactions is the influence of developments outside the universities which have impinged upon them. The increase in knowledge and in society's needs has required expansion in the curriculum, and this in turn has resulted in problems of various types. This chapter will also deal with the nature of these problems and the efforts made to solve them.

Throughout the English-speaking world there is great concern over the role of the university in these times. The comfortable ideal of a century ago will not suffice. In his *Higher Learning in Britain* (1955) Professor Kneller observed that "nowhere in British intellectual life is more soul-searching taking place than within the confines of the universities."[1] In the United States greater ferment and more widespread dissatisfaction with higher education have prevailed since 1945 than in any previous decade in its history. The nature of the program that should be developed in the new universities of India, and in the older ones as well, is a matter of vast concern, not only to educators but to the leaders in government as well. A commission, including representatives from England, has recently made a study of the universities of Australia at the request of the Commonwealth Government. Its recommendations, which have been applauded by the educators, have been accepted by the government and are now being implemented. Some of the reasons for the discontent with higher education among English-speaking peoples may be revealed in the pages that follow.

Learning for Learning's Sake

Professor Kneller[2] makes the point that this ideal did not originate in the medieval university as is generally assumed. For some centuries students gathered at the centers of learning to improve their professional status. They were not motivated by the abstract ideal of learning for its own sake, any more, perhaps, than their successors in modern times. In the early centuries the universities were tied in closely with the religious, political and cultural life of their times. They recognized their obligation to serve society perhaps as clearly as modern universities, though the framework within which they worked was different because the goals of society were different. The salvation of man was the conscious goal of social institutions and social endeavor. The universities were dedicated to the pursuit of that goal. They were not so concerned about acquisition of knowledge as about the development of rational thought proceeding from given hypotheses. When the objectives of society changed, the methods and purposes, along with the content of the curriculum, were modified to conform. Thus the difference between the medieval and modern university derives chiefly from the fundamental difference in the spirit of medieval and modern thinking, outlook and aspiration.

It was the institutions of the seventeenth and eighteenth centuries that developed the concept of learning for its own sake. In this period they passed from church to state control, and the new master was afraid of the new knowledge which threatened the social order following the Renaissance. University expansion in Britain practically ceased for more than two centuries, and those institutions already established were dominated by secular authorities who were concerned with maintaining social discipline. They required licenses for school masters, sought out possible heretics in the church, and inspected textbooks to insure against aberrations from accepted moral virtues. This attitude on the part of the state resulted in the universities concerning themselves with inherited knowledge rather than attempting to extend its frontiers. Thomas Hobbes declared that state security required universities to be supervised. It was in this atmosphere that the conception of "learning for learning's sake" found expression.

In practice this ideal has never been prominent as a working principle of the university. It represents the spirit of the true scholar, and insofar as the academic atmosphere contributes to the development of scholars the ideal may be thought of as a goal of the university. It is not, however, in conflict with training for a profession. Indeed, the classical curriculum was itself designed as preparation for the learned professions. Whatever one's activity, the love of learning for its own sake is a chief asset, hence education for vocations and professions, as well as for scholarship, should be dominated by that attitude.

These facts should be borne in mind as we examine the nature and aims of higher education. Otherwise when one discovers the vast array of professions and vocations for which universities provide preparation today, he may conclude that the character of true university education has been lost. If it has been lost, it is not because it seeks to serve utilitarian purposes but because the spirit of scholarship has ceased to dominate instruction.

Some courses are more stimulating to the imagination and to the desire for knowledge than others. Also when the immediate goal is preparation for some useful work, it may be more difficult to stimulate the intellectual interests of the student because of preoccupation with what is the *most* useful information from the standpoint of the job in prospect. There are, too, occupations for which university education is not required. Whenever training for such occupations is attempted at the university level, it results in a distortion of the character of education. In the examination of the nature and aims of higher education these facts are important, for whether or not the spirit of learning is more, or less, prominent now than it was in earlier periods depends not so much upon the changes in the curriculum as upon the nature and aims of the instruction. Likewise, discrimination is essential in the choice of vocations for which college courses are designed to prepare.

While vocational objectives may be distracting to the learner and retard his intellectual growth, they are not the only offenders. When passing final examinations becomes a major consideration of the students and attention is focused on that as the chief purpose of study, the results may be equally distracting. Or again, if the accumulation of credits becomes the obsession of the student, he may acquire a degree but not real education.

Expansion of the Curriculum

The most striking change in higher education in the past century is the growth of the curriculum. The seven subjects embodied in the trivium and quadrivium which prevailed in the middle ages have given way to offerings numbering a hundred times seven, and the end is not yet. A single example will illustrate. Natural philosophy, one subject in the curriculum a century ago, has evolved into the natural sciences, biology, botany, zoology, chemistry, physics, geology, biophysics, biochemistry, physical chemistry, geophysics and a wide variety of technological subjects that are based on these sciences. Not only has the increase in knowledge contributed to curriculum expansion, but specialization has multiplied the areas of investigation and study. The technologies which stem from the sciences represent in the main the demands of society for useful applications of scientific knowledge. With the progress of science and technology continued expansion is inevitable unless some new criteria for selection of subject matter should evolve.

To make explicit the variety and complexity of curricula in the English-speaking world it will suffice to cite examples of the offerings found in the calendars of representative universities in the Commonwealth countries and in the United States. In the United Kingdom the University of Manchester is reasonably typical of the full-grown civic institutions. It is located in a large center and is in its seventy-eighth year as a university. It is more complex than many of the younger institutions of this group, but it may be thought of as representative of the objective toward which the younger universities are moving. An alphabetical listing of its offerings displays the pattern of instruction now in force:

Accounting, adult education, American studies, anatomy and histology, anthropology, Arabic, architecture, art, botany, chemistry, comparative literary studies, Coptic, crystallography, dentistry, economics, education, education of the deaf, Egyptology, engineering, electrical engineering, English language and literature, French studies, geography, geology, paleontology and petrology, German language and literature, government and administration, Hebrew, history, horticulture, Italian, law, linguistics, mathematics, mechanics of fluids, Mesopotamian studies, metallurgy and metallography, music, Near Eastern archeology, palaeography, Persian studies, philosophy, physics, physiology, psychology, romance philology, Russian studies, Scandinavian studies, Semitic studies, social anthropology, social studies, Spanish and Portuguese studies, technology, town and country planning, zoology.[3]

Under medicine, dentistry, engineering and theology an equally impressive array of topics for study are listed. As one scans the modern calendar or catalog it is difficult to see the forest for the trees. The complexity of the modern multipurpose curricula makes it hard to discern the underlying unity of the university.

The same impression results from an examination of the postgraduate offerings. The University of Calcutta furnishes an example. It is an affiliating institution with college councils that conduct postgraduate education in arts, commerce, law, science and technology. In addition, the central university provides postgraduate programs in the following:

English, Sanskrit, Pali, Arabic, Persian, Hebrew, Syriac, Greek, Latin, French, German, Bengali, Modern Indian language other than Bengali, comparative philology, mental and moral philosophy, history (including ancient Indian history and culture and Islamic history and culture), economics, political science, commerce, mathematics (pure and applied), physics (pure and applied), chemistry (pure and applied), physiology, botany, geology, zoology and comparative anatomy, psychology and applied psychology, anthropology, statistics, geography, radio-physics and electronics, education and law.[4]

The University of Sydney, the oldest and largest institution in Australia, will serve to illustrate the breadth of the interests of higher education in the Antipodes. Its calendar indicates the variety of its instruction. It lists the following:

Agriculture, anatomy, anthropology, archaeology, architecture, biochemistry, botany, chemistry, divinity, economics, education, engineering, English, forestry, French, geography, geology, German, Greek, history, Italian, Latin, law, mathematics, medicine, mining, music, Oriental studies, pharmacology, pharmacy, philosophy, physics, physiology, psychology, Semitic studies, social work, veterinary science, zoology, dentistry, ceramics, dental anatomy and dental histology, dental bacteriology, dental jurisprudence, dental materia medica and therapeutics, dental pathology, nutrition, operative dentistry, orthodontia, periodontia, preventive dentistry, prosthetic dentistry, ecclesiastical history, New Testament language and literature, Old Testament language and literature, philosophical and historical theology, aeronautical, chemical, civil, electrical, mechanical and mining engineering, bankruptcy, common law, company law, constitutional law, contracts, conveyancing, criminal law, divorce and domestic relations, equity law, industrial law, international law and jurisprudence, introductory jurisprudence, legal ethics, legal interpretation, lunacy law, mercantile law, pleading, procedure, property, Roman law, succession and admiralty, anaesthetics, bacteriology, child health, diseases of ear, nose, throat, diseases of the skin, embryology, gynaecology, gynaecology (clinical), histology and embryology, infectious diseases, medical ethics, medical jurisprudence, medicine, medicine (clinical), newborn (care of), obstetrics, obstetrics (clinical), ophthalmology, pathology, preventive medicine, psychiatry, surgery, surgery (clinical), tropical medicine and tutorial classes.[5]

In the United States some of the larger universities, both public and private, present even longer lists of offerings than their counterparts in the British Commonwealth. A listing of the special degree curricula as represented by the different kinds of degrees awarded in some 1,900 institutions will provide perhaps the best picture of the American program of higher education. The American colleges and universities award 227 different undergraduate degrees, 123 Masters' and sixty-nine Doctorates. They offer organized curricula designed to prepare for twenty-three professions. In addition a variety of courses in the community colleges is given as preparation for a host of vocations. There are five junior college degrees: A.A. (Associate in Arts); A.A.S. (Associate in Applied Science); A.Ed. (Associate in Education); A.F.A. (Associate in Fine Arts); and A.S. (Associate in Science).[6]

In the light of this great welter of courses, two questions constantly arise. Are universities justified in developing courses of study in such specialized areas as are represented by the offerings on both the undergraduate and graduate levels? Could not the quality of education be improved if there were a grouping of subject matter and a division of labor between the universities? Why should each university provide instruction in all fields whether or not there is sufficient demand to warrant it? When six Faculties of Forestry produce no more than twenty-five graduates annually, why shouldn't the six be reduced to one? Eight Mining Faculties in English universities over the past several years have together averaged about twenty graduates per year. If all these students were concentrated in one university, they would probably receive a better education at a fraction of the cost required to maintain eight faculties. Duplication of effort and the multiplication of specialized curricula in the English-speaking world are serious problems, the solution of which will require a high order of educational statesmanship.

In the United States recent efforts at eliminating unnecessary duplication have resulted in the formation of compacts between the states in three regions, the South, the Midwest and New England, whereby a division of labor is effected. The Southern Regional Education Board, the oldest of the three, comprises fourteen states. Medicine, veterinary medicine and social work are among the educational programs maintained on a regional basis. For example, a state which has no School of Veterinary Medicine sends its students to an institution in another state which has this program, paying not only the out-of-state tuition for the student but an additional sum to defray the cost of instruction, which is always more than the tuition charge. In this way great economies are effected.

The civic universities in Britain, and some institutions in other Commonwealth countries, have developed specialties which are not found in other universities in their respective areas, but this does not hold with respect to the well-established fields. For example, agriculture is taught in fifteen universities and in five non-university centers; archaeology in thirteen universities; architecture degree courses in nine universities, and diploma examination courses in eleven; medicine in all except five universities in the United Kingdom, and mining and mining engineering curricula in nine universities. Eight other non-university institutions, such as technical colleges, provide instruction in the same fields. This type of duplication is found in every Commonwealth country, and the United States is not without similar examples. Closer scrutiny of the organization of subject matter, and a reasonable division of labor among the institutions to the end that unnecessary duplication is eliminated, are much-needed reforms.

Basic Postgraduate and Professional Education

The universities of the English-speaking countries provide three types of education: basic education, postgraduate work in a variety of fields, and professional education, both on the undergraduate and graduate levels. In the United States the College of Arts and Sciences is the division of the university which provides the general studies program. As the name indicates, this college requires work in both the arts and the sciences for the first degree.

In England, South Africa, Australia, India and Pakistan the undergraduate degree of Bachelor of Arts normally is given for courses only in arts subjects. In some instances optional courses in sciences are available, but apparently are not usually taken by the arts students.

The Bachelor of Science degree in both pure and applied science fields likewise has no provision for courses in history, literature and philosophy.

In American and Canadian Universities both arts and science students must have general courses designed to give them an understanding of their heritage, of the social forces at work in their society, and of the role of science and technology in the modern world. By the same token students taking certificates for teaching or the Commerce Degree will be taking 30 to 40 per cent of their work in the Arts and Science College. Even in Engineering and Applied Science Faculties students are usually required to devote 15 to 20 per cent of their time to humanistic-social studies.

A marked difference between British and American patterns is in the humanistic-social studies requirement in scientific, technological and professional curricula in American Universities. This is absent in most of the Commonwealth countries.

The emphasis upon professional education in the English-speaking countries is a characteristic development of the twentieth century. Though the arts college in most institutions is the largest single division of the university, the scientific, technological and professional faculties usually attract more students. For example, in England, excluding Oxford and Cambridge, according to the *Commonwealth Universities Yearbook* for 1956, arts faculties enrolled 16,947 students, whereas science (including technology), medicine and commerce attracted 32,696 students in 1956. In Wales comparable figures were 2,169 and 2,697; in Scotland 5,057 and 8,791; in Belfast 656 and 909; in Australia 9,455 and 11,031; and in South Africa 6,099 and 9,473. Only in India and in Canada did arts college students appear to outnumber those in the scientific and professional fields.

In the United States the B.A. originally outnumbered all other Bachelor's degrees, but this is no longer true. The B.S. degree is now more popular. However, the arts college provides courses for students not only in the science degree courses but in engineering, commerce, education and other professional fields. In a multi-purpose state university of about 8,500 students in the 1956–1957 session, the arts college faculty did slightly more than one-half the teaching in all undergraduate courses.

Degrees and Their Curricula

There is great confusion in the meaning of the several degrees awarded in the universities in the English-speaking world. The B.A. degree in the United States represents two years of general studies, followed by an additional two years which include some concentration in one or two fields, whereas in the British Commonwealth countries the B.A. may be taken in one, in two, or in three subjects. Even more confusion exists with respect to the M.A. degree. At Bristol and Liverpool it normally requires a thesis and at least two years of advanced work under direction. At Birmingham and Manchester it may mean, under certain conditions, no more than one year spent in advanced studies. At Glasgow or Edinburgh it is the first degree, corresponding roughly to the Bachelor of Arts in the English university. At Oxford and Cambridge it denotes neither advanced study nor examination, but simply that the B.A. graduate has paid certain fees to his college and to the university and has received his Bachelor of Arts some two to three years earlier. In Australia and New Zealand the M.A. denotes one to two years' work beyond the B.A. This is true, also, in the United States, South Africa, Canada, India and Pakistan. A still further complication is the fact that in Scotland only three years are required for the ordinary M.A., but four years for the M.A. with honors. In Canada, South Africa, Australia and New Zealand, and in some Indian universities, the B.A. requires three or four years, whereas the B.A. with honors requires an additional year.

In addition to the degrees which are awarded after three or four years' attendance at the university, there are degrees awarded through the external examination plan, which require no attendance. This is true of the University of London and of the University of South Africa. Some institutions also in Australia and New Zealand have such a plan.

In the United States there are no honors or pass degrees, though in some universities a degree cum laude, magna cum laude or summa cum laude is awarded. These distinctions are based upon the quality of work and not upon the character of the course pursued. While degrees "with honors" are conferred by all Commonwealth universities, there is great variation in the several countries with respect to student interest in pursuing honors work.

At Oxford and Cambridge most students pursue honors degrees; indeed, the pass degree has become almost obsolete. On the other hand, in Australia practically everyone takes the pass degree, and very few go in for honors. In New Zealand there are no Bachelor of Arts programs which give an honors degree, save in one subject in one of the constituent universities.

On the other hand, first and second honors are given in the Masters' degrees awarded by the University of New Zealand in addition to the ordinary M.A. At Oxford and Cambridge the mode is special honors, with a student taking only one subject for the three-year period, whereas in the provincial universities the pattern usually is general honors, involving two or three subjects.

Requirements for the several degrees vary in the different countries. In the University of Liverpool, which is perhaps typical of the civic universities (p. 224, 1956–1957 calendar), the Bachelor of Arts in general studies requires nine courses. A subject taken for two or three years counts as two or three courses. One subject at least shall be studied for three years, and another for two years. Candidates who shall have attained a sufficient standard in the subject so studied and in the examination as a whole shall receive the degree with honors in general studies.

In Scotland the curriculum for the ordinary degree consists of five subjects, two of which must be studied for two full years.

The degree examinations on these two subjects must be of higher standard than the examinations in the other three subjects. A full course consists of not less than seventy-five meetings of the whole class on separate days, with additional meetings for tutorials or other supplementary instruction.

In Canada students entering the university on junior matriculation, corresponding normally to the termination of grade eleven, must have four years in order to complete degree requirements, while those who have a twelfth year (or thirteenth in Ontario and British Columbia), and have attained senior matriculation, may complete the degree in three years. The M.A. requires normally one year beyond the Bachelor's degree.

In Australia nine qualifying courses are required for the pass B.A. degree. They must include either three subjects studied in three consecutive years, or some combination in which one or more subjects are pursued two or three years. The B.A. *with honors* is a four-year program. The M.A., pass or honors degree, requires normally one year beyond the B.A.

In South Africa ten courses are required for the B.A. pass degree. The honors B.A. requires an additional year. The honors B.A., or its equivalent, is necessary for admission to the M.A. program. The Master of Arts degree requires one to two years beyond the honors Bachelor's degree.

In New Zealand nine units (year courses) are required for the Bachelor of Arts degree. The Master of Arts usually requires a minimum of one year beyond the B.A. A candidate must take an examination in one or more of the subjects and, in some cases, present a thesis. When a thesis is required, the combined results of the written examination and the thesis will be the basis on which the candidate is judged. The M.A. may be a first or second honors, or a pass degree.

In India the undergraduate program in the university is ordinarily four years in length. At the end of two years there is an intermediate examination. One who has successfully passed this examination may proceed to the Bachelor's degree, which usually requires two additional years. The successful candidate obtains a pass or an honors degree, according to the courses taken or the marks obtained. Some universities, in addition to the two-year courses, provide separate honors courses requiring three years beyond the intermediate examination. The Master's degree is usually awarded for one or two years of study beyond the Bachelor's.

In the Universities of Annamalai, Andhra, Madras and Kerala (formerly Travancore) honors graduates in arts and science who obtain their honors degrees after three years' study may be awarded an M.A., after a lapse of time, without further examination, following the plan at Oxford and Cambridge.

Aims of Liberal Education

The role of the liberal arts appears to be conceived differently in the United States and in the United Kingdom, and hence also its purposes. This could perhaps be best illustrated by quoting from two distinguished sources.

President Griswold of Yale, in his little book entitled *In the University Tradition* (1958), says:

They (the liberal arts) are not a body of revealed truth or logical absolutes or a quantum of knowledge. They are studies designed to develop to capacity the intellectual and spiritual powers of the in- dividual. Their aim is to make the most of a man, in order that he may make the most of his calling, his cultural opportunities, and his responsibilities as a citizen. Such was the meaning of the liberal arts in Plato's time, and such is it today.[7]

In commenting on the general courses provided in the British universities, the UGC Report (1958) on University Develop- ment, 1952–1957, reads as follows:

The fact that many of the subjects grouped together under the rather misleading title of "arts" have an immediate vocational utility only for the intending teacher or scholar may cause their value for other students to be called in question. These subjects, however, are concerned with man as a thinking and social being, and such subjects cannot but be of great importance at a time when the constant advance of science and its application creates ever more pressing problems in the social and political field. On the other hand, the importance of these subjects is not a sufficient reason for a great increase in the number of undergraduates studying them.

Further on it says:

we think it important that University departments, in deciding whether to admit a student for a course in a subject which he does not propose to apply vocationally, should consider with particular care whether his response to the course is likely to be such as to justify the cost of his university education.[8]

The broad difference between the institutions in the Commonwealth and the United States may be summed up by saying that in the former, the aim seems to be to produce a scholar, a kind of specialist in one or two fields of study, whereas, in the latter, breadth and balance in scholarship is the goal. In the special honors programs a single subject is covered intensively; whereas, general honors, which combine two or three subjects, correspond more nearly to the American pattern. The Scottish university plan is not far different from the general honors pattern so far as the subjects covered are concerned.

In recent years dissatisfaction with the courses, methods and purposes of the undergraduate program is a characteristic of universities in both the Commonwealth and the United States. In Britain a host of critics, Moberly, Livingstone, Baillie, Truscot and others, have found educational results disappointing. In the United States the general education movement represents a widespread discontent. Neither aims nor methods have proved satisfactory. Both are confused and unsatisfying.

Moberly, for instance, diagnosed the difficulty in the modern university as follows: "Most students go through our universities without ever having been forced to exercise their minds on the issues which are really momentous. Under the guise of academic neutrality they are subtly condemned to unthinking acquiescence in the social and political *status quo* and in the secularism on which they have never seriously reflected."[9]

Sir Richard Livingstone suggests that higher education is ineffective when it fails to give the student "a philosophy of life, however provisional; a definite view of the ends to which it should be directed, and of the principles by which it should be ruled; a clear idea of good and bad in conduct."[10]

Bruce Truscot said: "We must try to clarify in the undergraduate's mind the concept of general culture, and to urge upon him the adoption of a definite policy of self-education. Dilettantism must be vigorously deprecated and its deleterious effects made plain. . . ."[11]

Mr. Baillie concludes that "never in any culture has intellectual life so much lacked a sense of direction as in the Western world during the last several generations."[12]

Educational Experiments—England, Australia, India and the United States

ENGLAND

The most notable innovation undertaken in England during the past decade is the North Staffordshire University College, established by Royal Charter in 1949. Its novel feature, and one of its chief purposes, is to impart to both science and arts students an understanding of the fundamental concepts of the humanities and of the sciences. It is authorized to grant the degree of Bachelor of Arts. It has a Court, Council and Senate, with the usual powers and duties found in other English universities. In addition it has an academic council which is composed mainly of representatives from the universities of Oxford, Manchester and Birmingham, whose responsibility is to approve all matters of academic importance.

Lord Lindsay, who for many years had been master of Balliol College, Oxford, and before that was at Glasgow University, designed the College. His long experience had suggested certain weaknesses in the traditional program of British universities which he sought to avoid in the new institution. The significance of the experiment is enhanced by this fact.

This institution has a four-year instead of the three-year curriculum common in British universities. Another special feature is the fact that the first of the four years is compulsory and identical for all students. Tutorial work is given to provide for individual needs, but the course is common for all first-year students. It is concerned with "Man and His Environment," the "Heritage of Western Civilization," and the "Industrialized Society." It deals particularly with the methods and influence of the experimental sciences on our culture.

In the last three years at least four subjects must be taken, and these must include one from the humanities and social sciences, and at least one from the natural sciences. Two of the four subjects must be studied throughout the whole of the three years. The entire four-year program is an integrated whole designed to provide a balanced educational menu. If the work of the student shows sufficient merit, the degree of Bachelor of Arts *with honors* is awarded. There appears to be genuine interest in this experimental program on the part of faculty members in other universities of Great Britain. The general attitude is one of approval of the project. It should be stated, however, that it is not considered of such merit or importance as to influence the programs of the older institutions in the United Kingdom.

AUSTRALIA

The Australian National University at Canberra is worthy of special mention. It is the only university in the English-speaking world devoted exclusively to graduate and research work. It has research schools in medicine, physics, the social sciences and Pacific studies. It is little more than ten years old, but has already demonstrated considerable potentialities.

This institution has moved slowly in order to make certain that it would not antagonize unduly the older institutions. Even so, one hears comments to the effect that the funds spent on this institution might have served a better purpose if divided among the older universities. Though such a point of view is natural, it does not seem to be warranted.

It seems to have the possibilities of developing a research center of a high order and thus be able to attract capable scholars from other parts of the world who would otherwise not be available in Australia. If this proves to be true, it would then be in a position in time to draw the most promising scholars from other Australian universities and thus develop a center of learning on that continent. Though in time it may prove to be advantageous to establish an undergraduate alongside the graduate program, it would nevertheless seem wise for it to have begun as a research institution. Recent legislation has authorized National University to incorporate Canberra University College but it has not seen fit to exercise that authority.

INDIA

Two programs in India are worthy of mention. The Shreemati Nathibai Damodar Thackersey Women's University is the only degree-granting university in the Commonwealth exclusively for women. It was modeled on the Women's University of Tokyo.

There are two special features borrowed from the Japanese institution worthy of note in the program of this university. In the first place the curriculum is built on the philosophy that courses of study for women should be different from those for men, because they play different roles in the life of the community. The medium of instruction is the vernacular. It is the only Indian university in which instruction is wholly in a language other than English.

There are both degree and diploma courses. The Bachelor of Arts degree, requiring three years, is built around home science, including elementary biology and hygiene; home making; home management and cookery; food and nutrition; physiology; psychology and child psychology. All these subjects are compulsory, that is, must be taken by all students. Ethics, philosophy, music, drawing and painting are optional.

In addition to the B.A., there is an ordinary and an honors B.Sc. degree in nursing, the one pursued for three years and the other for four years. In the nursing program the theoretical work is carried on in the university, while the practical demonstrations and training are conducted at a Bombay hospital.

Postgraduate courses leading to the degrees of Master of Arts, Bachelor of Teaching and Master of Education are provided. In addition to the Bachelors' and advanced degrees, a diploma course in home science has been introduced. It is planned to establish a full degree course in this subject.

The second experimental university program in India is that of Visva-Bharati. It grew out of an experimental school started by Rabindranath Tagore in 1901. It was raised to university status in 1951. The institution is designed to serve all of India, and draws students and teachers from abroad as well. All the colleges and institutions affiliated with the University are coeducational and residential.

In view of the unusual character of this institution, it may be well to state the aims as set out in the *Commonwealth Universities Yearbook,* 1957:

The aims of the University are to study the mind of man in its realization of different aspects of truth from diverse points of view; to bring into closer relationship with one another through study and research, the different cultures of the East on the basis of their underlying unity; to approach the West from the standpoint of such a unity of the life and thought of Asia; to seek to realize in a common fellowship of study the meeting of the East and the West and thus ultimately to strengthen the fundamental conditions of world peace through the establishment of free communication of ideas between the two hemispheres; and with such ideals in view, to provide at Santineketan a cultural center where research into and study of the religions, literature, history, science and art of Hindu, Buddhist, Jain, Islamic, Christian and other civilizations, may be pursued along with the culture of the West, with that simplicity in externals which is necessary for true spiritual realization, in amity, good fellowship and cooperation between the thinkers and scholars of both Eastern and Western countries, free from all antagonism of race, nationality, creed or caste.

Besides the academic programs, Visva-Bharati has two departments: (1) Rural Reconstruction and (2) publication of books of educational and cultural interests. The rural reconstruction project provides for a comprehensive study of the problems of rural life in all its aspects, social, cultural, economic, etc. A rural institute of higher education is being gradually developed in connection with this program.

THE UNITED STATES

In Chapter III attention was called to the importance of the general education movement. While this will not be repeated here, it is relevant to describe a recent development in the field of general education which has considerable significance.

Chicago, Columbia, Harvard and Yale, with substantial foundation help, have administered for several years a program of internships in general education. Brown University was added to the program in 1955. Each selected three younger professors from other institutions and invited them to spend a year on their campuses studying their programs of general education and participating in the instruction. The grant was sufficient to provide not only full salaries but an additional sum to cover the cost of living away from home. Several assistant professors from all sections of the country have spent a year each studying the program and the possibilities of adapting it to their respective institutions.

Each year the interns, along with members of the teaching staffs of their institutions, have met for several days to consider together the problems of curriculum and methods, the differences in approaches in the four institutions involved, and the ways in which the several programs might be improved.

For five years President James B. Conant conducted an experimental course on the teaching of science to non-science majors. This program was built around the notion that if students could know something of the ways in which the great discoveries had been made, they would sense the importance not only of science, but of scientific method. This was another approach to general education in a limited field through a single experimental course. The fact that it was conducted by the President of Harvard, formerly a leading scientist, enhanced its significance.

Four of the ranking technological institutions of the country, Massachusetts Institute of Technology, Case Institute, Carnegie Institute and California Institute of Technology, conducted five-year experiments designed to develop more adequate courses in the humanistic-social areas for technology students. Those efforts were concerned not only with the curriculum, but with methods of teaching the subject matter in the humanities and social sciences.

These programs ran concurrently and elicited unusual faculty interest. They were motivated by a deep concern that the students should have a vital contact with the basic studies. The faculties believed that students of science and technology must be given an opportunity to acquire some understanding of the concepts underlying the humanistic-social disciplines if they were to achieve effective careers in their chosen fields.

Efforts in the United States have also been directed toward strengthening professional education. Since 1950, studies in medical, dental, legal, nursing, pharmaceutical and theological education have been conducted by the relevant professional associations. These efforts have resulted in significant reforms in the standards and in the content and methods of instruction in these several fields. The focus has been on *education* rather than training, on individual growth rather than professional skill.

One of the boldest experiments in the history of medical education has been in progress in Western Reserve University since 1948. It involves drastic changes, not only in curriculum but in methods. One of its chief purposes is to integrate subject matter in the basic sciences with that in the clinical fields, and at the same time to develop better integration of subject matter, laboratory experience and clinical activities. Back of this program has been the conviction that the traditional education in medicine has often been but a collection of disjointed parts, whereas it could and should be an integrated whole. Even though excellent training may be given in the basic science classrooms, in the laboratories, and in the clinics, the result may be far from satisfactory if the relation between these three activities is not made real to the student.

Though this experiment has been in progress for several years, its success or failure will not be readily determined. There is little doubt, however, that it will have many useful results, whether or not the program as a whole proves to be generally feasible.

Conclusion

It is clear from the foregoing discussion that the pattern of higher education in the universities of the English-speaking world is difficult to define. The variation in curriculum, in methods, in terminology, in degrees awarded, and in the conception of the function of higher education and of its role in society makes it doubly difficult.

The multiplicity and diversity of offerings is the most notable characteristic of modern university education. With the rapid expansion of knowledge and of social needs, the complexity of the program is likely to increase. Perhaps the time has come to take stock of the situation and to formulate criteria for the selection of subject matter. The distinction between education and training should be clarified. There should be a sharper focus on the aims of university education in all its phases and at all levels. It applies not only to basic education, usually provided for in the undergraduate program, but also to postgraduate and professional education as well. Greater clarity of aims, particularly in the field of basic education, is imperative before there can be a more discriminating selection of subject matter. The broad goal of professional education is clear, whether it be medicine, law, education, engineering or theology. It is to produce effective practitioners in these respective fields. Nonetheless, great diversity of views exists with respect to the best means of achieving this result. Likewise, in postgraduate education, the production of scholars, university teachers and research scientists is the broad objective, but views differ widely on the program best adapted to attain the objective.

In the field of basic education there is no common understanding with respect to the objectives to be sought. Thorough scholarship in a limited field, such as Oxford and Cambridge and other Commonwealth universities provide through the special honors program in a single subject, is a worthy purpose, but surely not the same purpose as that of the pass degree. The Scottish and civic university undergraduate programs and those of other Commonwealth countries contrast sharply with those of the American and Canadian colleges of arts and sciences.

Without commenting on the merits of the several programs found in the universities of the Commonwealth and of the United States, it may be useful, in concluding this chapter, to consider in some detail the historical and philosophical backgrounds of education as they are revealed in early societies. These considerations may provide a perspective for appraising the merits of the developments outlined in an earlier section of this chapter.

One of the original objectives of education was orientation of youth. In the puberty rites of primitive peoples, one of the aims is to acquaint youth with the traditions of the tribe, or clan, and with its ideals and aims. The ordeals by fire and water are designed, not merely to test the stamina of youth, but to teach him what his society expects of him. Likewise, the test of skills found in such rites not only indicates his achievements, but his abilities to make his way in the society into which he is entering as an adult.

This, in miniature, is a picture of what education is designed to accomplish in civilized society. Orientation of youth is provided through courses in history, literature and philosophy, those subjects which aid him in understanding his heritage. Likewise, social studies assist in adjustment to his society through giving him some knowledge of its motivations, of the social, economic and political currents and countercurrents which operate within it. Knowledge of nature and of man's relation to it, which science and technology provide, corresponds to the achievements in skills which enables the primitive to take his place as an adult member of his community.

The purpose of basic education, the orientation of youth to its environment, is of special importance in a highly specialized and industrialized society. While the market value of such education may not be demonstrable, its potential value in developing intelligent citizenship cannot be questioned. Much of the frustration in modern life results from the difficulty in understanding what is taking place, and in adjusting to the changes which our society is constantly undergoing. Unless the college graduates who, in the main, furnish the leadership, are able to interpret social change in terms of its cause and effect, even greater confusion may be anticipated.

The goal of university education is threefold: (1) to assist growth of the individual, his adjustment to his environment, the development of his intellectual powers and interests; (2) to prepare students for useful occupations or professions through assisting them in the acquisition of specialized knowledge and skills; and (3) to provide society with intelligent leaders and qualified workers in all those fields of endeavor, preparation for which requires higher education. If any one of these three purposes is neglected or overemphasized the program becomes unbalanced. For some centuries higher education was concerned chiefly with developing the faculties of the minds of the students. Gradually, professional education assumed greater and greater prominence in curricula until it is now the largest segment. Its incorporation into the university was originally primarily to meet the desires of students, and secondarily the needs of society. In recent years the needs of the state seem to be the primary motivation of governments in subsidizing the universities. This changing focus of interest has affected the nature and aims of university education in a variety of subtle ways, and will probably affect it still more profoundly in the future if educators fail to sense the dangers in present trends.

V

Organization of Higher Education

❖❧❧❧❧❧❧❧❧❧❧❧❧❧❧❧❧❧❧❧❧❧❧❧❧❧❧❧❧❧❧❧

University organization in the English-speaking world presents
a varied pattern. Throughout the British Commonwealth the
university may be an affiliating, a teaching or an examining
body, or it may combine all three functions. In Great Britain
most universities are unitary-teaching, though an outstanding
exception is the University of London, which has some seventy
federated and affiliated units. Elsewhere in the Commonwealth
one finds the three types of universities. Canada, Australia
and South Africa, for example, have affiliating and unitary-
teaching institutions. The University of South Africa, one of
the nine universities in that country, is only an examining body,
the only one of its type in the British Commonwealth. The
others are chiefly unitary-teaching and examining bodies. The
Universities of Wales and New Zealand are alike in the fact
that each is composed of four constituent colleges located in
different geographical areas. In both the university coordinates
and supervises the programs of the several institutions incorporated within it. In India most of the universities have
affiliated, constituent or "recognized" units. For example, the
University of Calcutta has 111 such units.

Traditionally the colleges and universities of the United
States have been single-campus institutions. Recently a new
pattern has been developing which involves a single control
for units within a given area. Twelve of the forty-eight states
now have boards of control governing all state tax-supported

85

institutions. These are Arizona, Florida, Georgia, Idaho, Iowa, Kansas, Mississippi, Montana, New York, Oregon, North Dakota and South Dakota. In three others a state board coordinates and controls, in some respects, the policies and practices of boards which have charge of individual institutions. These three states are New Mexico, North Carolina and Oklahoma. The board of trustees of the State University of New York, for example, has a total of forty-two units under its jurisdiction.

The effectiveness of the organization of higher education is measured first of all by its influence on the functioning of the university as a teaching and research agency. This is not, however, the sole criterion. It may also serve to interpret the university to its community and thus be a factor in stimulating interest and support. The effectiveness of a university program may be aided or hindered by the nature of its organization.

Boards of Control

The boards of control in different sections of the British Commonwealth employ different methods of operation. Even within Great Britain there is diversity of organization. In general the function and purpose are the same, but the details of organization vary. A few examples will illustrate.

The University of Bristol has a Court of Governors totaling 360, providing the widest representation. It includes the chief officers of the University; life members who have subscribed £1,000 or more; members appointed by various corporations, ranging in type from an Oxford College to a tobacco manufacturer; representatives of the city and its various interests, of county councils and county boroughs, of learned societies and professional organizations, and of Parliament. Members of the Court include also mayors, bishops, heads of nonconformist bodies, chairmen of county councils, chairmen of educational committees, chairmen of local hospital associations, heads of the leading schools in the counties, the University Council, the deans of faculty, professors and professors emeriti, the librarian, the registrar, twenty-five representatives of graduates, two representatives of the readers and lecturers, nominees of affiliated colleges and a small group appointed by the Council.[1]

Clearly, such an unwieldy group could not be effective in determining policy, but it may, on occasion, be useful in interpreting the role of the university, its needs and its problems, to the public. Though somewhat bewildering in size and diversity of membership, such a court has the merit of giving a large number an official connection, which carries with it some sense of responsibility as well as of belonging to the university. For the purpose of transacting business the number required for a quorum is twelve.

The active executive body of the civic university is the Council, with thirty to fifty members, most of whom are appointed by the Board of Governors and by local authorities. One-fifth to one-sixth of the whole is appointed by academic bodies. The fact that the academic members constitute so small a minority means that the founders thought the academic voice should not be dominant in determining matters of policy. The powers of the Council are tremendous. In essence, it has charge of the conduct of practically all the affairs of the university.

While the Council is the overall governing body, the Senate has jurisdiction over academic matters. There is always rivalry between the Council and the Senate. When a new vice-chancellor is being considered, the question is frequently raised as to whether he is a Council or a Senate man. Very few vice-chancellors succeed in being equally popular with both bodies.

The Court of the University of Wales is also widely representative. It includes the chief officials of the university, appointees of the Lord President of Council, of the county councils, county borough councils, the Courts of the constituent colleges, their Councils and their Senates, and of the Councils of other constituent colleges. The membership includes also the Senate and Council of the School of Medicine, the Association of Theological Colleges and Schools of Theology, the Guild of Graduates, the Students' Representative Council, the University Tutorial Classes, head teachers of secondary and elementary schools in Wales, etc., etc. The executive body of the University is the Council, and the academic board replaces the Senate, which is common in English institutions. This academic board is made up of the vice-chancellor, the principals of the constituent colleges, the provost of the School of Medicine, one representative from each faculty including new ones when established, and three elected members.[2]

The University of Glasgow, as representative of Scottish universities, has a Court, a General Council, and a Senatus Academicus. The Court is charged with administering the property and the revenue of the University and consists of the rector, the principal, Lord Provost of Glasgow; an assessor nominated by each of the following: the chancellor, the rector, the Lord Provost, Magistrate and Town Council of Glasgow; four assessors elected by the General Council; and four assessors elected by the Senatus Academicus.

The Senatus regulates and superintends all matters relating to teaching and discipline. It appoints two-thirds of the members of the Standing Committee on Libraries and Museums. It is composed of seventy-one members, one-third of whom constitutes a quorum.

The General Council (corresponding to the Court in English universities), on the other hand, consists of the chancellor, members of the University Court, and professors of the University, all ex-officio; Masters of Arts and those holding any degree awarded after an examination given by the University. A quorum of the General Council is ten for each 1,000 graduates, or fraction thereof, a total of more than 300 members. It elects the chancellor and four assessors, takes into consideration all questions affecting the well-being and prosperity of the University and makes representations to the Court. Ordinances, and changes in ordinances proposed by the Court, are to be submitted to the Council.[3]

In the civic universities there are three major bodies: the Court, the Council and the Senate. The supreme governing body is the Court, consisting of professors, representatives of graduates, heads of schools, persons nominated by the university, local authorities, educational organizations, religious denominations and learned societies. It is often composed of 300 to 400 members. The Council administers the finances of the university, confirms recommendations of the Senate for academic appointments, and authorizes academic regulations proposed by the Senate. In most universities it appoints the vice-chancellor. Though the Council is composed mainly of lay members, many are graduates of the university.

The Senate is subject to the powers of the Council. It approves and coordinates the work of the faculties. It is responsible for the teaching and discipline of the undergraduates. Under the constitution of University College of North Staffordshire, the Council may not make appointments, except on the recommendation of the Senate and the approval of the academic council.[4]

In contrast with these institutions the ancient universities of England have simplified their organizations. For instance, Oxford is governed by two bodies: (1) a congregation composed of Doctors and Masters in residence, and (2) The Executive Committee, which is called the Hebdomadal Council. Likewise, the University of Cambridge is governed by a Senate and an Executive Committee, called the Council of the Senate. The government at both Oxford and Cambridge evolved from the corporations or guilds of teachers and students. They have no lay members as the civic universities have.[5]

Bruce Truscot, in his *Red Brick University*, contrasts the methods of transacting business in the ancient universities with those in the civic universities. He says, if a professorship becomes vacant at either Oxford or Cambridge the appropriate body appoints a committee to make the selection. It meets and makes the appointment and the next day announces its action. At "Red Brick University," on the other hand, he says when a vacancy occurs the faculty board must first ask the Council to allow the chair to be filled, and then submit a comprehensive report from the faculty, which may be debated for weeks or months in the Senate. If the Council agrees in principle that the chair should be filled, the Senate or the faculty, or both, appoint a large selection committee made up of members of both the Council and Senate and of members from other faculties. The committee, after advertising, interviewing and making the selection, reports its findings to the faculty board and then to the Senate. If the faculty board and Senate approve, it goes to Council. He asserts that it usually requires about a year to fill a vacancy.[6]

The organization of the boards of control in Commonwealth countries is less complicated than that of the civic universities. In Canada, for instance, there are usually two bodies, the Board of Governors, which has control of the property, the staffing and financing of the institution, and the Senate, which is autonomous in matters academic. The Board of Governors usually consists of not more than fifteen or less than nine people. The Senate has some twenty-five members and is a more powerful body in Canada than in the civic universities. In academic affairs it has been known to overrule the Board of Governors.

The University of South Africa, which is purely an examining body, has a Senate composed of two members appointed by the Council, the principal, those professors and lecturers who are heads of departments recognized by the Council for representation on the Senate, two representatives of the Senate of each of the other universities in South Africa, and not fewer than eight other professors or lecturers in other universities.

The governing body of each of the other universities in South Africa consists of a Council, made up of members appointed by the Governor-General, and representatives of the benefactors of the university, its graduates, Senate and certain public bodies. It has general control over all university affairs, purposes and functions and administers its property. The Senate normally consists of the principal or rector, the professors and heads of academic departments, the librarian, representatives of the council and of the lecturing staff. It is responsible for instruction, examination and discipline.

In Sydney, Queensland and Western Australia the governing body is called the Senate; in Melbourne, Adelaide, Tasmania, New South Wales University of Technology, Australian National University, New England and Canberra University College, it is known as the Council. The pattern of control is the same, though the terminology differs. The state is represented on governing bodies in three cases by ex-officio representatives from the State Department of Education. Melbourne University has not only representatives of Parliament, but also of manufacturing and commercial interests on its Council. Most governing bodies in Australian universities have representatives from among the graduates and from the academic staff; some have student representatives. The size of these bodies varies from nineteen to thirty-five.

The professorial board is the body that is concerned with the educational program. Discipline is in the hands of a proctorial board. In all Australian universities, except the New South Wales University of Technology, there is a body known as the Convocation, Council or Senate, composed of the general body of graduates. This body appoints its representatives on the governing board and, in some instances, is asked to express its views on matters of policy and practice, though it is never expected to initiate legislation.

In the University of New Zealand the governing body is the Senate. It has representatives of each of the colleges, of the government, and of the graduates. The Court of Convocation is the senior body, but its chief duty is to select representatives to the governing body. New Zealand has a University Grants Committee composed of nine members, the chairman of which is the vice-chancellor of the University. This Committee does not have the powers of its counterpart in Britain, but serves only in an advisory capacity to the government.

In India there is considerable variation in the constitutions of the different universities, but the general pattern of control is the same. The authorities are the Executive Council (called the Syndicate in some universities), the Court or the Senate, the Academic Council, and the faculties. The Executive Council formulates the statutes and regulations and has a powerful voice in the administration of the university. It represents various interests of the university and of the community in which it is located. Most members are elected by constituencies, but some are nominated by the chancellor.

The Academic Council is concerned with matters academic, including the courses of study, organization of teaching and examination. It coordinates the work of the various faculties. In Calcutta affiliation is handled by the Senate. In other instances affiliation is subject to the approval of the government.

The University Grants Commission provides funds for research and graduate work in most of the universities. Its organization and function are similar to those of its counterpart in the United Kingdom. It has a chairman and eight members. It allocates funds and gives advice on matters referred to it. It is a permanent, statutory body.

In the United States the governing body is called a Board of Trustees, a Board of Regents, or a Board of Directors. The original board is usually provided for by the charter of the institution, which also prescribes the method of filling vacancies as they occur.

In church-related colleges and universities, the original boards were composed chiefly of clergymen. Now, business men, lawyers, and other laymen more commonly constitute the Boards of Trustees. Service on these boards involves no compensation, though traveling expenses to and from meetings are usually, though not always, allowed.

The Board of Trustees is legally the corporation in most institutions. In some, the corporation is a separate and much larger body, which holds title to the property. It has complete control over the institution. All educational policies, though formulated by the administration and faculty, must be passed upon by it.

Often, the Board of Trustees in the United States takes more interest in financial affairs, and in buildings and grounds, than in the educational program. This is usually left to the president, who recommends policy, sometimes without full faculty collaboration in its formulation. Throughout the British Commonwealth the faculty voice is more influential than in most American universities. In Canada the Senate has overriding powers in matters academic, though the faculty has no representatives on the governing board. In New Zealand the academic board is given wide jurisdiction over academic affairs by delegation of the Board of Control. The civic university of the United Kingdom and the universities of Australia, South Africa and India have faculty members on their governing bodies. Oxford and Cambridge are governed entirely by scholars; Canadian and American universities, by lay boards; and the other institutions in countries under review fall between these two extremes.

There is great diversity in the size of boards of control in the United States. They range from three to more than one hundred. Normally, privately-supported institutions have larger boards than state institutions. Most of the privately-controlled institutions have at least fifteen board members, whereas 52 per cent of the publicly-controlled institutions have nine or

fewer members. In the case of the larger boards there is a
tendency to delegate authority to committees that study and
report on various aspects of the institution's problems and
needs.

It is clear from this brief sketch that there is little uniformity
in the composition of boards of control in the English-speaking
universities. There is no less diversity in the relations that exist
between faculties and boards. One practice is common to the
Commonwealth and the United States, that of having representation of the graduates on the board.

Organization of Faculty

In the British Commonwealth the usual divisions within the
university are known as Faculties. Occasionally the term
"School" is used. In the United States the terms "Schools" and
"Colleges," representing organized curricula in various fields,
are characteristic of university organization. The active administrative head in British Commonwealth universities is usually
the Vice-Chancellor or Principal. In most of the American, and
in some Canadian universities the term most generally used
is President, though in a few universities in the United States
the chief executive officers are known as Chancellors.

Faculties in the British universities comprise both students
and faculty within a given field of study. There are departments within the faculty, but the professor in charge of the
faculty, or the department, is usually known as Professor,
though sometimes he is called a Dean. In British universities,
the deanship is a temporary assignment, the professorship a
permanent one. The organization of the entire university into
Faculties on the British pattern is the simplest form of university organization, and admirably suited to the small institution,
but it is not adequate for the larger institutions. In Australia,
where some universities have 7,000 to 8,000 students, there is
considerable feeling that a new faculty organization should be
inaugurated providing for a larger administrative staff.

In the American universities there are not only the schools and colleges, with separates deans, who frequently devote their entire time to administration, but also personnel officers known as Deans of Students, who take responsibility for extra-curricular activities, personal and social counseling and problems of discipline.

The dean of the college or school is usually a permanent official and is responsible directly to the President. In his own division he is responsible for the organization of the curriculum, for procuring staff and for the quality of instruction. The student, therefore, will normally have more dealings with the dean than with the president. The academic dean supervises his program, checks the courses to insure that degree requirements are met and, upon occasion, permits minor variations from regulations in order to meet special needs.

Each division of the university, subject to the approval of the president and the board of control, formulates its own curriculum and, under the general regulations of the university, exercises control over its internal affairs, including the selection of its faculty. Many universities also have extension divisions for part-time students. Their counterparts in Commonwealth universities are usually styled Extra-mural Studies. American universities often have one or more research institutes as well as other units.

Faculty ranks in the British Commonwealth countries are Professor, Reader, Senior Lecturer, Lecturer, Assistant Lecturer and Demonstrator. Sometimes the term Instructor is used; less often the titles Assistant and Associate Professor. In the colleges and universities of the United States, there are four recognized ranks: Professor, Associate Professor, Assistant Professor and Instructor. It is possible for one to be admitted to the teaching staff with the rank of Assistant Professor, Associate Professor, or even Full Professor, provided his experience and maturity warrant it.

While many universities have Senates, or Councils, that serve the administration in an advisory capacity, they do not, as a rule, have the same influence as the Senates, or professorial boards, in the Commonwealth institutions. Beyond the teaching function and the development of the curriculum, the faculty plays little part in the formulation of university policy and practice. It is regrettable that broad educational policy in American universities and colleges does not receive the attention which it deserves. It derives partly from the fact that the teaching staff has no well-defined means of communicating officially its ideas to the administration or board of control.

The American Association of University Professors is a body concerned with faculty privileges, tenure, retirement, salaries, etc., but its interest in matters of basic educational policy is limited.

The teaching staff with the rank of Reader or Lecturer in some respects has less chance to become acquainted with educational practice in the Commonwealth than the Instructor, or the Assistant Professor in the United States. In the American university, schools and colleges, the faculties meet and discuss problems with all hands present, including the youngest Instructor. By that means the novice is introduced to the problems of instruction, its aims and purposes, as well as its methods. He also gains some knowledge of general university practices. In Commonwealth countries, where only the Full Professors share in decision-making, the younger men have less opportunity to know what is taking place or to participate in it.

Faculty-Student Relations

The tutorial system for honor students is common throughout the Commonwealth, but its form varies widely in different areas and in different institutions. Under the Oxford and Cambridge system, the tutor sees the student individually, or in groups of two or three, while in the Commonwealth universities, the student may be one of a group ranging from five to fifteen. Relatively few colleges and universities in the

United States have developed the honors plan on the British pattern. Swarthmore College and Princeton University provide the best examples of such programs.

The chief weakness of the British undergraduate program is not in its provision for honors students, though the tutorial groups may be large. It is rather in the lack of guidance furnished those who seek the pass or ordinary degree. Whereas the honors student is assigned a tutor at the beginning of his first term and can go to him for advice on any matter, the pass student has no one to whom he can turn. He therefore frequently feels neglected. Some of the civic universities have undertaken to remedy this situation by assigning a tutor to small groups of pass students. This is particularly needed in universities which have no student counselors.

In most American universities the freshman feels that he can approach the Dean of Students for advice on all types of questions. In addition, in many American colleges freshman students are assigned to members of the teaching staff who serve as advisers on academic and social matters throughout the freshman and sophomore years. At the beginning of the junior year the professor in charge of the subject in which the student is majoring serves as his educational adviser. The effectiveness of any system of advisers depends upon the talents and interests of the faculty members involved. Few institutions are satisfied with their counseling and guidance programs.

The Chief Executive Officer

The titles of the chief executive officers of universities are as varied as their duties. In general it may be said that the pattern in the British Commonwealth countries, except Canada, is to call the chief executive the Vice-Chancellor or Principal. Sometimes the titles are combined into Vice-Chancellor and Principal. In England, Wales, Australia and India, the title is uniformly Vice-Chancellor; in Scotland, Vice-

Chancellor and Principal, and in northern Ireland, President and Vice-Chancellor; in South Africa, Vice-Chancellor in English medium and Rector in the Afrikaans universities; in Canada, titles include Vice-Chancellor, Vice-Chancellor and Principal, President and Vice-Chancellor, President and, in the French-speaking universities, Rector.

The term of the Vice-Chancellors in the ancient universities, London and Wales, is two years. At Oxford and Cambridge, heads of colleges serve in the office; in London, a member of the Senate; and in Wales, the heads of the constituent colleges rotate in the Vice-Chancellorship.

In the Commonwealth countries, originally the Vice-Chancellorship was an honorary position. As late as 1957, this was true in the Universities of Bombay (India) and Queensland (Australia). The office now is generally a salaried, full-time position.

In the United States the title of the chief executive officer is usually President. This is not, however, uniform. Some institutions use the title Chancellor for the chief executive officers, such as Vanderbilt University (Tennessee), the University of Mississippi, the university systems of Georgia, Oregon, etc. On the other hand, in California and in North Carolina, the term Chancellor is used for the executive officer of a single unit of the consolidated university, whereas the head of the university is known as the President.

In general, the influence of the executive officer in the United States and Canada is greater than in other parts of the English-speaking world. He is more of a public figure. Public relations, money-raising, administration and educational leadership are included among his duties. Though some serve the same institution for forty years or more, the average length of term is only about five years in one institution, according to estimates.

Usually the executive officer of the university in Commonwealth countries has previously been a Professor and esteems the title over that of Vice-Chancellor. This has several advantages. It means that education has been his chief interest, that he is acquainted with the institution's problems, and that his first concern is likely to be the educational program. On the other hand, the scholar may find administrative details irksome, fail to sense their importance to the welfare and progress of the institution, and thus run into difficulties. Undoubtedly, administrative skill is important, but a genuine interest in education is a prerequisite qualification of a really successful university administrator. Scholarly interests, combined with administrative skill and wisdom, are basic qualifications for a successful university administrator.

It has been suggested that the presidency in American colleges and universities has more prestige than it deserves; that the quality of the institution is too often appraised in terms of its President. When this is true, it derives from a lack of full appreciation of the central role of the faculty. Instruction and research, the primary functions of institutions, depend upon the scholars and teachers. Obviously, their effectiveness is the measure of a university's success. The chief role of the President is to assist and encourage them in the achievement of these objectives. This involves a variety of responsibilities. He must see that the academic house is in order, and provide an efficient administration, good public relations, and plan for financing the operation. Frequently he is expected to assist in finding the funds. On the other hand, he is responsible for safeguarding academic freedom and maintaining an atmosphere conducive to scholarly activity in the university community.

American university Presidents vary in their interests and in the kind of contributions they make to their institutions. Some are essentially promoters, interested in growing enrollments, in adding to the physical plant, or in increasing the endowment. Others have special talents for public relations. They enjoy meeting with people, making speeches and singing the praises of their institution, and thereby arouse a wider interest in it. The stronger university executive frequently has a rare combination of qualities—scholarly insights, administrative ability and leadership qualities of a high order. The British universities have placed greater emphasis upon the educational qualifications of administrative officers, and the members of their boards of control usually have greater interest in scholarship than their counterparts in many American universities.

This does not mean that one must have been a Professor in order to make a good President, or to have been active in educational work to make an effective board member. The fact is, some businessmen who have had a life-long interest in education have provided distinguished leadership in universities. Members of other professions, such as lawyers and doctors, have been highly successful as Presidents of institutions of higher learning. Likewise, some of the most perceptive and effective trustees have been business executives whose devotion to education has been outstanding.

The Affiliating Function of British Universities

In American higher education, accrediting associations have played an important role. The Southern Association of Colleges and Secondary Schools and the North Central Association were created toward the end of the nineteenth century, and performed a highly useful service in establishing standards for degrees. Before their organization real chaos existed. Degrees from some institutions required less than the completion of the freshman year in others. Thanks to the voluntary accrediting associations, reasonably comparable minimum standards have been adopted. There are six regional accrediting associations covering every section of the country. These are now united in the National Commission of Regional Accrediting Agencies. These agencies were more useful in the early years of the century than they have been more recently, though they still perform a useful service.

No such organizations exist in Commonwealth countries. The universities serve that role through their affiliating functions. Those institutions desiring university affiliation are accorded that status only if their work is judged to be of standard quality. Even if standards are weak, the degrees obtained must be of comparable value since the university sets the examinations. Another vital element of the plan is the provision which it makes for the staff of the affiliated institution to be associated with members of the university faculty as colleagues. In most cases the faculty has the use of the library and other facilities of the affiliating university. This method of coordinating higher education and maintaining standards, as well, has great merit. It has resulted in greater uniformity of standards, though it may have served at times to stifle initiative.

British-American Organization—Contrasts

The universities in the United Kingdom, with few exceptions, have three central constitutional bodies, the Court, the Council and the Senate. The American university has only one, the Board of Trustees or Regents. While some universities have a faculty organization called the Senate or Council, it is not a constitutional body. The Court and the Senate of the British institutions have no counterparts usually in the United States.

Bruce Truscot, in *Red Brick University,* describes in detail the composition of the Court of one of the civic universities, which has a large membership. In concluding the description he suggests that it is a useless but harmless body. Perhaps it is useless, from the standpoint of its direct effect upon the management of the university, but in its public relations function it may serve a highly useful purpose. Not only the individuals, but the organizations which they represent as members of the Court have an official connection, and hence some concern for the institution's welfare.

In American institutions the alumni association performs

something of the same function, but since the association is not a constitutional body the relation of its members is not so close as that of members of the Court. The value to the university of a large membership in the Court is difficult to measure, but probably much greater than is usually supposed.

In the universities of Scotland the governing body is the Court, and the General Council corresponds to the Court in English universities. In Australia and South Africa there are the following constitutional bodies: the Board of Control, called the Senate or Council; the Professorial Board, sometimes called the Senate or Academic Council; and Convocation, which consists of the graduates. Institutions in Canada have a Board of Governors (Trustees or Regents) and an academic Senate. No salaried members of staff may serve on the Board of Governors. In India universities have Executive Councils (or Syndicates), Courts (or Senates), Academic Councils and Faculties. The Executive Councils and Courts are usually composed of those who represent various interests of the university and of the local community. Most of these are elected by different constituencies, but a few are nominated by the Chancellor.

In some British universities members of the faculty are included in the board of control; in others the teaching staff elects a limited number of the board of control members. Generally speaking the faculty has a closer affiliation with the board of control and greater influence on its thinking than their counterparts in the United States.

The British plan is more cumbersome and less flexible than the American. In the employment of staff, for example, the Dean of the division and the President can act with great dispatch. Even in the addition of new courses the dean's recommendation and the approval of the President are frequently all that is required. While in some instances there may be merit in having the Senate and the Council consider such matters before action is taken, it involves delay and frequently

unwarranted effort on the part of the teaching staff. Furthermore, because of the time and effort required to get action,
both the faculty and the administration may be discouraged
from suggesting changes that are needed.

The affiliating function of British universities is not found in
the United States, and accreditation by voluntary associations
does not exist in the Commonwealth countries. The two have
one purpose in common: insuring quality of performance in
institutions of higher education.

Determination of Educational Policy

The responsibility for directing the course of educational
change belongs to the administration and the faculty. There
are pressures within these groups, and also pressures from
outside that seek to bring about change. Some are wholesome
and some are not. The administration and faculty have the
responsibility for judging which have merit and which should
be resisted. A great weakness in higher education in both the
United States and the Commonwealth countries is the failure
to give adequate attention to this and other vital policy matters.
It was dealt with in the 1957 Report of the Committee on
Australian Universities, Sir Keith Murray, Chairman. In Section 340 it stated the problem succinctly:

If it were made possible for the academic people concerned to
play the part they should play in handling our plans and programs
and in examining the relative urgency from the educational research
points of view of the various projects, the problem of communication
would in large measure solve itself. Knowledge of what the university intends to do and why would inevitably become very much
more widely spread among the active teaching body, greatly to the
improvement of the plans and policies concerned and of the morale
of the whole working community. It is the proud boast of the
universities that the relationship between the university council
or senate and the university teachers is not an employer-employee

relation, but that universities have manners and methods of their own of conducting their affairs, safeguarding their academic liberty, maintaining their special way of life as a community of scholars. But clearly, these manners and methods have to adjust themselves to the necessities of the modern world if the universities are to play their proper part. It seems to us that this adjustment has not at present been achieved.[7]

Both the administration and the faculty are usually so preoccupied with matters of immediate concern that they devote little thought to the long-range needs, or the impact of the institution as a whole. Are there weaknesses in the educational program which could be corrected? Are there needs in the region which the institution is not providing for but could appropriately supply? Are there programs in operation that could be eliminated without serious loss? Does the institution serve the needs of the gifted student as it should? Does it require too much or too little of its students? These and a multitude of other questions need systematic and realistic study. The present organization does not provide adequate machinery for such study in either the American or Commonwealth universities.

Perhaps the major burden in the formulation of educational policy should be borne by the faculty. But it cannot effect changes without the sympathetic cooperation of the administration. Under the present organization of universities the Senates or professorial boards discuss policy questions from time to time, but they are not subjected to the same painstaking investigation that the scientist devotes to problems in his field of scholarship. Basic research in the methods and purposes of higher education is a critical need in the modern university. A chief difficulty is that faculty members rarely feel a responsibility for attacking those problems that underlie educational efficiency. Changes in the United States, and in the Commonwealth countries as well, have frequently resulted from the pressures exerted by the community. Public demands deserve serious consideration, but changes desired by the community may involve violation of the proper function of the university, or may be less important than other needs which the public does not understand.

In view of the prospective expansion in numbers and the consequent demands for new courses and programs, it is of crucial importance that machinery be designed to insure adequate consideration of fundamental educational problems. A standing committee or commission, made up of representatives of the faculty, the administration and the board of control, could serve a highly useful purpose in the critical days ahead. Such planning committees have been set up in many institutions to deal with the problems involved in the expansion of physical facilities. By a careful analysis of the institution's educational services, with reference not only to their effectiveness but to those provided by neighboring institutions, it should be possible to improve the quality of the program and to eliminate wasteful duplication. Attention has been called to the small size of faculties, or schools, in some universities which could be eliminated by absorption of their students into other institutions. This situation prevails to a greater or less extent in all the countries under review. Economy in staff, in educational effort, and in costs could be effected by a realistic consideration of institutional offerings and a reasonable division of labor.

The most serious gap in the organization of higher education in the English-speaking world is the lack of provision for realistic and systematic attention to broad educational problems, policies and practices. Neither the administration nor the faculty, under the present organizational framework, has the opportunity to scrutinize the program as a whole and to study it in its relation to the offerings of other institutions in the region. When new courses of study are proposed, some review of overall policy may take place, but only in a limited context as it relates to the particular problem under consideration. The broader issues are neglected, because the machinery for research and study of them is not provided.

In the Commonwealth universities, where the Senate gives more or less constant attention to matters academic, there is probably more discussion of broad policy questions than in the average American university. But even there the consideration is general rather than specific, and rarely based upon systematic study. Furthermore its functions rarely, if ever, include that of suggesting reforms which may involve the abolition of faculties and the addition of new ones. Since the board of control and the administration should share in the responsibility of formulating broad policy, the Senate is not sufficiently representative to be effective in initiating basic changes in policy and practice. Any committee or commission to be effective in this field should be representative of the board of control, the administration and the faculty, and should consist of the most influential members of these three groups.

If this suggestion should appear to be a radical departure from tradition, and as such unwelcome, it is well to remember that the present crisis in higher education throughout the English-speaking countries is without parallel in history. Within ten to fifteen years in most of these areas a doubling of enrollments is anticipated. The mounting demands for new courses, new emphases and new services will doubtless keep pace with the swelling tide of youth clamoring for admission to universities. In such a situation, unless comprehensive and realistic efforts are made to retain the basic values of the university tradition, they could be lost in the chaos and confusion that could result from an unwise handling of the pressures of the next decade or two.

VI

Financing Higher Education

✢✿✪✿G

Individuals and private groups provided the original support for higher education in the English-speaking world. Gifts and grants made possible the first buildings and the meager equipment they contained. In the earliest days of Oxford and Cambridge instruction was given in houses provided by the community. Many of the colleges that constitute these two ancient universities bear the names of men whose generosity made possible their establishment. Throughout the United Kingdom the story is the same. Voluntary donations were the seeds from which the colleges and universities in England, Wales, Scotland and Ireland have sprung. The story of higher education in other Commonwealth countries follows the same pattern. In Canada religious denominations, through the gifts of their members, gave birth to most of its colleges and universities. A small number of state universities of more recent origin were established under government sponsorship. Even in those cases the affiliated institutions, the nuclei around which they usually developed, were privately-established and privately-supported.

Though the universities of Australia were not founded until after the middle of the nineteenth century when state support for higher education was becoming common, private benefactions have been a chief factor in the development of higher education in that Commonwealth. The same holds true in New Zealand and the Union of South Africa.

In India three universities established by the British in 1857 were only examining bodies throughout the nineteenth century. The affiliated institutions which provided the instruction were established by private enterprise.

In the United States Harvard was founded more than 150 years before public support was provided for an institution of higher learning. As late as 1879–1880 only 7.9 per cent of the total income of higher education in the United States came from governmental sources. There was limited tax support of higher education in the United States, Canada, Australia and South Africa at the turn of the present century, but higher education depended mainly on voluntary gifts for its buildings and equipment, and, except for student fees, for its maintenance. In these times, when higher education is so dependent upon government support, it is well to remember that for more than six centuries it was supported entirely by voluntary gifts.

The present program of higher education derives its income from four souces: student fees, endowment income, gifts and grants and governmental support. The proportion of total income derived from each of these sources has varied through the years. In the early history student fees constituted the major source. While the colleges of Oxford and Cambridge in some cases had considerable endowments, a substantial part of the total cost of education at these institutions until very recently was borne by student fees.

Student Fees

Charges to students in the universities in each of the Commonwealth countries vary. For example, in the United Kingdom the tuition fees in the Arts Faculty range roughly from £33 to £41 per year; in Commerce from £30 to more than £50; in Medicine from £47 to £60. In the university colleges of Wales there is a uniform charge of £30 per year for students in the Arts Faculty. At McGill University (Canada) the students in the Arts Faculty pay $350 per year; at St. Joseph's, $135; and at other institutions fees range between those figures for instruction in this faculty. In Australia the variation is not quite so marked. In Adelaide the charges in the Arts Faculty amount to £75, whereas in Tasmania they are less than £45. In New Zealand the charges range from £18 in Victoria and Octago to £22 in Canterbury. In the Union of South Africa the charges to Arts College students in Rhodes University are £44 per year, while in the University of the Witwatersrand they are £75 plus additional fees for honor students. Charges in the universities of India range from Rs.120 to Rs.250 for arts and science courses and from Rs.250 to Rs.400 for professional and technological courses. Figures on financial assistance to students are not available, but it is roughly estimated that about 10 per cent receive some aid.

In the United States tuition charges vary more widely than in the British Commonwealth countries. They range from $1450 per year in one private university to less than $150 in some state universities. There is a movement among some private institutions to require students to bear a much larger share of the cost of their education through tuition fees.

There has been great fluctuation in the percentage cost of education borne by student fees. This is illustrated by the experience in the United States. In 1900 student fees produced 36.7 per cent of the total income; in 1920, 25.1 per cent; in 1940, 35.1 per cent, and in 1953–1954, 18.7 per cent. Even this figure for the United States is higher than that in the United Kingdom. Fees there in 1954–1955, including Ministry of Education grants for training teachers, provided only 11 per cent of the total income for recurrent purposes of the universities.

In Canada students' fees bear a larger proportion of the cost of education than in most other Commonwealth countries or in the United States. They range from 20.4 per cent in a state university to more than 60 per cent in a private university. The average is approximately 29 per cent. In Australia, in 1957, the percentage of income from fees in all Australian universities was 15.6 per cent; in the constituent institutions of the University of New Zealand, from 9 to 12 per cent; in South Africa, from 20 to approximately 35 per cent. While data on the Indian universities are incomplete, the variation in the percentage of income derived from student fees is from 11 per cent in Visva-Bharati to 53.8 per cent in Andhra University. In Great Britain the proportion of income derived from student fees in 1954–1955 was the lowest found in English-speaking countries.

Endowments—Gifts and Grants

Income from endowments and from gifts and grants, next to that derived from fees, was the major source of university funds in an earlier period. For example, in 1879–1880 slightly more than one-half the income for higher education in the United States came from endowment. The proportion in 1939–1940 was 12.5 per cent, and in 1953–1954 only 5.4 per cent, with gifts and grants accounting for an additional 6.4 per cent. In British Commonwealth countries the same downward trend is noted. Since 1919, when the University Grants Committee was established, it has been marked. A brief glance at the picture will suffice to indicate the extent to which endowment income is currently supporting higher education.

While many institutions in the British Commonwealth have no endowments and the figures for the overall endowment income in all these areas are not available, it is possible to gain some idea of the part endowment plays in the support of higher education by citing a few examples.

Birmingham University has an endowment providing a little more than 7 per cent of its overall income; the University of London, .8 per cent; Aberdeen University, 5 per cent; St.

Andrews, 3.43 per cent. For the United Kingdom as a whole the figure in 1954–1955 was 4.1 per cent. In Canada endowment plays a considerably larger part: at Acadia University, 15.3 per cent; in British Columbia gifts and grants, along with endowment, provided 18.34 per cent; Carleton College, 1.93 per cent; McMaster, approximately 15 per cent; Queens University, 13 per cent; St. Mary's, 15 per cent; University of Western Ontario, 9 per cent. In Australia endowment income in Adelaide provided 4 per cent of the overall income in 1954–1955; in Melbourne, Sydney and the University of New Zealand, 2 per cent each. In South Africa the income from endowment in Cape Town provided 3.9 per cent of the total income. In India Andhra University derived 1.1 per cent of its income from endowment; Baroda, 4.4 per cent; Gauhati, 17.7 per cent; Gujarat University, 1 per cent; University of Bombay, 8.69 per cent.

In 1953–1954 the aggregate endowments of all institutions in the United States amounted to $3,312,565,000. This represents approximately a twentyfold increase since 1900, when the aggregate of all endowments was approximately $170,000,-000. Despite that fact, as already noted, the percentage of income from endowment has dropped from 12.5 per cent in 1939–1940 to 5.4 per cent in 1953–1954. This situation stems partly from the fact that the rates of interest on endowment have been declining for a number of years. However, inflation and the expansion of public support for higher education in the United States have been the chief factors.

Government Support of Higher Education

In all English-speaking countries, with the exception of Canada and the United States, government support is the major source of income for higher education. It was not true before 1900. Though colleges and universities derived considerable support from government in the United States and in some parts of the British Commonwealth prior to the twentieth century, it was a minor factor in their maintenance before 1900. Since it is now such a major source, it is necessary to deal in some detail with developments in each of the countries under review in order to understand the full significance of the changes which have taken place.

THE UNITED KINGDOM

As noted earlier, the first government grant for university education in Britain was made in 1889, but before 1919 the treasury made no systematic contributions to its universities. It was in July, 1919, that a standing committee of the treasury was appointed, called the University Grants Committee, the purpose of which was "to inquire into the financial needs of university education in the United Kingdom and to advise the government as to the application of any grants that may be made by Parliament towards meeting them."

Under this plan the treasury contributed £916,000 in the 1919–1920 session to the universities and independent university colleges. This was boosted to £1,800,000 by 1929–1930, to £2,224,000 by 1939–1940. At that time it was somewhat more than one-third of the entire income of the universities. During the Second World War the annual grants were maintained at the 1939–1940 level.

Toward the close of the war consideration was given to the anticipated needs of the universities in the post-war period. It was clear that there would be a greater demand than ever for support from government. As a result, in 1943 the University Grants Committee was reconstituted and its purposes elaborated. As stated in 1946, they were as follows:

To inquire into the financial needs of university education in Great Britain; to advise the Government as to the application of any grants made by Parliament towards meeting them; to collect, examine and make available information relating to university education throughout the United Kingdom; and to assist, in consultation with the universities and other bodies concerned, the preparation and execution of such plans for the development of the universities as may from time to time be required in order to insure that they are fully adequate to national needs.

Under this new mandate treasury grants were greatly increased. By 1957 the total for recurrent expenses had reached approximately £30,000,000, with the expectation that by 1962 it would be in excess of £39,000,000. Government has been contributing not only to the maintenance of universities, but to their plant funds as well. For example, between 1947 and 1956 non-recurrent grants amounted to about £32,000,000, and the committee in 1957 recommended, for the quinquennium beginning that year, a total of approximately £72,000,-000 for buildings and equipment chiefly in the science and technology fields. In this connection it is a matter of interest to note that the Ministry of Education in the same year recommended grants totaling about £72,000,000 for the same five-year period to expand the plants of the technical colleges in the United Kingdom.

In addition to the sums allocated for general purposes of the university and for buildings, the Ministry of Education in 1954–1955 made substantial grants for the training of teachers.

In February 1952 the recurrent grants for 1952–1957, as announced by the Chancellor of the Exchequer, totaled £111,750,000. They are expected to approximate £170,000,-000 during the current quinquennium in addition to the grants for buildings and equipment. Though the universities of the United Kingdom are privately controlled, they receive a larger proportion of their support from the government than the institutions of other countries which have "state universities." This unprecedented development derives from the need for trained men and women, particularly for scientists and technologists. Government's recognition of its dependence upon universities for achieving essential social objectives is a recent phenomenon of great significance for the future of higher education in Great Britain.

CANADA

Education has been traditionally considered a provincial responsibility in Canada. The first federal government grant to the Universities was made in 1951. This was done without the benefit of a university grants committee. The treasury appropriated the funds to the provincial government directly on the basis of population and the aggregate enrollment of the universities within the province. The purpose in making the grant was to assist in defraying the increased cost of university education. It was not earmarked for science and technology exclusively, but included specifically the Arts Faculties. "The declining value of endowment and the effect of taxation and inflation" were additional factors recognized by the government in making the appropriation.

The original grant was for $7,000,000. The amount was increased in 1954–1955 to $9,000,000. In August, 1958, a 50 per cent increase brought the total to approximately $15,000,-000. In addition to the yearly grants for recurrent purposes, the government appropriated the sum of $100,000,000 to the Canada Council for the promotion of the arts. One-half serves as an endowment for strengthening Arts Faculties and for promoting the arts generally. Much of the income from this source is spent on projects outside the universities. For example, in 1957–1958, less than $20,000 went directly to the universities. The other $50,000,000 for capital grants goes to universities for buildings and equipment in the arts and social sciences.

The Council has interpreted its powers to make grants for university buildings for the arts and social sciences as extending to grants for the construction of halls of residence, if adequate library and reading room facilities have already been provided.

The government has encountered two difficulties in the administration of the grants to the universities. In the Province of Quebec all of the universities have refused federal funds, lest by accepting them they endanger the autonomy of the universities. The government has deposited the amounts allocated to these universities with the National Conference of Canadian Universities, awaiting the time when they may see their way clear to accept them. The second difficulty derives from the basis used in making the grants: "according to the population of each province and the number of full-time students in each university within the province." This has resulted in inequities. For example, based on this formula, the per capita student amount is larger in Newfoundland than in Manitoba and Nova Scotia, because the proportion of youth attending the university is less. The result is that the Newfoundland University receives a disproportionately large share, while in Manitoba and Nova Scotia the institutions receive relatively meager amounts.

In addition to grants received from the provincial and federal governments and from the Canada Council, the universities in all sections of the country have been securing substantial sums from business and industry. Bishop's University, for example, began a campaign in late 1957 for $3,000,000, two-thirds of which had been raised within a few months. The University of Western Ontario secured $4,600,000 from private sources, which made possible a $20,600,000 building program. The University of British Columbia raised in excess of $7,500,000 from business and industry, which will enable the university to launch a $30,000,000 building program. The University of Toronto has recently acquired new acreage near the present site of the university and has plans for raising a substantial sum from private sources to enable it to take advantage of funds available through the federal and provincial governments and the Canada Council for a building program that will cost approximately $55,000,000. The University of Manitoba has plans for doubling its student body within the next few years through funds which it confidently expects from government and private sources by 1960. The University of Ottawa, already engaged in a large building program, contemplates steady expansion over the next several years. Carleton University in 1957 was developing a plant on a new site, which is not only beautifully situated but will care for double the present enrollment. McGill University does not contemplate as great an expansion of plant as some other institutions, since it has decided to limit its enrollment to 9,500.

The response of business and industry to the campaigns for funds throughout Canada has been extraordinary. The result is a spirit of optimism and enthusiasm among Canadian institutions that is perhaps not equalled in any other English-speaking country. Progress is noted not only in plans for increasing physical plants, but in efforts to improve the educational programs. At the McGill University, for instance, studies were in progress in some five or six Faculties looking to reforms in instructional programs and improvement in salary scales. At Toronto the Council in 1958 adopted a new salary scale providing for a minimum salary of $12,000 per year for full professors and proportionate amounts for other ranks.

A significant phase of the Canadian program is its emphasis upon the arts. Though great expansion was noted in science and technology, with enrollments in these fields expanding twice as rapidly as the general enrollments of the universities, the arts were not being neglected. No program comparable to that of the Canada Council, with $100,000,000 for the arts, is found elsewhere in the Commonwealth or the United States. This grant was recommended by a Commission on National Development in Canada of Arts, Letters and the Sciences (1949–1950), headed by the Hon. Vincent Massey. This expression of interest in the arts is heartening at a time when science and technology generally claim the lion's share of attention and support.

The private institutions in Canada receive federal but not provincial support for higher education. For example, Acadia University receives 14.6 per cent of its total income from the central government; Assumption University, 32.9 per cent; Carleton University, 56.2 per cent; McMaster, approximately 40 per cent; Queens, 39.9 per cent; the University of Western Ontario, 40.5 per cent.

The provincial universities receive their major support from the provincial governments but are not precluded from sharing in federal funds. The University of Alberta, for example, receives 57 per cent of its income from the Province and 16.5 per cent from the central government. The University of British Columbia receives 44.54 per cent from the Province and 9.74 per cent from the central government. The University of Saskatchewan receives 47.1 per cent from the Province and 11.1 per cent from the central government.

In Canada the percentage of funds coming from the government is not as high as in the United Kingdom. This fact probably derives from the early history of the development of Canadian higher education. Except for the Western part of Canada, practically all of the universities began under church auspices. While the majority now are independent of church control, they still have a connection with the denominational body that established them. The church connection of so many colleges and universities probably accounts for the fact that the central government made its first grant for their support in 1951, while in England such support began in 1919.

University endowment funds in Canada are greater than in other Commonwealth countries; likewise, the proportion of the university education burden borne by student fees is higher. This means that government support in Canada has been substantially less than in other English-speaking countries. The increase from $1.00 to $1.50 per capita of the population for support of the universities, authorized in 1958, will modify substantially the relative support of the government.

To summarize, the sources of university income in Canada in 1954–1955 were as follows: endowment income, 6.1 per cent; tuition fees, 29.6 per cent; governmental grants, 42 per cent; miscellaneous, 22.3 per cent. This latter figure included research grants of $7,112,751, largely from government sources. In the period 1935–1936 to 1954–1955, the percentage of university income from endowment dropped from 14.7 per cent to 6.1 per cent, while student-fee income kept pace with the increase in university operating costs.[1]

AUSTRALIA

The picture in Australia differs markedly from that in Canada, chiefly in the higher proportion of tax funds that support its institutions. There are nine universities and two university colleges in the Australian Commonwealth. The Australian National University and the Canberra University College are federal institutions and receive no state funds. All others are state universities; none are privately controlled.

Until the Second World War all government support came from state sources. After the war the central government began to provide funds for research. In 1953 it adopted the policy of making grants for current operations. The first was for A£877,130. In 1955 this was increased to A£1,705,930. Grants were made on the basis of one pound for each three pounds contributed by the state.

The Australian government in 1957 requested Sir Keith Murray, Chairman of the University Grants Committee in Great Britain, to head a committee appointed to make a study of the universities in the Commonwealth. This committee, after spending several months visiting the institutions, submitted a report in September 1957. It recommended that a University

Grants Committee be set up and that the central government increase substantially its support of university education.

The Prime Minister, in a speech to Parliament, indicated the government's acceptance of the recommendations. He agreed to set up a permanent Australian Universities Committee (with the functions of the proposed University Grants Committee) and to provide emergency grants for a period of three years to allow the new committee time to be prepared to function. He recommended that, for the period 1958–1960, Commonwealth grants on the same terms, one pound for three pounds from the states, be raised 10 per cent each of the three years, bringing the total grant from the central government to A£3,107,900 in 1960. This would require A£8,501,800 during the three-year period, compared with a total of A£6,040,930 provided in the preceding three years, 1955, 1956 and 1957. In addition, he proposed to increase the grants to Canberra University College 10 per cent each year and to raise support of Australian National University from A£2,804,-500 in 1955–1957 to A£4,396,000 in 1958–1960. He agreed further to make emergency capital grants totaling A£4,500,000 during this period.

The central government had not made grants for capital purposes prior to 1958. The government accepted the recommendation of the Committee that it support the building program over the next three years on the basis of pound for pound in all universities except Western Australia and Tasmania, where it would provide a twenty-five shillings per pound contribution from the state.

In brief, the Prime Minister agreed in a speech on January 11, 1958, to raise Commonwealth expenditures for the three-year period, 1958–1960, to A£22,000,000 compared with A£6,040,-930 for the period of 1955–1957, and to increase provision for the Australian National University and Canberra University College along similar lines.[2]

The Prime Minister urged the universities to make an

appeal to business and industry and other non-state sources, as well as to the states, for building funds. He agreed to assist in the building of hostels, to the extent of A£200,000 per year for three years, matching state funds.

This account of the Murray Report and the reaction of the government to it has been given in some detail in order to make it clear that the picture of university support in 1957 will be substantially changed by 1960.

In 1957 student fees accounted for 15.6 per cent of the income to the universities; the state appropriations, for 50.3 per cent; and the Commonwealth government, for 29.2 per cent. This makes a total of 95.1 per cent. The balance of the income for the support of higher education comes from endowment and miscellaneous sources.

The expansion which lies ahead for the Australian universities is suggested by the fact that in 1957 only 4.4 per cent of the seventeen- and eighteen-year-old youth in New South Wales, for example, were in the university of that state, whereas 16 per cent were judged qualified to enter the university. It is anticipated that within the next ten years there will be an increase of 120 per cent in the number of students attending the universities of Australia over that of 1957.

NEW ZEALAND

The University of New Zealand, in 1955, received approximately £1,750,000 for its operation: £1,250,000 from the government; £25,000 from endowments; £165,000 from fees; and the remainder from miscellaneous other sources, according to the 1958 *Commonwealth Universities Yearbook*.

THE UNION OF SOUTH AFRICA

In South Africa there are eight teaching universities, one that functions only as an examining body, and the University College of Fort Hare. The picture there is different from that in Canada and Australia, where the provincial, or state, government has the major responsibility for higher education. The provinces may occasionally engage universities to provide services on a contract basis, but they do not assume responsibility for higher education. That is the function of the central government in South Africa.

The income of the residential universities in 1956 was estimated at £3,886,149. Of this amount 29.3 per cent was derived from student fees; 65.7 per cent from government subsidy, and 5 per cent from other sources, such as interest on investments, rents, annual grants from public bodies, etc.

The University of South Africa (an examining body) had a total income of £219,080, derived as follows: fees, 57.6 per cent; government subsidy, 41.69 per cent; and other sources, 0.71 per cent. University College of Fort Hare had an income of £113,339, of which 11.47 per cent came from fees, 79.1 per cent from government subsidy, and 9.43 per cent from other sources.

South Africa has no University Grants Committee, such as is found in the United Kingdom, in India, and as is recommended for Australia. Instead, subsidy funds are allocated by formula, the amount depending partly on the number of basic departments, and partly on the number of students in the university. The wide variation in the percentages of income provided by the government (from 76.8 per cent at Potchefstroom to 53 per cent at Rhodes University) suggests the need for some revision of the plan for making grants.

Through the years business and industry have provided substantial assistance in the development and maintenance of the universities of South Africa. It is not now, however, as important a factor as it is in Canada, the United Kingdom and the United States. This is, perhaps, due to the fact that while normal expansion is expected in the universities, the increase in enrollments anticipated in the other Commonwealth countries is not expected in South Africa. The degree of expansion to be expected has been estimated at about 40 per cent.

INDIA

Four universities of India are supported by the federal government and twenty-eight by the states. While the federal universities receive support only from the central government, the state universities often receive grants from the federal government, though they look to the states as the primary source of support. There are no privately-supported universities in India.

Federal funds for the support of higher education are distributed by a University Grants Commission. This was set up in November 1953, formally inaugurated by the Prime Minister on December 28th of that year, and began to function as of that date. This Commission has a full-time chairman and eight members. In Britain its counterpart has twenty-three instead of nine members. It has the responsibility for advising the Government of India on the funds to be allocated to the universities. It is also charged with advising the government on problems of university education which may be referred to it and with allocating and disbursing grants for various purposes to the universities out of the funds placed at its disposal by the government.

Funds allocated to the state universities are usually for postgraduate studies and research activity. The Commission also makes grants for capital purposes, particularly for the erection of libraries and scientific laboratories and for the purchase of equipment and books.

The Government of India, in setting up the University Grants Commission, hoped that through its grants to the universities it might be able to assist them in maintaining and developing high standards, in providing facilities for research, and in promoting coordination of their work.

In addition to tuition fees, governmental support, endowment income and gifts, examination fees in many cases provide a substantial proportion of the university's revenues. For example, in 1955–1956 the University of Agra, which had a government grant of Rs.123,700, received Rs.1,900,660 from examination fees; the University of Calcutta, 35.7 per cent of its income from examination fees; Rajasthan, approximately one-half its total income from this source; and others, substantial amounts but in smaller proportions.

In 1957 the University Grants Commission announced the allocation of 50 Crores of Rupees (Rs.500,000,000) for buildings and equipment in the field of science and technology for the period 1957–1962. While it was originally planned to establish a large number of new institutions, it was later decided to devote the major portion of these funds to the expansion of existing universities.

PAKISTAN

Pakistan has six universities, one of which (Karachi) is supported by the central government, and the others by the state governments. The central government makes occasional grants to state universities on the basis of *ad hoc* committee recommendations. It has no University Grants Committee but is considering establishing one. In Pakistan half the universities have been established since partition in 1947, if the University of Sind, which was founded that year, is included.

Data on the income of the universities in Pakistan are incomplete. Information is available only on Dacca University, which in 1954–1955 derived somewhat more than one-half its income from the government and about 40 per cent from student fees; the rest it received from endowment and miscellaneous funds. According to the estimate given in the 1958 *Commonwealth Yearbook*, more than one-half the operating income of Pakistan universities was derived from the government.

Comparisons and Contrasts

In all the countries under review there has been an increase in the number of students attending universities and colleges and a consequent increase in demands for financial support. Of the four sources of support, endowment income, gifts and grants, student fees and governmental aid, the first three, in most instances, have declined in the percentage of the burden which they bear, though each is larger in dollar, pound or rupee amount. It is only government support at local, state (or province) and central government levels that shows an increase in the percentage of income provided for higher education. The only exception is the gifts and grants income in the United States, which has increased markedly in recent years. Generally speaking, voluntary sources of income, including student fees, have not kept pace with the expansion in enrollments and in the financial needs of higher education.

In the United Kingdom the endowment income in 1935–1936 was 14.5 per cent of all income for the support of higher education. By 1946–1947 this had declined to 9.3 per cent, and in 1954–1955, to 4.1 per cent. In Canada comparable figures are for 1935–1936, 14.7 per cent; 1946–1947, 7 per cent; and 1954–1955, 6.1 per cent. While the figures available for the United States are not for the same years, they indicate the same trend. For instance, in 1929–1930 endowments yielded 16.3 per cent of all university income; in 1939–1940, 12 per cent; in 1949–1950, 5.5 per cent; and in 1954–55, 5.4 per cent.[3]

Gifts and grants in the United Kingdom in 1935–1936 amounted to 2.5 per cent of the total educational income in universities, whereas in 1946–1947 it had dropped to 2.2 per cent, and in 1954–1955 to 1.1 per cent. In the United States gifts and grants in 1929–1930 amounted to 5.6 per cent; in

1939–1940, to 6.6 per cent; in 1949–1950, to 6.2 per cent; and in 1953–1954, to 6.4 per cent. Canadian gifts and grants in 1954–1955, in twenty-three universities, amounted to 5.8 per cent of their total income.

The decline in percentage of the burden borne by tuition fees has shown the same trend as endowment income and gifts and grants. For example, in the United Kingdom tuition fees provided 32.5 per cent of the income of the universities in 1935–1936, 23.2 per cent in 1946–1947, and 10.7 per cent in 1954–1955. Comparable figures for Canada are 33.5 per cent in 1935–1936, 41.4 per cent in 1946–1947, and 29.6 per cent in 1954–1955.[4]

In the United States tuition fees in 1929–1930 provided 36.4 per cent; in 1939–1940, 34.7 per cent; in 1949–1950, 21.4 per cent; and in 1953–1954, 18.7 per cent. The difference between the percentage of the burden borne by student fees in the publicly-supported and in the privately-supported institutions is worth noting. For 1951–1952 student fees accounted for 22.1 per cent of the income of all institutions; 10.4 per cent in publicly-controlled institutions, and 36.6 per cent in privately-supported institutions. Endowment earnings provided 1.1 per cent in public institutions and 11.2 per cent in private institutions; and private benefactions, 2.3 per cent in public, and 13.7 per cent in private institutions. The distinction between public and private institutions which prevails in the United States is not observed in the British Commonwealth countries, with the exception of Canada.

Tax support has been required to make up the deficits represented by the decline, percentage-wise, of student fees, endowment and gifts and grants as sources of income. The increase in the amounts provided by government has been startlingly rapid. In the United Kingdom, for example, parliamentary and local authorities made grants totaling 43 per cent of the income of higher education in 1935–1936, 58.3 per cent in 1946–1947, and 73.6 per cent in 1953–1954. Plans announced for the 1957–

1962 quinquennium will result in the government's bearing a still greater share of the cost of higher education.

In Canada the government grants in 1935–1936 amounted to 40.3 per cent; in 1946–1947, 41.8 per cent; and in 1954–1955, 42 per cent. While the increase was very rapid in Great Britain during the twenty years from 1935 to 1955, there was only a slight increase in Canada. The United States followed a somewhat similar pattern: state and federal government grants in 1929–1930 amounted to 41.7 per cent; in 1939–1940, 34 per cent; and in 1949–1950, 39.5 per cent plus 16.2 per cent for veterans' education. In 1953–1954 it was 42.4 per cent.[5]

To summarize, in the United Kingdom government funds in 1954–1955 bore 73.6 per cent of the burden of university education, whereas for 1935–1936 it was only 43 per cent. In the United States in 1954–1955 government sources provided 42.5 per cent of total revenues, about the same as in 1929–1930, though the amount in dollars was four times larger. In Canada, government grants totaled $5,359,000 in 1935–1936 and $22,281,000 in 1954, yet the percentage was approximately the same throughout the period.

In addition to the grants to the universities, governments have also contributed scholarships and bursaries. In 1954–1955 in Great Britain 72.9 per cent of all students registered in universities received some kind of scholarship or bursary aid. A comparable figure in Canada, according to the best estimates, was 14 per cent.

Figures for the number of students receiving scholarship funds are not available for the United States, but according to the Council for Financial Aid to Education, 55.9 per cent of all students were enrolled in state universities and colleges in 1951–1952 where fees are low. It was estimated, though doubted by some, that 20 per cent of students enrolled in private institutions received scholarships that paid at least the cost of tuition. Thus, some three-fourths of the students in the United States received directly or indirectly, financial assistance. This is strikingly similar to the British figure.

It is of interest to note that the percentage of revenues derived from endowments in all private institutions in the United States is slightly greater than in the ancient universities of Great Britain—11.2 per cent as compared with approximately 10 per cent for Oxford and Cambridge.

In Australia the situation with respect to sources of support compares more nearly with that of the United Kingdom than with that of any other Commonwealth country. At the present time the tuition fees bear a larger share of the burden, 15.6 per cent as against 10.7 per cent in Great Britain, but this will be changed in the early future, due to the increased support of government resulting from the Murray Committee report. The income from endowment and gifts and grants is less than in Great Britain, and much less than in Canada. The sources of support in South Africa correspond more nearly to the Canadian than to the United Kingdom pattern. In India and Pakistan the fees for tuition and for examinations bear a larger proportion of the cost of higher education than in the other Commonwealth countries, while the support from endowment, gifts and grants is much less. It should be remembered, however, that almost one-half the universities in India and Pakistan in 1957 were ten years old or less.

Government Support and University Autonomy

Since government support has become such a major factor in the building and maintenance of universities, the question of the effect of this policy on university autonomy has been frequently raised. The attitudes on this question vary greatly in the different countries under review. In some special devices have been developed to insure against interference.

In the United Kingdom the University Grants Committee, made up largely of educational leaders, serves this purpose. The Grants Commission in India and the proposed Universities Committee in Australia will doubtless serve similar purposes. The highly satisfactory experience in Great Britain for almost forty years has encouraged the belief that government support need not interfere with the autonomy of universities.

In Canada, with the exception of the Province of Quebec, universities have no hesitation in accepting funds from the federal government. Indeed, the Canadian philosophy is that diversity of sources of income is a safeguard against interference. Thus private gifts and grants, endowment income, provincial and federal grants mean that no one source has a controlling interest.

In the United States the federal government has made grants to higher education since the Land-Grant College Act was passed in 1862. It has provided increasing support for these institutions each decade since their establishment. These grants are made to the states, earmarked for these institutions. No serious difficulties have arisen in that long period. Yet some fear that if American colleges and universities should receive substantial funds from the federal government their autonomy might be jeopardized. This apprehension, however, seems to be diminishing in view of the British experience and as the needs increase.

In South Africa, where government legislation is aimed at segregation of the races, there is much concern among the English-speaking universities, which have traditionally admitted students irrespective of race. More than half the funds of those universities that oppose Apartheid are provided by the government. In an excellent document entitled "Open Universities," presented to the government by these institutions, it is contended that for the government to attempt to say who shall be admitted is an invasion of the rights of the university.[6]

In Australia, India and Pakistan the fear of government's interference, because of its overwhelming support of their universities, does not appear to have arisen, though from time to time complaints have been registered in India against the tendency of government to overstep the boundaries of its jurisdiction in dealing with universities.

The University Ideal and Government Support

The major role which government is playing in the support of higher education in the English-speaking world has overtones that need analysis. They suggest that the university has a position of prestige unprecedented in the past; that governments have higher expectations of results from the universities than ever before; that university education must be more sensitive to utilitarian ends; and that basic changes in the goals of higher education are possible as a result of the new role which it is called on to play.

It is encouraging to note the confidence which governments exhibit in the universities. They recognize that the advance of science and technology is basic to economic health, and in these times to national defense as well. Likewise, there is a new appreciation of the importance of the gifted individual. The cry is for more and better scientists, pure scientists as well as technologists. The search for talent in the scientific field is afoot everywhere. At no time in the past has there been so much concern that those who have special talents shall find a way to develop them. To achieve this purpose the universities are indispensable. They are essential to the development of those talents most needed in our time. The recognition of this fact has given new prestige to universities and a new challenge for the future.

Governments and the peoples which they represent demand results when they invest so largely in higher education. Hitherto, universities have been corporations chiefly engaged in private enterprise. For more than seven centuries of British history this was true. It was forty years ago that systematic support of higher education by the British government was instituted. Public support means that what the universities do is a matter of public concern. As this support expands the demands and pressures on the universities will grow. Thus, the faith in education expressed by vast support is a two-edged sword. It means undreamed-of expansion and development of institutions of higher learning, but it may also involve changes in the traditional ideal of the university.

Increasing government support means that universities must concentrate increasingly on utilitarian ends. If 80 per cent of their income is derived from public funds, it is natural that the public should expect results in accordance with its interpretation of needs. Thus the pressures and demands for realistic, practical considerations as understood by the public will grow. "Knowledge for its own sake" may be supplanted by "useful" knowledge as the goal. This could involve a change in the spirit of university education. Historically and traditionally universities have dealt with the moral, philosophic and spiritual issues of man and his society. These still are as important as in the past, yet they receive less and less attention and emphasis in modern education. Pursuit of knowledge for purposes however worthy is not synonymous with "pursuit of truth," the prime goal of the university according to earlier standards. In the light of these facts the dangers of losing autonomy through overt acts of government appear less serious than those which threaten the future of the university ideal and purpose. A new and vital reinterpretation of education in the light of present conditions may be indicated.

VII

Student Life—Services and Organizations

❖❘❮

The task of higher education does not end with providing classrooms, laboratories, libraries and teaching staff. Facilities for housing and boarding students proved early in the history of the ancient universities to be essential to their stability and effectiveness. To achieve this, colleges were founded at Oxford and Cambridge. For several centuries these sufficed to furnish the necessary organization and services of student life. As new universities were founded, hostels and dormitories took the place of the colleges in providing room and board, and a form of social life, for students. Some institutions had separate residential colleges affiliated with them that supplied similar facilities. Little beyond this was considered necessary until well into the nineteenth century.

When student enrollments increased and university communities expanded, new services were required. Recreational facilities had to be added to cater to the physical and social needs of youth. Thus, athletics and sports programs were early recognized as essential to the welfare of the university community. Physical education soon followed, though usually on an informal basis. The voluntary service of coaches in the various sports and in gymnastics was a common arrangement. Playing fields of various types were then necessary, as well as gymnasia and other facilities for indoor games. As time went on stadia and field houses were required to provide for spectators.

These provisions for the great body of students did not care for those suffering from the minor and major ailments to which youth is subject. The ill, as well as the able-bodied, student must be served by the educational institution. Thus health services developed. Sick bays, infirmaries or hospitals became essential equipment, together with nurses and doctors, part-time or full-time, depending on the size of the institution and the state of the health of the students.

Counseling of students was given by the faculty in the small institution, whatever the type of problem. Since the ratio of students to faculty was small, the teacher could know each student and counsel him on personal, social or vocational matters. With growth in enrollments and in the ratio of students to faculty this became more difficult. As interest in research grew, the teacher had no time for student counseling, since instruction and research required all his energies. This gave rise to a new kind of staff member, the student counselor, guidance officer, dean of men, or dean of women, etc. In the larger American universities these officers have large staffs who are fully occupied with extra classroom duties such as discipline, individual and social adjustment problems and vocational guidance.

Another need of student life was early recognized as essential to the development of youth, the encouragement of students to participate in the organization and management of their own extra-curricular activities. A variety of student activities is found on every campus. In the larger universities the number and variety of these organizations are bewildering. One British university, for example, had seventy-odd student organizations to cater to some 3,500 students. Another, with 700 students, listed fifty-three student organizations.

In recent times another element of student life has grown to the point that it deserves special consideration. For many years an international exchange of students has played a minor role in university life. Since World War II this has taken on new significance. The numbers of students and countries involved have no parallel in the previous history of education. Its importance does not, however, lie simply in the numbers involved, but in its influence on present-day university students and the effect upon the future of international understanding which this development can have.

This chapter, then, will deal with facilities found in the Commonwealth countries and in the United States under the headings: (1) Student Housing; (2) Athletics and Recreation; (3) Health Services; (4) Personnel Services; (5) Student Organizations, and (6) International Student Exchange.

Student Housing

In the United Kingdom there are great differences between the universities in the percentage of students cared for in residential halls and hostels, or colleges. They range all the way from the ancient universities, where until recently a large proportion of the students was housed in the colleges, to King's College, New Castle, which provided housing for the smallest percentage of its students in 1956–1957, with 241 residential places for 3,011 students. The overall picture for all universities and university colleges in Great Britain as of 1955–1956 showed slightly more than one-quarter of the students cared for in colleges and halls of residence. In that year 27.5 per cent resided in colleges or halls; 44.7 per cent, in lodgings; and 27.8 per cent, at home.[1]

In the Commonwealth countries the percentages housed by the universities are usually lower than in Britain. In most instances the universities depend upon affiliated residential colleges for the housing of students. In some cases hostels have been constructed by the university for the housing of its own students, but this is not common: in Australia, 9 per cent; in Canada, more than 50 per cent; in India and Pakistan, 10 to 20 per cent; and in South Africa, 31.8 per cent of students are in halls of residence.

In 1957 great interest was exhibited in all Commonwealth

countries in developing housing for university students. The educational advantages have loomed as a highly important element in their desire to provide more residential accommodations.

While the overall figures for the United States are not available, the picture there is considerably brighter than in the British Commonwealth countries. Residential halls have been popular elements in the building program of both the private and public universities. Much housing has been constructed on borrowed funds, to be repaid through rental charges to students. The federal government has provided loans to be used for this purpose. A majority of the American university and college students, excluding the junior colleges, live in dormitories or in fraternity houses, which usually are located on the campus and are under the general supervision of the university authorities.

The fraternities are a unique feature of the American colleges and universities. They sprang from the early literary societies of the late eighteenth and early nineteenth centuries. In the beginning they were local, independent groups, but in 1780–1781 Phi Beta Kappa of William and Mary granted charters to groups at Yale and Harvard. From this beginning has grown a vast array of national fraternities and sororities. Seventy-seven national fraternities and forty-five national sororities now sponsor from five to 110 chapters each.[2] Sororities were patterned after the fraternities, and began to be established about the middle of the nineteenth century. Phi Beta Kappa has become exclusively an honorary society. Most of the contemporary fraternities that sprang from it are concerned now with social life and extra-curricular activities. After the Civil War, 1861–1865, the fraternities and sororities began to purchase houses in which their members could live. Thus they provided a part of the physical equipment of the universities and colleges. Their influence has so permeated every phase of college life that it is not possible to understand American higher education without taking them into account. It is not the purpose, however, at this point to discuss their importance as student organizations, but rather to call attention to the role which they have played in the solution of the housing problem on campuses throughout the United States.

The doubling of enrollments anticipated before 1970 in all the countries under review brings into sharper focus the acute problem of housing. In India, where almost half the universities are less than twelve years old, this problem is more critical than elsewhere. It is true that the new universities there acquired some residential facilities through the colleges which they incorporated as affiliated institutions, but only 10 to 20 per cent of Indian students live in university housing.

The fact that student housing is income-producing makes it somewhat easier to finance than other types of university buildings. However, building dormitories, hostels or residence halls on borrowed money is not satisfactory. The cost of maintenance, repair and replacement is too great to make it feasible. To attempt liquidation of the total cost of such construction through rental charges is a dangerous policy, since the rates would have to be prohibitively high. Some American states provide one-third to one-half the funds required for construction and equipment of dormitories, permitting the institutions to borrow the balance, and have found it reasonably satisfactory. This plan of borrowing for hostel construction has not been tried to any appreciable extent in the Commonwealth countries.

Athletic and Recreational Facilities

English-speaking peoples have traditionally been fond of competitive sports. From the early days of Oxford and Cambridge emphasis on games and sports has been more marked than in the universities of Europe and Asia. They are considered important as recreation for youth, but that is not the only reason for the emphasis. There is a common belief among the English-speaking peoples that sports make a real contribution to the education and character development of youth. The old saying that the battle of Waterloo was won on the playing fields of Eton echoes a belief that is prevalent among Anglo-Saxons. This conception of games and sports has been a significant factor in the development of the athletic programs found in the countries under review.

It is of interest to note the variety of sports that are listed in the *Commonwealth Universities Yearbook* of 1957. They are as follows: soccer, Rugby, football, boxing, rowing, golf, LaCrosse, netball, basketball, badminton, cricket, tennis, hockey, swimming, table tennis, squash racquets, fencing, gymnastics, polo, yachting, shooting, ju-jitsu, billiards, judo, shinty, harrier, Gaelic football, jukskei, wrestling, archery, skiing, horseback riding and cross-country running.

Not all but many of these sports are found in each of the universities of the British Commonwealth. In the beginning sports were spontaneous and informal, engaged in merely for fun and physical exercise. Such intramural sports still exist. Larger and larger numbers of students are attracted to some form of sport on the purely local and intramural level. As interest grew, competition with other colleges and universities developed. Most of the Commonwealth universities have inter-university sports programs which are attracting spectators in larger and larger numbers. Even in India this is an important feature of a number of the older universities. The Oxford and Cambridge cricket match dates from 1827; the boat race from 1829. Association football, Rugby, cricket and basketball, along with rowing, are popular sports in all Commonwealth countries. All these have value for the spectators, as well as for the players, but the wider the student participation, the more value a sports program has. In this respect, British universities have set an example for other countries. This is notably true of Oxford and Cambridge, where practically all students take part in some sport.

In the United States the program of athletics and physical education has developed as a prominent division in many institutions. Football and basketball have been highly commercialized and so popular that they fill the largest stadiums. There are regional and national collegiate athletic associations that undertake to maintain high standards of sportsmanship and to promote the educational values inherent in sports. The commercial aspects of the program have, however, brought it into disrepute in some areas. The over-emphasis upon games and sports in some high schools, colleges and universities is little short of shocking when football holidays are declared, and all hands are encouraged to attend the game. Such over-emphasis is much more common in the United States than in the Commonwealth countries. The reputation of some universities as educational institutions has suffered seriously from it.

At one time baseball was the major American university sport. It is now football, followed closely by basketball, that attracts the largest numbers. With the growing interest in professional football, there are some indications that campus excesses may be on the wane, though the evidence is not yet convincing. All who are interested in educational progress cannot but be concerned about the evils resulting from the commercialization of university sports.

Medical and Health Facilities

A wholesome development in the modern university has been the growing emphasis upon the health of students. In the major universities regulations require all students to be examined on admission and in some cases annually as long as they are students. In Britain the universities generally require X-ray of chest, inspection of teeth, eyes and a general physical examination. Birmingham, Bristol and Leeds have such examinations annually. Sheffield requires the examination only on entrance. In the University of Wales the Welsh National School of Medicine gives examinations to all students. North Staffordshire, Leicester, Edinburgh, St. Andrews and Queen's University (Belfast) have compulsory medical and health examinations. In Canada, McGill, McMaster, Manitoba, New Brunswick, St. Mary's, the University of British Columbia and Dalhousie require physical examinations or physical training of all students. In India the same program is developing. Baroda, Mysore, Osmania, Travancore, and in Pakistan, Dacca University, all require that students be subjected to health tests of various kinds.

Institutions in the countries under review generally provide sick bays, infirmaries or hospitals, part-time or full-time medical officers and nursing and dental service. Some institutions check students before their participation in strenuous sports. Some have special programs for the control of communicable diseases and a follow-up on physical defects found in the matriculation check-up. In Melbourne University, Australia, the student union has developed a blood bank. Weekly lectures on physiology, health and hygiene are frequently provided. In Calcutta there is an arrangement for inspection of hostels and halls of residence. In Osmania students are examined before they are admitted to hostels. At Visva-Bharati there is a leprosy clinic.

The health program is financed in a variety of ways. In some instances there are small charges, but in most universities there is an overall fee which includes the medical examination and limited treatment in case of illness. While some of the newer universities in India have not yet developed health programs, the concern there, as in the other Commonwealth countries and in the United States, is to provide adequate health and medical care for all students as a primary responsibility.

In the United States, whatever the size of the college or university, facilities and personnel to look after the health of students are provided. In the larger universities a full-time medical staff, including doctors and nurses, and a well-equipped infirmary are characteristic. Provision is made not only for maintaining physical health, but in the larger universities psychologists and psychiatrists are also available for consultation on a full- or part-time basis and for treatment if necessary. For these health programs American colleges and universities usually require a special medical or health fee.

Student Personnel Services

In addition to provisions for housing, boarding, recreation and health, colleges and universities have recognized another need not met in the classroom, that of counseling and guidance.

At the ancient universities the college system was well adapted to providing the personal and social counseling needed by the students, when the groups were small. The faculty lived largely within the college. Thus there was constant and intimate contact between students and faculty at Oxford and Cambridge. The residential colleges of the universities in Canada, Australia and India, as well as of the civic universities, meet this need partially. Even in the residential halls there is a certain amount of supervision and contact between staff and students that assist the students in various kinds of extracurricular problems. But, as already noted, large numbers of students now live in lodgings or at home, and hence do not have the benefit of the close contact with staff which is provided for the majority of students who live in university housing. In Britain, for example, the 44.7 per cent in lodgings and the 27.8 per cent living at home frequently have little contact with the faculty except in the classroom. These percentages will increase as the enrollment expands. Thus, the problem of counseling, already serious, is bound to become more so as time goes on. Universities will be unable to provide the additional housing required for the increased number of students, which means that the percentage of those living in lodgings and at home will increase. For instance, in Britain, where plans in 1957 called for admitting 40 per cent more students during the quinquennium than in the beginning, provision for residence halls is not expected to keep pace with expanding enrollments.

In the universities under review counseling and guidance needs have generally been neglected. Even in the United States, where vast numbers live in dormitories and fraternity houses, the universities have been slow in recognizing the importance of this problem. While more has been done there than in the Commonwealth countries, the problem is far from being adequately solved.

The situation of the pass degree student in the civic universities of England, to which Bruce Truscot called attention, illustrates the nature of the need as student numbers increase. There, a form of counseling for freshman students is gradually being established, but in most cases the counselor has little preparation for the task. In the United States the faculty adviser system has been supplemented by full-time personnel officers, known as deans of students. Counseling and personnel problems of many kinds are concentrated in the one office. The University of Natal has established the office of student counselor following the American pattern. This officer serves the two branches of the university located at Pietermaritzburg and Durban, sixty miles apart. A few Indian universities have counselors, but they are not as common in the Commonwealth as in the United States.

Various patterns have developed in the United States in the field of student counseling. Counselors, living in large residence halls, or dormitories, work closely with the deans of students and their assistants to provide a variety of services, including job opportunities while in the university. They serve as advisers to student organizations, counseling with the officers and planning with them the activities and programs. In addition to full-time personnel officers, academic counselors are frequently appointed from the faculty, who help freshmen and sophomores with academic problems. At the beginning of the junior year the head of the major department or someone appointed by him frequently serves in this capacity.

In counseling, personality schedules or tests of emotional stability are frequently used. In the larger universities psychiatrists and psychologists confer with students referred to them by the personnel officers, and provide assistance in solving adjustment problems.

The vocational guidance field developed late, but is now highly organized in many of the stronger universities. Information on various careers and their requirements is a part of this guidance. Aptitude tests to determine the fitness of students for different types of work are part of the equipment used in vocational guidance work. Frequently placement is combined with guidance so that there are officers who assist the students in finding work, not only during college days, but upon graduation. After all, the choice of vocation is one of the most important decisions made by youth, and yet, the matter is often decided in a haphazard manner with little help from adults.

The problem of guidance will become more difficult as student numbers increase. The needs of society in special areas, such as science and technology, will require different levels of training—technicians, technologists, engineers, engineering helpers and pure scientists. Determining the type of training needed for each and acquainting students with these will make more complex the training and guidance programs.

Many difficulties lie in the way of meeting the need for student personnel services. In the first place, the shortage of staff is universal, too few professors for the number of students. Again counseling is a special field of education for which few are suited by temperament, training or experience. Furthermore, the absorption of the time of faculty members in teaching the larger classes will be greater than in previous years. In addition, there is more expected today by way of research on the part of the teaching staff than before. Thus, the problems of meeting the counseling and guidance needs of students will grow as student numbers increase and society's needs expand.

It should be remembered that the effectiveness of the entire educational program may depend largely upon the effectiveness of counseling and guidance. If a student has unsolved personal problems, or is maladjusted socially, his work is affected adversely. Many drop out as a result of inability to adjust. Frequently professional help could save them. Others choose fields of study for which they are not suited. Loss of time and discouragement are the result. Help in appraising aptitudes and understanding the requirements of the various vocations and professions would obviate much of that waste.

No other major problem in universities has received so little attention in the past as that of counseling and guidance. It is highly important, in view of the rapid expansion which lies ahead, that a new emphasis be placed upon this phase of university responsibility. Only meager attempts to solve this problem are in evidence in the Commonwealth countries. There is, however, a growing interest in the matter. A few universities in India have recently added student counselors to their staff. When the student bodies were small and highly selected, and from privileged homes, the need for student counseling may have been negligible, but the situation is now, and in the future will be, very different. It is highly important that this need be reckoned with in planning for the future.

Student Organizations

Student life in colleges and universities reflects, in its organization, the same tendency as community life outside. A great variety of societies, clubs, circles, guilds, associations, etc. characterize the student community in all the English-speaking universities. The story of higher education in these institutions would be incomplete without some analysis of this phenomenon and some appraisal of the way in which the organization of life on the campus affects the educational impact of the institution as a whole.

All are agreed that the interaction of students on each other is an important factor in the complex educational process. Young people learn valuable lessons from each other. They are also stimulated by association with their peers in significant ways. Sometimes fellow students have more influence on their colleagues than their teachers, especially in the area of motivation. In the give and take of the classroom, the playing field, the debating society, etc., tolerance and respect for the opinions of others are encouraged and developed.

In the light of these facts, the organization and activities of students function not merely to provide pleasant association and recreation, but also to furnish essential educational ingredients. For that reason they deserve attention. Too often the extra-curricular activities have evolved from poorly developed concepts, or none. The result has been that some organized groups serve little useful purpose and require much time and energy on the part of students. On the other hand, many values may be derived from the organizations of students if the purposes are worthy and the activities well planned.

In the first place they learn by actual experience the way in which democracy works. Through the debating of issues, through compromise where there is difference of view, and through learning the art of reaching sound conclusions, student organizations provide invaluable experience and lessons not taught in the classroom. In view of the role organizations play in modern society, it is highly important that one learns the effective means of securing results by group action. Students learn to judge their fellows, their motivations, capacities and methods of achieving results. By the same token they are able to measure their own capacities.

Qualities of leadership are developed through serving as an

officer in a group of one's peers. Positions of responsibility require those attitudes, qualities of character and skills in working with others that are essential to leadership if success is to be achieved. Learning to serve as a yeoman in the ranks may be as valuable as serving in an official position. Much can be learned by those who make up the rank and file of the group. One needs to learn how to compromise on detail without involving principles. Both the leaders and the members of groups learn the lessons of tolerance as they participate in the discussion of issues where the differences of opinion are sharp.

Student organizations are educationally important in that they provide a basic incentive for the development of individual talents. In the wide variety of activities every kind of ability is called for. The debating societies, the dramatics clubs, the musical organizations of various kinds are examples of groups in which the expression of special gifts is sought. Frequently students discover talents in themselves that had not been recognized before. Those who have acquired skills in various forms of expression before entering the university have an opportunity to refine them as they participate in undergraduate activities.

There are two broad types of student organizations: (1) those that represent the entire student body, and (2) those that are of interest to particular groups. Types of university-wide organizations are student unions, guilds, student government associations, dramatics and debating societies, choral clubs, glee clubs, bands, orchestras, etc., and major honor societies, such as Phi Beta Kappa, Sigma Xi and Omicron Delta Kappa.

The second broad classification might be styled departmental clubs. Mathematics, physics, English, history, indeed almost every major department on the university campus has a club which promotes interest in the subject and provides stimulation through associations with others of like interests.

Departmental clubs also provide informal contacts with teachers, which frequently result in a new appreciation of their qualities. This type of student organization is not found as frequently in Commonwealth countries as in the United States.

Student representative councils, guilds and associations are common elements of student life in well-established universities. Their purposes and methods vary in detail in different countries and in different universities, but the general aim is the same. They coordinate student activities, foster a fuller and more vigorous life and serve as a liaison body between student societies and organizations and the university authorities. In some universities these groups operate more or less independently; in others they cooperate closely with the faculty. Most of the universities throughout the Commonwealth have a guild or students' representative council, and these have organized national student unions to which the local organizations belong.

This is not true in South Africa, where since 1933 the Afrikaanse Studentebond has enjoyed the support of the Afrikaans medium universities, while the English medium universities support the National Union of South African Students.

In the United States there is a federation of Student Government Associations, organized in 1947, that has a membership of some 500,000 students. Among its purposes are: (1) to stimulate and improve democratic student government; (2) to improve student welfare; (3) to promote international understanding, and (4) to maintain academic freedom. This organization holds annual meetings and has a monthly publication called *Student Government Bulletin*.[3]

The purposes of student government associations in the United States are twofold: to assist the administrative authorities of institutions in maintaining smoothly-functioning relations with students; and to provide for students firsthand experience in democratic government. Though student government asso-

ciations and unions normally work in cooperation with faculty
and administration, they sometimes assume great authority.
In India, when the seizure of the Suez Canal resulted in
British and French troops being sent there, the student union
in one of the universities declared a strike, which lasted more
than a week, in the course of which the students held protest
meetings. In other cases student organizations have been
known to oppose administration policies, thereby creating
problems of some magnitude. Fortunately such actions are
exceptional. Generally a good relationship exists between the
unions and university administrations in the countries under
review. In Canada several student unions have raised substantial funds for buildings and equipment. In most institutions
they make real contributions to the stability and progress of
the university community.

The interests of student unions, and student government
associations, cover all phases of student life. They have made
pronouncements on such important issues as the value of the
lecture-system; on various matters that touch on the welfare
of students as a whole; on special problems that arise on the
campus; on the needs for better housing, better food, better
communications, etc. The wishes of students are usually trans-
mitted to the administration through the officers of the organization. In some instances disciplinary problems are handled
by the students without reference to faculty or administration.
In others they make recommendations to the administration which takes responsibility for the final decision. It has
many advantages, not only in the training of the students who
participate, but also in the regulation and control of student
life.

Another organization found in the United States is the
"honor society." The best known are Phi Beta Kappa in the
arts and Sigma Xi in science—both emphasizing scholarship—
and the O.D.K. Society, which recognizes leadership as well
as scholarship. In addition to these, honor societies have been

established in most of the major divisions of the university, all designed to foster high standards of scholarship. Schools of commerce, education, engineering, medicine, law, pre-medical studies and military training have such societies. While these societies are student organizations, the faculty cooperates in the selection of members and in the planning of programs, without relieving students of the major responsibility.

The social fraternities referred to earlier in this chapter have been the subject of controversy throughout their history. Some institutions have banned them; others have welcomed them and assisted them in developing chapter houses. A chief objection is that they develop snobbishness and other un-American attitudes in students, since membership is only by invitation. Such procedure, it is alleged, is undemocratic. Some are excluded who would like to be members. Some complain that students devote too much time to the social life fostered by fraternities, though the scholastic records of members compare favorably with those of non-fraternity men and women. Lack of discipline, excessive drinking, and low standards of conduct generally, including social irregularities, have sometimes occurred, which have brought these organizations under criticism. Through the cooperation of the national headquarters, the standards of fraternity chapters have been steadily raised in recent years.

On the credit side of the ledger there are significant values accruing from the social fraternity and sorority. As already suggested, they provide housing for many students. The small groups provide an opportunity for students to become well-acquainted with each other, which is important in institutions with large enrollments. They also afford students an opportunity to learn something of business management through the handling of their own affairs. While there is usually supervision of the management of the chapter house, the responsibility is on the shoulders of the members. Not only the universities, but the national organizations are concerned with efficient management. The chapter houses provide meals for the members who desire it and, in most cases, rooms for a majority of the members.

Despite the opposition which these organizations have encountered, they have continued to expand. In the decade ahead, when student numbers will be expanding, fraternities and sororities will doubtless experience still greater growth. The interest of the national society in the scholastic achievements of its members has been an encouraging development. This has resulted in raising standards of scholarship. On many campuses the average scholarship record of fraternity men and women is higher than that of non-fraternity students. The national organizations have also been concerned frequently about the reputation of their chapters on the various campuses. Through stimulation from that source, many fraternities and sororities have been encouraged to improve living and social as well as academic standards.

In both the Commonwealth countries and in the United States the student union building has become a recognized essential in the well-run institution. It serves as the focus of student social life, providing headquarters for the various student organizations, and snack bars or dining rooms for students. As a popular social center it serves the highly useful purpose of creating a sense of unity in the college or university community. In 1951 student unions were operating, under construction, or in the planning stage in 293 institutions in the United States.

In most cases there is administrative supervision of union buildings. Often a staff member will be quartered there charged with the responsibility of seeing that it is efficiently managed and that the proper atmosphere is maintained. Though the modern student union building is a comparatively recent development, it has proved so valuable that it has a high priority on the list of university housing needs.

A final phase of student organization which deserves special mention is that of student publications. On the large campuses in the United States daily newspapers are sometimes provided; on others it is a weekly that gives news of the happenings in the university. These publications are usually popular with students, and they perform the highly useful function of focusing attention on problems that concern the community as a whole in addition to their news reporting. Conflicts occasionally arise over news stories or editorial comments. Through bad management the publication may be below standard, or the financing may be inadequate. To meet such contingencies there is usually a publications board made up of both faculty and students, to whom such matters may be referred. The student staff, however, carries the burden of the enterprise.

Most colleges and universities produce yearbooks that give information about student organizations, individuals, particularly members of the senior class, and the administration. Pictures of the campus, its buildings, administrative staff and students largely make up this publication. It assists in developing an understanding of the various phases of student life and also in developing a sense of unity among students. Though these publications are expensive, they are popular with students and are usually financed largely or wholly by sales to them. Indeed some enterprising and energetic students have been known to make a handsome profit in the production of the yearbook, through local advertisements and subsidies from student organizations and sales.

A third publication found on many campuses is known as the "humor" magazine. In the effort to provide the kind of humor which the editor thinks will satisfy his clientele he sometimes fails to exercise good taste, with the result that he incurs criticism, sometimes of students, but more often of faculty and administration and frequently of outsiders as well. The most famous of the humor magazines in the United States is the Harvard *Lampoon*, which has been published now for many decades, and has established a wide reputation for its wit, its rashness and its satirical humor.

A fourth student publication is the literary magazine. This is more unstable than other student publications in the United States. Its success seems to depend largely on an individual faculty member, or on some unusually able and persistent student who is willing to give the time and effort required to develop an acceptable product. Consequently many literary magazines in American universities are short-lived. Few are found in British universities.

It is obvious that student publications provide excellent training in a variety of fields. The editor and business manager of each publication have highly practical experience in organization, management and financing their enterprises. The reporters have valuable experience in newsgathering and in presenting facts through stories or pictures. Perhaps the greatest value, however, is the stimulation which it provides to learn the art of writing and to develop a sensitiveness to the problems of student life to which the newspaper in particular calls attention. The yearbook provides for the exercise of a wide variety of talent in design, in selection of pictures, in displaying of student organizations and in producing a book which will win the approval of fellow students. The humor and literary magazines provide for the expression of other kinds of gifts.

In the Commonwealth universities student publications are less numerous, less frequent and less varied in character. Newspapers are usually issued weekly or fortnightly. Other publications appear once, twice or three times per year. Typical examples are the University of Birmingham, which issues *Guild News* weekly, *The Mermaid* twice annually and *Carnival Magazine* once a year. The University of Alberta (Canada) has an annual (*Evergreen and Gold*), a weekly newspaper (*Gateway*), and two quarterly magazines, *Western Theatre* and a literary quarterly. Melbourne in Australia publishes an annual magazine, a weekly newspaper and five departmental magazines representing medicine, commerce, law, science and engineering. Orange Free State University (South Africa) issues an annual and a monthly magazine. Indian university student publications are rare. Occasionally the student union publishes an annual or semi-annual magazine.

Foreign Student Exchange

A phenomenon of great significance is the unprecedented international exchange of students which has occurred in the universities of the British Commonwealth and of the United States since 1945. Since earliest times students have migrated to other lands. It was the refugees from the University of Paris that played an important part in the founding of Oxford University in 1167. Similarly the return of students from the continent made possible the founding of the first university in Scotland, St. Andrews, in 1411. The migration of students in pursuit of learning is as old as organized higher education itself. However, the volume of the exchange since 1945 is of such magnitude in the universities studied as to merit special consideration.

Table 9 will give a picture of the foreign students in British Commonwealth universities in the 1956–1957 session.

TABLE 9

Country	Total University Enrollment	Foreign Student Enrollment	Percentage Foreign Students
United Kingdom	81,705	9,962	12 per cent
Canada	72,000	3,484	4 per cent
Australia	33,327	1,569	4 per cent
New Zealand	5,215	183	3 per cent
South Africa	28,010*	1,078	3.8 per cent
India	563,901	2,067	.3 per cent

* Including 6220 external students. Source: *Commonwealth University sities Yearbook 1957*.[4]

Table 10 shows the distribution by fields of study of those students attending universities in Britain (239 unclassified).

TABLE 10

Subject	Student Number
Agriculture and Forestry	247
Arts	3,982
Dentistry	368
Medicine	1,711
Pure Science	1,302
Technology	2,046
Veterinary Science	67
Total number	9,723

Source: *Commonwealth Universities Yearbook 1957*.[5]

In the United States 34,232 students from 129 different countries were studying in the colleges and universities in 1954–1955. Of this number 19,124 were enrolled as undergraduates, 12,110 as graduate students, 2,205 with special status, and 793 whose academic interest was not given. In 1957–1958 more than 40,000 foreign students were enrolled in the universities of the United States.

Approximately 30 per cent of the foreign students in the United States in 1954–1955 came from the Far East, 25 per cent from Latin America, 15 per cent from Europe, 13 per cent from Canada and the remainder from the Near and Middle East, Africa and Oceania. Those from Jordan, Cuba, Venezuela, Colombia, Jamaica, Greece and Korea were chiefly undergraduates; those from India, the United Kingdom, the Philippines and Thailand were chiefly graduate students.

More than half of all these students were under twenty-five years of age; 12 per cent were under twenty; almost 25 per cent, between twenty-five and thirty; and 17 per cent, over thirty. Somewhat less than 25 per cent were women. The area with the largest percentage of women was the Philippine Islands, a total of 46 per cent.[6]

The fields of study attracting the largest number of foreign students were engineering and the various branches of the humanities, more than 7,000 students in each. The social, natural, physical and medical sciences, business administration, education and agriculture followed in that order. Every state, the District of Columbia, Alaska, the Canal Zone, Hawaii and Puerto Rico enrolled students from abroad. Almost two-thirds of the total number, however, were concentrated in New York, California, Massachusetts, Michigan, Illinois, Pennsylvania, Texas, Indiana, Ohio and the District of Columbia, with more than 25 per cent in New York and California.

The institutions having the largest percentage of foreign students were M.I.T., with 11.6 per cent; Cornell and Harvard, 7 per cent each; Columbia, 5 per cent; and the University of Michigan, 4 per cent.

It is frequently assumed that foreign governments, along with the American Government, furnish most of the funds for students from abroad. Actually in 1954–1955 only 12 per cent of foreign students in the United States reported either American or foreign government aid as the source of their support. On the other hand, it was estimated in 1952–1953 that approximately 25 per cent of the foreign students in the colleges and universities of the United States had full or partial tuition grants from the institutions which they attended.

Where the number of foreign students is small, a faculty member, assisted by a small committee, serves as adviser to them, usually on a part-time basis. In the larger institutions it is common to find someone giving full time to this work. London University has had an adviser to overseas students since 1946. In a few instances universities provide an "International House" which serves as a center for foreign students and for the advisers who work with them. Few institutions have made adequate provision for the counseling and guidance of foreign students since the influx of such large numbers. There is, however, great interest in this matter, and increasing efforts are being made to assist them in their adjustment to the end that their American experience will have maximum value.

In all British Commonwealth universities somewhat less than 20,000 foreign students were enrolled in 1954–1955, while in the United States the number was in excess of 34,000. On the other hand, the percentage of foreign students in the university population of Commonwealth countries was much higher than that of the United States. Foreign students in the United States accounted for only 1¼ per cent of the 2,720,000 college students, whereas in the Commonwealth (excluding India) they constituted some 7 per cent of the university population.

The influence of the foreign student population on the college and university campuses can have a far-reaching effect on the future of international relations. The fraternization of American students, for example, with young men and women from 129 countries should make a real contribution to international understanding. If the foreign students in the English-speaking universities find their association pleasant and profitable and the kind of instruction which they seek, they will be powerful factors in the promotion of international good will. More than 50,000 men and women each year are pursuing higher education in English-speaking countries. This means that a great army of leaders will have an opportunity to become acquainted with the ideals and motivations of the Western world. At the same time students from other lands provide American and Commonwealth students with an opportunity to understand their hopes and aspirations. Perhaps the most important contribution which foreign students make to campus life is the atmosphere of interest which they create in what is going on in other lands. This may prove to be one of the most valuable by-products of the unprecedented international exchange of students which has characterized the post-war period.

Summary

In the foregoing pages the nature and variety of student services, organization and activities have been described, with some comments on their effect upon the development of the student. It remains to suggest that the tone and atmosphere of campus life is a matter of primary importance. What are the concerns of students and faculty? What are the prevailing topics of conversation in their informal sessions? What provision is made by students, faculty and administration to stimulate interest in matters intellectual, ethical, esthetic and spiritual? The climate of campus life may be the chief asset of a university, transcending all others in its contribution to the development of youth. Is there a conscious effort to promote its development?

At Dartmouth College, for some years, a program called the Great Issues Course has been required of all seniors. This program, which acquaints students with some of the significant issues of their time and brings them into contact with American leaders of thought and action, is perhaps the most imaginative, serious and sustained attempt to create an atmosphere and climate conducive to the stimulation of mature social and intellectual growth among the universities in the United States.

Proper guidance and stimulation of student organizations and activities can affect profoundly the spirit and attitude of the university community. The ideals of sportsmanship on the playing fields, the spirit of tolerance and respect for others in the debating clubs or in the day-to-day collaboration in organizational activities, and the habit of meticulous honesty and sincerity may accomplish far more than classroom instruction in developing personality and teaching the art of effective human relations. The nature of programs sponsored by the dramatics, music or art clubs may do more to develop taste and discrimination than any other influence in the university. The character, quality and interests of visiting lecturers may stimulate the spirit of inquiry and learning in ways which are not available to the classroom instructor. Few institutions realize the full potential of the educational impact of student activities and organizations, but there is a growing awareness of their importance.

VIII

Women and Higher Education

❖❧❧❧❧❧❧❧❧❧❧❧❧❧❧❧❧❧❧❧❧❧❧❧❧❧❧❧❧❧❧❧❧❧❧❧❧❧❧

The past century has witnessed phenomenal growth and change in higher education. Enrollments have increased unbelievably, new types of programs have been added, the scope of instruction has expanded and the goals of university education have been transformed. Among the many changes which have occurred, the admission of women to the universities is by all odds the most significant. It is difficult to realize that it was only eighty-one years ago that women were first admitted to a British university. London took that step in 1878, and some decades later the older universities followed the lead. Indeed, it was 1948 when Cambridge finally accorded women full privileges. It is the purpose of this chapter to sketch the development of the higher education of women in the English-speaking countries, and to comment on its significance and on various aspects of the university curriculum as it relates to the opportunities offered.

Before outlining the story of colleges for women and of coeducation, it is appropriate to present a few facts about the early history of women and higher education. It is seldom realized that in the middle ages, between the sixth and tenth centuries, competent scholars and Latinists were to be found among the nuns of Europe. They not only achieved a high standard of scholarship, but gave classical instruction to younger women. Thus, before the Universities of Paris or Oxford were founded a program of higher education for women had developed. After four centuries, however, the record indicates a decline in scholarly interests and academic achievement among women in Europe.

As a result of the enthusiasm for higher learning during the sixteenth century a few women among the aristocracy became scholars, but the vogue was short-lived. There is no evidence that during the seventeenth and eighteenth centuries there was any emphasis upon, or concern for, the higher education of women. Indeed, it was during this period that the universities in Britain were at their lowest ebb.

The first signs of the revival of interest in women's education appeared in the second quarter of the nineteenth century. It was a part of a larger movement that resulted in the founding of the University of Durham in 1832 and the University of London in 1836. Interest in women's education was expressed in various forms, and in different quarters. For example, Queen's College, established in 1848, led the way in providing scholarly training for girls in England. It was followed by Bedford College in 1849; North London Collegiate School in 1850; and Cheltenham Ladies College, 1854, which was the first to provide a sound education under a boarding school system similar to that given to boys of corresponding ages in the great public schools such as Eton and Harrow.

While these changes were taking place in Britain there was a similar movement in the United States involving the development of colleges for women and provision for women to attend other colleges. Oberlin, founded in 1833, signified in its charter its intention to admit women, and did actually admit them in 1837. Wesleyan College in Georgia was founded in 1836; Judson College (Alabama) in 1838, and Mary Sharp College (Tennessee) in 1852. This last institution began under good auspices, but after about forty years it ran into difficulties and finally closed in 1895. Elmira College (New York) had a happier experience. It had perhaps the strongest foundation of any women's college established to that date, 1855, and is still serving the people of that section. Thus, one hundred years ago the formal higher education of women was just emerging. The ancient universities of England had been operating for more than 600 years, and Harvard was in its third century before women were recognized as capable of profiting from the higher learning.

The United Kingdom

The last half of the nineteenth century witnessed great advances. Between 1860 and 1870 the British expressed an interest in this matter in a variety of ways. The Schools Enquiry Commission (1864–1867), in its report, emphasized the inadequacy of educational opportunities for girls. The North of England Council for Promoting the Higher Education of Women, the London Schoolmistresses Association and the Association for Promoting the Higher Education of Women in Cambridge were formed in this decade. Local examinations were opened to women at Cambridge in 1865 and at Oxford in 1870. In 1867 Edinburgh formed an association for the higher education of women. The plan was for certain professors to give winter courses of lectures in their particular subjects for ladies. This experiment had been tried in other places, but had failed. In Edinburgh it stood the test. By 1884 professors and their assistants were giving instruction to women students in English literature, Latin, Greek, Biblical criticism, logic, moral philosophy, political economy, theory of education, fine art, mathematics, experimental physics, botany, zoology and physiology.

As early as 1877 an association for the higher education of women was formed in Glasgow at a meeting presided over by the principal of Glasgow University. In 1883 the association was incorporated as Queen Margaret College. This institution added a medical school in 1890.

At first Queen Margaret College hoped for affiliation with

the University in such a way that while it would retain its separate existence and management, it would provide instruction that would qualify for university graduation. When the negotiations over affiliation were nearing completion in 1891, the commissioners issued a draft ordinance proposing to empower the University authorities to admit women to the ordinary classes or to establish separate classes for them. When this was voted, Queen Margaret College, instead of seeking affiliation, proposed that its real property, with the endowments of the college, be made over to the University, which would undertake the instruction of women with the stipulation that buildings and grounds and the endowment should be used exclusively for the university education of women.

Under this arrangement Queen Margaret College was dissolved and the house and grounds were given to the University along with an endowment of £25,482. In the beginning its students were taught separately, but they were gradually admitted to the regular classes, starting with the honors group.

After 1870 the movement for the education of women gained momentum in England. The Education Act of that year made instruction in the three R's and domestic arts for girls compulsory. Girton College came into being at Hitchin in 1869, and was established close to Cambridge in 1873. Merton Hall, Cambridge, established in 1872, became Newnham Hall in 1876 and Newnham College in 1880. At Oxford, Lady Margaret Hall, Somerville College, St. Hugh's Hall and St. Hilda's College were established in the period 1878–1893. The Women's Education Union, the parent of the Girls' Public Day School Company, started in 1873, had by 1901 founded thirty-eight day schools for girls providing an education comparable to the best afforded to boys. The Education Act of 1902 included girls in all its provisions for new secondary schools.

As a result of these efforts, there were 160,022 girls in grant-earning schools by the end of the first quarter of the twentieth century, whose average age of matriculation was sixteen years, two months. The development of these schools was greatly aided by the opening of the universities to women, first for lectures and examinations and later for full membership. By 1926–1927, 7,873 women were enrolled in the universities of Great Britain—800 at Oxford, 472 at Cambridge, 3,136 at the University of London, and 3,465 in the provincial universities. The Scottish universities had kept pace with those in England in the admission of women. Indeed, Glasgow had the largest number of women students of all British unitary-teaching universities in 1926–1927, a total of 1,464. By that time, too, teaching posts were nominally open to women in all the universities, but only London and Wales actually had women professors.

The United States

The first settlers in the United States brought with them the traditional European attitude respecting the education of women. Little was needed since marriage was their only respectable vocation. A few dame schools were established in the Colonial period, but up to the end of the Revolution practically the only place in which girls could secure elementary instruction was in the home, though schools for boys and nine colleges had been provided by that time.

There were some exceptions. In Hampton, New Hampshire, when the school teacher was employed in 1649, and at Dover in 1658, it was understood that instruction should be given to all the children, both boys and girls. In Philadelphia, as early as 1689, the Society of Friends established a school (predecessor of the William Penn Charter School) open to all classes and to both sexes. At Nazareth, Pennsylvania, the Moravians organized a school for girls in 1750. In 1784 Dorchester, Massachusetts, permitted girls to attend school from June 6 to October 1, and in 1789 a private school for girls was established at Medford, Massachusetts.

A female seminary was established by Emma Willard in

Troy, New York, in 1821, and Mount Holyoke Seminary, South Hadley, Massachusetts, was opened in 1837. By the middle of the nineteenth century secondary schools were opened to girls, largely displacing the early academies and seminaries.

Higher education for women in the United States began with the founding of Wesleyan College in 1836 and the admission of women to Oberlin in 1837. The story of its development may be conveniently divided into five twenty-five-year periods, beginning with 1835. During the first period, 1835–1860, coeducation began, and four colleges for women were founded. Though authorized to grant degrees, these institutions were not of university grade.

The first college of unquestioned quality was Vassar, chartered in 1861, at the beginning of the second period 1860–1885. Other ranking colleges for women in the Northeast followed in rapid succession: Smith, Wellesley, Wells, Bryn Mawr, Goucher and Mount Holyoke. Mills Seminary in California became Mills College in 1885. All these were liberal arts institutions patterned after Harvard and Yale.

In the third period, 1885 to 1910, a new type of institution developed in the South which is little known within the United States, and scarcely known at all outside. They were the state colleges for women. Their chief characteristic was the emphasis upon studies designed to equip young women for homemaking and for gainful employment outside the home. All of them provided elementary teacher training and technical courses of various kinds. Domestic science, secretarial studies, music and art were among the subjects found in the curricula. Each provided a core of liberal arts studies around which the vocational courses developed. Mississippi, Alabama, Florida, Georgia, South Carolina, North Carolina, Texas and Oklahoma established such institutions. Mississippi State College for Women, opened in 1885, was the first to be established; the Oklahoma College, founded in 1908, was the last.

It is relevant to note that the Land Grant College Act was

passed twenty-three years before the opening of the first state college for women. It was the growing popularity of these technical, agricultural schools for men which encouraged a similar plan of education for women. Just as agriculture, engineering and other practical subjects were popular in the land-grant colleges, so domestic science, secretarial studies, music and art were common subjects of study in the new institutions for women.

The original names of these institutions indicate something of the objects which motivated their founding. In North Carolina, for instance, the institution was first styled the Normal and Industrial School. In Alabama, the Girls' Industrial School, later the Technical Institute and College for Women, and finally, Alabama College; in Oklahoma, the Industrial Institute and College for Girls. In Texas it was referred to as the State College for Women. The new type of women's college followed the lead of the land-grant colleges, which were frequently called "state" colleges.

While technical and vocational courses designed to open these fields to women was a central purpose of these institutions, there was another reason for their establishment. The women's colleges in that period were far more expensive than the men's colleges. Few families in the South could provide the funds necessary for the education of their daughters in the well-established colleges for women. The region was still suffering from the effects of the War Between the States, and there was great need for low-cost education, especially for women. This probably accounts in part for the fact that the independent state-supported college for women developed only in the South. New Jersey established a state college for women in 1918, but it was a department of Rutgers University. New York City established Hunter College, which was supported by city taxes. But with these two exceptions, tax-supported colleges for women developed only in the Southern section of the United States.

The eight state-supported women's colleges in the beginning provided substandard courses. In some instances it was twenty-five years after their founding before the first degrees were awarded. As time went on they raised their standards, developing graduate as well as undergraduate programs. The proportion of work in the liberal arts was increased and strengthened. Two of these institutions have opened their doors to men since 1945, but the distinctive technical and professional courses designed to cater to women have been continued.

In the Northeast Simmons Female College was chartered in 1899 "as an institution in which instruction may be given in such branches of art, science and industry as would best enable women to earn an independent livelihood." Its name was changed in 1915 to Simmons College. This institution sought to provide technical and vocational courses for women along lines similar to those developed by the state-supported colleges in the Southern area. In 1957 it had schools of business, home economics, library science, science, social work, nursing and retailing. Skidmore and Russell Sage Colleges, founded in 1911 and 1916 respectively, followed much the same pattern.

In addition to the separate college for women and coeducation, which began in 1837, there is another type of woman's college in the United States known as the coordinate college, a department of a university. The first of this type was the H. Sophie Newcomb Memorial, opened at Tulane University in 1887. This was followed in 1888 by the Woman's College at Western Reserve University in Cleveland, Barnard College in 1889 at Columbia, and Pembroke at Brown University, which was authorized in 1892 to confer the Brown degree and was made a department of the university in 1897. Radcliffe College was incorporated in 1894 and authorized to confer B.A., M.A., and Ph.D. degrees, subject to the approval of the president and fellows of Harvard College. It dates from 1879, when it began as The Society for the Collegiate Education of Women, "for the purpose of providing systematic instruction for women by professors and other instructors in Harvard University."

The following state universities were coeducational from the beginning: Utah, 1850; Iowa, 1856; Kansas, 1866; Minnesota, 1868; Nebraska, 1871. Other state universities opened their doors to women in the last half of the nineteenth century: Missouri, 1869; Michigan, California and Illinois, 1870; Ohio State, 1873; Wisconsin, 1874. All state universities now admit women to some parts of their program. The privately-controlled institutions followed the spirit of the times. Cornell admitted women in 1872; M.I.T. in 1883; Tufts in 1892. Boston, Stanford and the University of Chicago were coeducational from their founding. In 1956 there were 123 colleges and universities exclusively for men and 181 colleges for women only. Thus women have access to fifty-odd more institutions of higher education in the United States than men.

The period 1910 to 1935 was marked by consolidation of gains. The state colleges for women and many of those which were privately supported were recognized by accrediting associations. The older ranking colleges for women conducted successful campaigns for funds and in many other ways strengthened their positions. New programs introduced by Vassar and Smith attracted wide attention. Stephens Junior College in Missouri evolved a new curriculum for women based upon their vocational and avocational needs in modern society. Numerous other experimental programs appeared during the boom days of the nineteen twenties and the depression years of the nineteen thirties.

During this period, too, the numbers of women students increased more rapidly than in any other. The technical, professional courses, particularly in the state universities, were vastly expanded. The popularity of coeducation reached a new high while at the same time several new colleges for women appeared: Sarah Lawrence (1929), Bennington in Vermont, and Scripps College, California. The period 1910–1935 was the most significant in the history of the higher education of women in the United States. It came of age during this period.

Commonwealth Countries

The pattern of higher education in the British Commonwealth countries is very different from that in the United
States. There are only two institutions in the British Commonwealth exclusively for women authorized to grant degrees.
They are Mount Saint Vincent College in Canada and Thackersey Women's University in India. Most of the institutions in
all Commonwealth countries admit women. Many colleges for
women are affiliated with universities. In Britain itself Oxford
and Cambridge have a total of seven colleges for women, five
at Oxford, two at Cambridge. London University has four
partially segregated colleges for women: Bedford, Westfield,
Queen Elizabeth and Royal Holloway Colleges. There are no
women's colleges affiliated to the provincial universities or to
the Scottish, Welsh or Irish universities. In Canada there are
five colleges for women affiliated to the universities; in
Australia, six affiliated or associated residential colleges; in India and Pakistan, between forty and fifty. Many of the latter
institutions, however, are quite small.

Table 11 indicates the full-time enrollment of women in
various sections of the Commonwealth *in the years designated.*

TABLE 11

Country (and Year)	Enrollment of Women	Total Enrollment[1]
Britain (1954–1955)	20,410	81,705
Canada (1955–1956)	19,131	71,927
Australia (1956)	4,408	18,320
New Zealand (1955–1956)	1,206	5,215
South Africa (1955–1956)*	5,210	21,790
India (1955–1956)	77,489	563,904
Pakistan (1955–1956)	4,251	47,181
United States (1955–1956)	936,771	2,720,929

* These figures do not include 6,220 external students enrolled in the
University of South Africa.

In Commonwealth universities outside of India and Pakistan approximately 25 per cent of all students enrolled are women. In India and Pakistan the proportion is substantially lower. In the United States in the fall of 1955 women students constituted 34 per cent of the total enrollment.

The difference between the programs of higher education for women in the Commonwealth and in the United States lies in the greater number of specialized courses in the latter. As suggested in earlier sections of this chapter, technical and professional courses designed to prepare women for gainful occupations have been developed in a number of women's colleges and in most of the state universities.

The question has been raised in Britain as to whether the university should provide courses limited to the early concepts of the needs of women in preparation for homemaking. Sir Ernest Barker suggests that possibly in justice to women there should be further provision for their special needs. He is aware of the fact that opinions differ on whether women have special educational needs, which differentiate them from men, but he admits that the provision of university education for women, whether along with men or in separate courses, is not yet perfect. It is of interest to note that the proportion of women in United Kingdom universities was lower in 1957 than in 1922, as brought out in the U.G.C. Report submitted to Parliament in 1958.

The percentage of women students in American colleges and universities is distinctly higher than in Commonwealth universities. But this is misleading with respect to the percentage of women who take post-secondary school work. A large number of women in training for elementary school teaching are enrolled in training colleges which require two years beyond the secondary school, but are not counted in Britain or in any other Commonwealth countries as university students. In the United States teachers colleges award degrees, hence their students are counted in college and university statistics. Since elementary teachers are in the main women, if those in training

for this work were added to the university enrollment the
picture would be very different. Hence, in attempting to
appraise the difference between the United States and the
Commonwealth in their provisions for post-secondary school
education of women statistics are of little significance.

The fact that women are admitted to practically all degree-
granting institutions in the Commonwealth countries is also
relatively unimportant. This does not mean that women have
equal educational opportunities. A simple analysis of the
curricula in the universities will reveal this fact. The basic
educational program represented by the arts college is perhaps
of equal value to both men and women, and if the universities
confined their offerings to the liberal arts and science subjects,
as was the case a hundred years ago, all English-speaking
countries could claim to make equal provision for its men and
women. But since more than half the university students in
most countries are enrolled in courses other than those of the
Arts Faculty, it becomes necessary to examine the nature of
the offerings outside the arts field. These are, of course, mainly
professional and technical in character.

Faculties of law, medicine, theology, teaching, engineering,
commerce, science and veterinary science provide for the
majority of university students not enrolled in the Arts
Faculties. These prepare for the professions which chiefly
enlist men. Though women are enrolling in increasing numbers,
they constitute a relatively small minority in all professional
fields except teaching. An examination of the curricula of
universities in Commonwealth countries with a view to determining the extent to which they offer educational opportunities
to women will indicate the status of the provisions for women
in university education.

Those programs of training designed to fit women for homemaking and allied vocations, and for those professions in which
the majority of practitioners are women, will be considered
as especially adapted to meet women's needs. For example,

the home sciences, nursing, social work, library science would be classified as programs for women. Using this as the criterion, it will be our purpose to sketch briefly the situation which prevails in the English-speaking countries respecting women's educational opportunities.

In the United Kingdom—England, Scotland, Ireland and Wales—only one university gives a degree course in household science and in nutrition. A number of men take the degree in the latter. This is the University of London. However, domestic science training courses are found in the training colleges affiliated with the Universities of Birmingham, Bristol, Durham, Leeds, Liverpool, London, Manchester, Leicester and Aberdeen. A home science course is also provided by National University of Ireland in one of its constituent university colleges in the adult education division. Diploma courses in nursing are found in Birmingham, Leeds, London and Manchester. There are also courses in social work, but no organized curriculum such as is found in the United States and Canada.

In South Africa domestic science degree courses are found in each of the Afrikaans-speaking universities: Orange Free State, Potchefstroom, Pretoria and Stellenbosch. There is also a diploma course in nursing of one year's length in Cape Town University; a Bachelor of Science in nursing, a four-and-a-half-year course; a Bachelor of Arts in nursing, a four-year course; and a diploma in psychiatric nursing. In Witwatersrand there is a nursing program leading to a diploma. There are no domestic science courses found in the English-speaking universities of South Africa, and no courses in nursing in the Afrikaans institutions. These are apparently the only programs of training designed with particular reference to women in the entire higher education system of South Africa, except such courses as the training colleges give for those who plan to enter the field of elementary teaching.

In Australia no special programs for women are listed in the curricula of the universities or in their affiliated institutions.

The one possible exception is the course in industrial nursing established within the School of Public Health and Tropical Medicine which is found in the University of Sydney. In New Zealand the University of Otago provides a diploma and a degree course in home science, the aim of which is "to provide a thoroughly scientific education for women in subjects concerning the organization and conduct of home life." The program emphasizes the sciences in the degree course and house crafts in the instruction leading to the diploma. There are home science residence halls attached to the School of Home Science in which house crafts are practiced by home science students.

India's provision for the higher education of women presents an unusual picture. It supports the only university for women in the Commonwealth. The Shreemati Nathibai Damodar Thackersey Women's University emphasizes training of women for homemaking. The required courses leading to the Bachelor of Arts in home science include elementary biology, hygiene, home making, home management and cookery, food and nutrition, physiology, psychology and child psychology. Among the optional courses provided by this institution are ethics, philosophy, music, drawing and painting. In addition to the B.A. degree course, the women's university provides both the ordinary and the honors B.Sc. in nursing. The ordinary degree requires three years, the honors degree, four. The University of Baroda also places strong emphasis on programs that are designed to train women for home making. It has a Faculty of Home Science, with a pre-primary school for teaching child development and allied subjects. It also has a Faculty of Social Work with a mental hygiene and psychiatric clinic attached.

Two other universities in India, Allahabad and Delhi, provide degree programs in home arts and sciences. Allahabad gives both the Bachelor of Arts and the Bachelor of Science, the one emphasizing the arts, and the other the sciences that underlie home making. The Universities of Bihar, Calcutta,

Madras, Mysore, Nagpur, all have diploma courses in home sciences and household arts. One of the affiliated institutions of the University of Karachi is a College of Domestic Science. The B.Sc. in nursing is provided at Delhi and Madras. Lahore University (India) has a College of Home and Social Sciences among its affiliated institutions.

In 1958 the Government of India appointed a National Committee on Women's Education, with responsibility for suggesting ways and means to accelerate the pace of women's education in the country.

More courses of special interest to women are listed in Canadian colleges and universities than in other Commonwealth institutions. All of the provincial universities provide such courses and some of the private institutions.

For example, the University of British Columbia has three departments or schools enrolling chiefly women students—a school of nursing, a department of social work and a department of home economics. The departments of home economics and social work are organized within the Faculty of Arts and Sciences; the school of nursing under the Faculty of Applied Science. The University of Manitoba has a graduate professional school of social work, a School of Home Economics, and grants both the B.Sc. and M.Sc. degrees in home economics. It also provides diploma courses in home making, both practical and cultural. The offerings in home economics include five courses in art, nine courses in clothing and textiles, two in education, seven in foods and nutrition and seven in home and family living. In addition to these there are three courses in institutional administration. This range of offerings is typical of the provincial universities. The University of Toronto provides a course in household science, a faculty of music, a graduate school of social work, a school of nursing and a library science school. The University of Saskatchewan has home economics and nursing.

Among the privately-supported institutions, the University

of Western Ontario provides a school of nursing and an affiliated music teachers' college. McGill University has a program in household science, library science and nursing. Twenty degree-granting institutions offer work in home economics or household science; nineteen give nursing; twelve offer social work courses; and seven give library science training, two of which have organized schools of library science.

In the universities of the United States there are six professional schools in which the majority of students are women. There are approximately 500 institutions that provide curricula in home economics; thirty-three have library schools; 193 have fully-accredited schools of music. A large number of other institutions also provide for degrees in music, though they are not fully accredited by the National Association of Schools of Music. There are thirty-nine collegiate schools of nursing on the mainland of the United States, with one in Hawaii and one in Puerto Rico. There are fifty-two graduate schools of social work in the universities of the United States, and approximately 1,200 colleges and universities provide programs of teacher education which qualify students for entering the profession.

As evidence of the popularity of programs which enroll a majority of women students, it will suffice to indicate the distribution of degrees earned in 1954–1955: of 103,709 women students who received first level degrees in that year, 35,790 were in the field of education; 8,711 in fine arts; 8,000 in basic social sciences; 7,978 in English; 7,169 in home economics; and 5,179 in nursing. Thus approximately 70 per cent of the Bachelor's degrees awarded women in 1954–1955 were in fields particularly popular with women. The basic social sciences and English are included in the College of Arts and Science, where women are enrolled in larger numbers than men. Thus, with the single exception of English, the six programs of study which proved most attractive to women students in the United States are rarely found in the British universities.

As one analyzes the picture of university education for women in Britain, its status appears to be about the same as that for men one hundred years ago. In the middle of the nineteenth century colleges and universities were mainly concerned with basic education. The Arts Faculties provided the majority of the offerings. Theology, law and medicine were taught in some institutions, but without emphasis on their professional aspects. Professional training was usually provided by independent proprietary institutions, both in the United States and in the Commonwealth countries. Many of these were later affiliated with universities, and later still became organic parts of universities. The university curricula today differ from those of the nineteenth century in that they emphasize general social needs rather than the needs of the individual for personal growth and development. The languages, mathematics, science and philosophy of the classical curriculum were disciplinary subjects, the aim of which was to develop the intellectual powers of youth. Today the great stimulus to university development is society's need for trained men and women to meet the urgent demands of the present and the future. Science is emphasized not because it is essential to training in method and accuracy of thought, but because it prepares youth to meet the requirements of a scientific and technological age. The economy, as well as national defense, is involved in more and better scientific and technological training. Thus university education has shifted its goals from that of supplying the basic needs of individuals as intelligent human beings to supplying the needs of a society in which science and technology are requisite to stability and progress.

This goal of university education applies equally to women, insofar as they have an interest in scientific and technological careers, but few have that interest and there are relatively few opportunities for them in those fields. In most Commonwealth countries outside of Canada there was no more emphasis upon home sciences and occupations of special interest to women in 1958 than there was on engineering, commerce and technology in 1858. It is in that sense that the higher education of women is a century behind that of men and that opening universities to men and women alike does not mean giving them equal opportunities.

Not only in Commonwealth countries, but also in the United States there is a growing concern about the adequacy and effectiveness of the educational program for women.

The current period (1935–1960) has been characterized by widespread interest in and questioning of the offerings of higher education as they relate to one-third of the population of the colleges and universities—the women students. Several books and numerous articles have appeared since 1945 on the subject of women's educational needs. All have been critical of the provisions now being made. The American Council on Education in 1952 established a Commission on the Education of Women which has been actively engaged in a comprehensive study of the role of women in modern society and the kind of higher education needed to help them play that role effectively.

For the first time in American history women outnumber men in the total population, but only about half as many have opportunity for higher education. In a report of the American Council Commission on the Education of Women, issued in 1954, this significant paragraph appeared:

In this rapidly changing scene, questions are being raised as to whether the basic personal values of Western civilization are being applied as fully as possible in relation to the women of the United States. Are women encouraged to achieve their highest potentialities? Do they hinder their own development and advancement through a lack of clear purposes? Is the education women receive effective in terms of their varied roles? Such questions are becoming increasingly insistent as women assume greater prominence than ever before in the total life of the nation.[2]

Almost one-third of the labor force in the United States is

composed of women. Sixteen members of the National Congress are women. In four million homes, one in ten, the woman is the chief breadwinner as well as home planner. They hold posts in various departments of international, state, county and city government as well as civil service positions at home and abroad. In addition, they are "increasingly enriching and strengthening the cultural life of the nation by their growing prominence in the fields of art, literature, journalism, drama, music, radio and television, religion, science and social work as well as in the professions of teaching, law, medicine, engineering and business." And yet almost unanimously women think of "marriage, home making and child rearing as major goals and responsibilities."

In the light of this background it is obvious that education for every type of vocation and profession should be open to women as they are in the English-speaking universities. But is this enough if little or no education is provided in some areas for those vocations which women generally consider "major goals and responsibilities." If the needs of society are the criteria which guide in curriculum emphasis, what are more fundamental to social stability and progress than those studies which look to strengthening the basic unit of society—the home, child rearing and family solidarity?

The real problem in modern society is that of human relations. Two world wars and a world-wide depression in one generation is proof enough of the fact. The first and most lasting lessons in human relations are learned in the family circle. In the last analysis the aggregate of the attitudes developed by its tone and atmosphere determines the spirit of the international community. In the short run atomic stockpiles and missiles may be our best insurance against war, but in the long run it is only social understanding, tolerance and positive good will that can ultimately insure peace in the world.

It has been suggested that the content of the sciences and arts which underlie home making is not such as to warrant university recognition, that it may be appropriate in a training college but not in a university. Plant genetics, poultry raising, glass technology, brewing and veterinary science currently appear in university calendars, and are accepted as appropriate elements of the curriculum, but not the home sciences and arts.

The home is not merely an agency which provides food, raiment and shelter for the young. It is the incubator of human personality, the generator of human values and the progenitor of community attitudes. What more basic subject could adorn the curriculum and what is more needed in this revolutionary period in the world's history? Those studies which could throw light on the problem of making home life more effective would involve a wide variety of sciences and arts. The biology, physiology and psychology of child growth and development and of adolescence, the chemistry of foods and textiles, the science of nutrition in all its ramifications, and the philosophy of home and family life are but a few of the elements of a curriculum that is slowly developing in some areas. The fact that such subjects have been so slow in finding a place in university education derives perhaps from the monastic origin and domination of universities in their early history.

In the great emphasis on science and technology in the modern curriculum the universities have broken with tradition. A new outlook prevails and new courses are constantly appearing. The boldness which has characterized universities in the development of curricula in science and technology may be needed in the areas which represent the "major goals and responsibilities" of women.

IX

Professional Education—The Learned Professions: Theology, Law and Medicine

❖❘❖

The seven liberal arts made up the medieval curriculum. These were grammar, logic and rhetoric (called "the trivium"), and arithmetic, geometry, music and astronomy (known as "the quadrivium"). The addition of the higher faculties of theology, law and medicine constituted the first expansion of the curriculum in the ancient universities of Great Britain.

For centuries the Faculties of Arts, Theology, Law and Medicine constituted the University. Some European universities began with one or more professional faculties. For instance, Bologna (1088) and Siena (1357) each began as a Faculty of Law; Ferrara (1391) began with Law, Medicine and Surgery; Paris (12th century) with Arts, Canon Law, Medicine and Theology; and Cologne (1388) with Law, Medicine and Philosophy. Oxford and Cambridge, which began with general studies, added Theology, Law and Medicine early in their history, and in recent decades other professional faculties. The civic university colleges in the nineteenth century began the emphasis on science and technology and have greatly extended their offerings in these and other professional fields since becoming universities. Following that pattern the Commonwealth and American universities added training in other vocational, technical and professional areas until professional curricula now occupy a dominant position in the list of university offerings. In addition, pre-professional courses in the colleges of arts and sciences have become so numerous in American universities as to prompt the suggestion that the central faculty of earlier times, the arts college, has become largely a service division. In the Commonwealth countries students enroll in professional curricula, such as law, medicine and theology, on admission to the university. This means that basic studies are either omitted altogether or occupy a minor place in education for the professions. For example, in 1956 the Arts Faculties in the universities of the United Kingdom enrolled only 43 per cent of the total student body, and in some of the universities law, divinity and commerce are included within the Arts Faculty.

With this general sketch of professional education in the modern university as a background, it is the purpose of this chapter to examine in some detail the nature of the program offerings in the older professions as found in the Commonwealth countries and the United States.

Theology

In the institutions which now provide programs in theology the Bachelor of Divinity, a graduate degree, is the most common. It is still found, however, as an undergraduate study in some universities. For instance, in Cambridge, Leeds, Manchester, Nottingham, Oxford, Sheffield and Wales Universities, among the courses leading to the B.A. degree are Biblical history and literature, or theology. The Master of Arts, the first degree in Aberdeen and Edinburgh, may also be taken in theology. A certificate, or diploma course on the undergraduate level, is found at the Universities of Durham, Hull, Glasgow and Leeds. The University of Wales has several affiliated theological colleges that provide instruction in theology for which the B.D. degree is awarded.

The Bachelor of Divinity degree is awarded by all universities in the United Kingdom except Bristol, Exeter, Liverpool,

Reading, Sheffield and Southampton. There is variation in the details of the regulations governing this degree, but the requirements are essentially similar. Usually two to four years of study, a thesis or published work and an examination are required. All universities except Cambridge grant the B.D. degree to graduates of other approved universities, as well as to their own graduates.

The requirements at Cambridge are five years' standing from admission to a first degree, after submitting a dissertation or published work. Queen's University in Belfast will confer the B.D. degree upon graduates of approved universities after two years of further study and examination. The usual requirement in other institutions is a minimum of three years beyond the first degree. The B.D. may be taken with honors at some institutions, though as an advanced degree it is usually granted without honors. The B.A. in Theology is given as an honors, or general degree course.

All the universities which grant the B.D. degree also grant the D.D. (Doctor of Divinity). In addition, the University of London awards the Master of Theology. Only the University of Manchester admits to the Doctor of Divinity degree graduates from other approved universities. There is variation in the length of time after receiving the B.D. degree before the D.D. may be awarded. At Cambridge it is three years; at Manchester, four for its own graduates, and six for graduates of other institutions; at Birmingham and Durham it is five years; at Nottingham, seven. At Oxford one must have completed his Bachelor of Divinity degree fourteen years before he may be granted the D.D. In the Scottish universities the D.D. degree is always honorary.

Manchester University has six associated colleges which are recognized for external lectures in theology. These are: (1) Manchester Baptist College, (2) Hartley Victoria Methodist College, (3) Lancashire Independent College, (4) Moravian College, and (5) Unitarian College. The sixth, The

University School of Theology, is non-denominational and provides courses in comparative religion.

The cooperation between the several denominational schools and the university school has proved mutually beneficial in many ways. The association of prospective ministers with the university students gives them breadth and perspective, and their presence in the university community also makes a contribution to its tone and atmosphere. Professors from the seminaries give lectures in the university school and find stimulation in this association.

The University of Wales has five associated theological schools and colleges. Some of these are located near the constituent colleges, which provide mutually beneficial associations.

In Canada some universities award the Bachelor of Divinity degree, usually through an affiliated theological college. In other cases a theological school is authorized to confer the degree. Trinity and Victoria colleges in Toronto, and St. Anne's in Halifax have such authority.

The major burden of training ministers in Canada is borne by seminaries. There are twenty-five Protestant seminaries: two Baptist, eleven Church of England, two Lutheran, two Presbyterian, and eight United Church. For the secular clergy, the Roman Catholics have ten seminaries, and for the clergy in communities, a total of twenty.

The late Sidney Smith, who for many years was president of the University of Toronto, in speaking of Canadian higher education (November, 1956), had the following to say about seminaries:

> The most numerous professional schools are those which train the clergy. Over two dozen theological colleges are associated either distantly or closely with the English-Canadian universities. They are not large or wealthy; it has been fashionable in some secular academic circles to deprecate their scholarship, yet they exert remarkable influence on university structure. They are not the

children of the university, but rather its godparents. Their theo-
paternal role has been to emphasize the tested educational values
of humane learning, of residential life, of the disciplined academic
community, of the Wykehamite motto: "manners makyth the man."
I do not suggest for a moment that they are the sole protagonists
of those values, but I believe that their contribution in this respect
is considerable.[1]

This tribute to the Protestant theological seminaries indicates
the unusual role which they play in the Canadian system of
education. A total of fifty-five seminaries are supported by the
Protestant and Catholic churches.

In addition to the work of the seminaries, the following
universities grant theological degrees: Acadia and Bishop's
University grant the degrees directly; Alberta, McGill,
McMaster, Queen's and Western Ontario grant them through
their affiliated colleges.

Australia, in contrast with Canada, makes relatively meager
provisions for training in theology. The University of Sydney
established courses in this field in 1937. It now awards the
Bachelor of Divinity degree for three years of work beyond
the first degree, and may also confer the Doctor of Divinity
degree. In 1953 the University of Queensland established
courses in divinity and now provides a three-year program
leading to the Bachelor of Divinity degree and a diploma
course requiring a minimum of two years. The University of
Melbourne is prohibited by Act of Parliament from conferring
degrees in divinity, but the Melbourne College of Divinity,
not a university institution, grants degrees of Bachelor of
Divinity and Doctor of Divinity. No seminaries are found
among the university affiliated institutions. This is in striking
contrast with the prevailing pattern in the United Kingdom
and Canada.

Otago University is the only unit in the University of
New Zealand which provides courses in theology. The enrollment in this division of Otago University is eighteen to twenty

students. The degree of Bachelor of Divinity is awarded by the University of New Zealand for the work done at Otago, one of its constituent units.

In South Africa four teaching universities provide instruction in theology and each grants the Bachelor of Divinity degree. They are: the Universities of Potchefstroom, which grants Th.B., Th.M. and Th.D. degrees; Pretoria, Rhodes and Stellenbosch, each of which grants the B.D. and D.D. degrees. The University of South Africa provides correspondence courses leading to the Bachelor of Divinity, Master of Divinity and Doctor of Divinity degrees, which are awarded as external degrees.

In the University of Natal theological subjects are included under the Arts Faculty. Two courses in Biblical studies, two in theology and a half course in comparative religion are available. The courses in Biblical studies and theology are recognized as two-year majors for the B.A. degree.

One of the difficulties encountered in the development of theological education in South Africa results from the divisions in the Afrikaans Church. In the Union the Dutch Reformed Church—largest of the dominant Protestant peoples—is divided into three major branches. Two of these have theological training in the same university, Pretoria, with two separate faculties having little formal interchange, although informally they do meet together when visiting foreign lecturers are entertained.

In India there are three religions for which theological training is given. The University of Banaras grants degrees in Hindu theology; Aligarh University provides courses leading to the Bachelor's, Master's and Doctor's degrees in Islamic theology; Osmania University provides Master's and Doctor's degrees also in Islamic theology; and Serampore College awards the Bachelor of Divinity and Master of Theology degrees and a diploma course leading to the Licentiate in Theology (L.Th.).

In the United States there are three roughly-defined periods in the development of Protestant theological education: the College period, the Tutorial period, and the Seminary period. Harvard was founded in part for the purpose of training ministers, and for some years about 50 per cent of its graduates went into the ministry. Other colleges provided training for ministers during the Colonial period. This represented the earliest form of theological training.

In the Tutorial period theological education was informal. A minister would take into his home one or more young men and provide them board and lodging, supervise their study, discuss theology with them, and give them practical experience in the work of the church.

Seminaries developed from the tutorial plan. The Rev. John H. Livingston, who was approved by the Dutch Reformed Church as capable of training ministers for that denomination, began his work in Rutgers University, New Brunswick, New Jersey. As student numbers grew he added others to his staff to share in the task. This resulted in the establishment of the New Brunswick Theological Seminary, founded in 1784, the first in the United States.

The Protestant seminaries remained small until toward the end of the nineteenth century, when numbers increased and the program expanded. There are now 109 seminaries in the United States, of which 73 are fully accredited. Of this number sixteen are units of universities and fifty-seven are independent. Theology is the only profession in the United States for which most of the training is given outside the universities.

In addition to the Protestant theological seminaries there are 119 under the Roman Catholic church. There is no formal accrediting agency for these seminaries, but most of them are affiliated with the theology department of Catholic University of America, and a number are accredited by the regional educational associations.

There are also Jewish Rabbinical schools, a total of thirteen. Except for these, only three institutions of higher learning are under Jewish auspices: Brandeis University, Waltham, Mass.; Dropsie College, Philadelphia; and Yeshiva University, New York City.

Theology suffers a hardship not experienced by other professions in the education of its practitioners. In some countries tax funds may not be used for theological education. In the United Kingdom, for instance, it is forbidden to use U.G.C. grants for the support of denominational institutions, yet the churches can no longer afford to pay stipends, equal to university salaries, to the teachers of their denominational colleges. In some cases the seminary professors are given university teaching posts. The University of London, in 1958, instituted several senior posts in King's College (a secular college incorporated into the University) to provide non-denominational instruction in theology. In Canada state universities grant theological degrees through affiliated or federated seminaries. In Melbourne, Australia, a seminary is permitted to grant the degree; likewise in India Serampore College grants theological degrees. Apparently, in South Africa, New Zealand and in some Australian universities this handicap is not experienced by theological education.

In the United States state universities often give credit for religious education courses given by denominational representatives, whose salaries are paid by the churches. No state institutions have affiliated denominational units, such as are found in Canada.

The curriculum for the Bachelor of Divinity degree differs markedly in the universities of the several countries. In England, South Africa and Australia there is no emphasis upon practical theology. The curriculum embraces the Bible, both Old and New Testaments; the history of the church, including early, medieval and modern periods; the theological field, covering the philosophy of religion, Christian ethics, early Christian doctrine, theology and philosophy. On the other hand, in the Scottish churches in Canada and in the United

States practical theology occupies an important place in the curriculum for the divinity degree. This is sometimes called liturgical and pastoral theology. It includes preparation for confirmation, baptism and marriage; personnel work and counseling; visiting; social service; church and parish organization; religious education; church music; guilds and societies; and homiletics.

Law

Law is not only one of the ancient and learned professions, but it is the most popular of the three, if we are to judge by the number of universities that provide preparation for it. For instance, all the universities in Great Britain, save one, have Faculties of Law. Reading is the one exception. In Australia the six older major universities likewise have legal faculties. Only Australian National University, a research institution founded in 1946; New South Wales University of Technology, founded in 1950; and New England University, chartered in 1954 provide no legal studies. In South Africa all nine universities have Law Faculties, including the University of South Africa, which provides correspondence courses and examinations for the external degree. Four of the constituent units of the University of New Zealand provide legal instruction. In Canada approximately one-half the degree-granting institutions have schools or Faculties of Law, including all the older universities. In India and Pakistan all but five universities list law among their offerings. These are Andhra, Jammu and Kashmir, Roorkee, Visva-Bharati and Thackersey Women's University, all special types of institutions in India.

In the United States there are 170 law schools, of which 129 are accredited by the American Bar Association. One hundred and twenty-three of these are integral parts of the universities. At the turn of the present century relatively few law schools were integral parts of universities. Many proprietary schools which subsisted largely on the fees paid by the students were operating in 1900. These institutions, with part-time faculties made up mainly of local practitioners, have gradually disappeared. Now all but six of the approved schools have university affiliation. Most of those entering law schools have completed a minimum of three years of college work, though some law schools require only two years of college work for admission. In 1956 two states required less than two years pre-legal work.

Not all those who take the law degree go into the practice of the profession. Legal training has great attraction for those who enter other fields: the banker, the industrialist, the politician, the businessman, indeed, the administrator in whatever field considers legal training a valuable asset. It is a common practice in American industry to promote the legal counsel to the presidency of the company. His knowledge of all aspects of the business, in addition to his knowledge of law, fits him admirably for the position.

No other professional group is quite so influential in American life. The majority of the state legislators and of the National Congress have usually had legal education, as have most of the Governors, all of the Judges, and many of the business and industrial leaders. It is the lawyer who is counselor and advocate when conflict arises, and the lawyer who guides business and industrial corporations to insure that they operate within the law. Thus those with legal training not only largely make, interpret and execute the laws of the land, but through the office of corporation counsel, steer the course of business and industry in many essential matters.

In the light of these facts, it is little wonder that law is found in the curricula of most well-established universities, in both the United States and the Commonwealth countries, and that many who study law enter other fields of endeavor. What then is the nature of the training which the lawyer receives in the countries under review?

In the first place, the length of course, the type of training and the steps by which one enters the profession vary widely in the several countries. Some examination of these programs will indicate the variety.

In Britain there are several different types of programs. First of all, law is one of the subjects of study in the Arts Faculty in Cambridge, Oxford and Southampton. Cambridge offers the LL.B. degree for a fourth year, one year after the B.A. Southampton also offers the LL.B. degree after a prescribed period of study beyond the Bachelor of Arts. Oxford does not offer this degree. At all other universities in Great Britain candidates may proceed to the LL.B. degree three years after matriculation, except in the Scottish universities. There they must be graduates of an approved university before being admitted to the course.

The advanced degrees, LL.D., LL.M., B.C.L. and D.C.L., are also awarded by the universities of the United Kingdom. The Master of Laws is awarded by Birmingham, Bristol, Cambridge, Durham, Hull, Leeds, Liverpool, London, Manchester, Nottingham, Sheffield, Southampton and Wales. The degree of Doctor of Laws is awarded by all universities except Durham, Oxford and Reading. The requirements of these two degrees differ in the several universities. At the Scottish universities the LL.D. is conferred only as an honorary degree. Durham and Oxford confer the degrees of Bachelor and Doctor of Civil Law, B.C.L. and D.C.L. At Durham these are restricted to graduates of the university, but at Oxford graduates of other universities may become candidates for the B.C.L. and apply for the degree after six terms of residence. Candidates for the D.C.L. must be Bachelors of Civil Law of the university of at least five years' standing.

Several specialized types of instruction in law are found in the British universities. For example, Cambridge awards a postgraduate diploma in comparative legal studies; Edinburgh, a postgraduate diploma in administrative law and practice;

London University, in addition to having an academic post-graduate diploma in law, has an Institute of Advanced Legal Studies to provide additional facilities for postgraduate students. The University of Southampton awards a postgraduate diploma in air law.

The University degree in Britain does not qualify one for admission to practice, though a good performance in the examinations leading to a degree in law exempts the holder from some of the examinations, both for the bar and for the solicitor's qualifications.

One who wishes to become a barrister at law must, in addition to his law degree, obtain admission as a student to one of the four Inns of Court: Lincoln's Inn, the Middle Temple, the Inner Temple and Gray's Inn; pass the prescribed examinations; and "keep terms" by dining in the hall of his Inn or Court on any three days in each term if a member of a British university, or on any six days if he is not. Normally a student will not be called to the bar unless he has kept twelve dining terms, there being four dining terms in each year.

In order to be admitted as a solicitor a candidate must have passed the preliminary, intermediate and final examinations of the Law Society. He must also enter into Articles of Clerkship with a solicitor for five years (three years if a university graduate), or have completed ten years bona fide service as a solicitor's clerk.

Although aliens may be permitted, with the approval of the Law Society, to serve Articles of Clerkship, only British subjects can be admitted as solicitors. Barristers at law of at least five years' standing and solicitors from the Dominions and Colonies are not required to serve Articles of Clerkship in order to be admitted as English solicitors.

There is a striking similarity between the curricula of the law schools in the various countries of the British Commonwealth and in the United States. A list of offerings and requirements as found in the calendars of several institutions chosen at random are shown in Table 12.[2]

TABLE 12

UNIVERSITY	Procedure-Pleading	Constitutional Law	Roman Law	English Legal System	Criminal Law	Law of Contract	Law of Torts	Property and Conveyancing	Equity	Jurisprudence	International Law	Domestic Relations	Evidence
Vanderbilt (U.S.)	X	X			X	X	X	X	X	X	X	X	X
Bristol (England)		X	X	X	X	X	X	X	X	X	X		
Sydney (Australia)	X	X	X	X	X	X	X	X	X	X	X	X	X
British Columbia (Canada)	X	X			X	X	X	X	X	X		X	X
Witwatersrand (S. Africa)	X	X	X		X	X	X*	X		X			X
Lucknow (India)	X	X			X	X	X	X	X	X	X	X	X
University of N. Zealand	X	X			X	X	X	X		X	X		X

* (Delict)

A glance at the listings will reveal that the main body of the curriculum in each of the countries is the same, though there is a greater emphasis on practical aspects of the law in the Commonwealth countries outside of Britain than in Britain itself. It is of interest to note that in the Lucknow curriculum there are courses on both Mohammedan and Hindu law. With those exceptions, the curricula are similar in most respects in all Commonwealth countries and the United States.

There are several unusual features about legal education in Canada. For instance, before February 1957, Osgoode Hall, established by the Law Society of Upper Canada, directed all training of lawyers in the Province of Ontario. This arrangement has now been changed. One is required to attend Osgoode Law School only six months and pass an examination on the courses taken there if he is a graduate of one of the Canadian law schools. This has given a new impetus to legal education in the province. The University of Western Ontario is planning to establish a law school in 1961. Ottawa University, which for some years has maintained a law school based on the Civil Code, inaugurated a program based on the Common Law in 1957.

Osgoode Hall was established because of the failure of the universities to provide the needed legal education. It served not only as a regulatory body, but as a school and as a court. There is a general feeling that the change in regulation effected in February 1957 will result in improving substantially the program of legal education in Ontario, and will also stimulate the universities to take a greater interest in providing it.

In the Province of Quebec the basis of legal training is the Civil Code rather than the Common Law. In the Law School of McGill University there is great emphasis on comparative law, which helps to some extent to bridge the gap between the law training in Quebec and that in the other provinces of Canada. It also gives considerable attention to the Common Law. McGill also has an International Air Law Institute, the only one of its kind in the Commonwealth.

One trained in the law in any other province of Canada finds it difficult to practice in the Province of Quebec because of the difference in its legal system. In some areas the courses are parallel, but there are marked differences in the Civil Law.

The University of Ottawa is the only university that operates the two types of law schools. It has also a school of canon law. Thus it provides training in three legal systems and in two languages, since it is a bilingual institution. There is considerable enthusiasm at Ottawa over its program in the Common Law. The size of the first entering class in September 1957 was somewhat larger than the average of classes in the Civil Law school.

With the exceptions noted, the curricula of Law Faculties in the Commonwealth and the United States are basically similar, though the requirements for entering the profession vary.

For the university graduate in Britain a minimum of three years is usually required for admission as a solicitor. A barrister who has eaten his dinners can take bar examinations and be called soon after he takes his degree, though most graduates wait a year. In Canada, Australia, South Africa and New Zealand one may enter the profession immediately after receiving the university law degree. The same is true in some parts of the United States. In India two years, based on junior examinations (two years beyond the secondary school), are required for the law degree and for the certificate to practice. The American Bar Association has expressed the view that all candidates for admission to the bar should be required to take an examination set by public authority after receiving the degree, but this is not required by all the states. The graduates of most state university law schools are allowed to practice in the state where the degree was awarded.

The pattern of instruction in most Commonwealth countries outside Britain includes the use of the case system, but the proportion of time devoted to case studies is less there than in the United States. On the other hand, the historical and philosophical aspects of law receive great emphasis. The average American trained lawyer has little background knowledge of Roman law, which is stressed in British universities, and little interest in the philosophy of law. This is the chief difference between the American and British systems of legal education. Labor law is more prominent in the American than in the British curriculum. Practical aspects of the law are like-

wise stressed more in the United States. Trial techniques,
trial and appellate practices, medico-legal problems, administrative law and other such courses, though common in
American law schools, are not found in the British faculties.

Medicine

Medicine in the countries under review requires a longer
period of training than any other profession, a total of six to
eight years beyond the secondary school and a minimum of
one to three years' internship, in all countries except India,
for admission to practice. For those who wish to qualify for
specialties, such as surgery, up to five years of internship and
residency are usually required.

Despite the exacting requirements, the number of qualified
students seeking admission to medical schools is greater than
can be accommodated in each of the countries included in this
study. The reasons for the attractiveness of the profession are
manyfold. Some analysis of these reasons is relevant in a discussion of medical education.

Medicine has outstripped all other professions in the variety
and quality of its achievements. The discovery of vaccines,
beginning with smallpox, is a dramatic story in itself. Typhoid,
paratyphoid, bubonic plague, cholera, tetanus, yellow fever,
diphtheria are among the plagues that have been conquered
by medical science. The latest of the marvels is the Salk
vaccine for poliomyelitis.

A variety of antiseptics has largely eliminated the perils of
infection in surgery. The treatment of diseases such as dia-
betes, pneumonia, tuberculosis and various types of heart
trouble have prolonged the lives of millions. Nutrition research
to which medical schools have contributed has not only
lengthened life but made it more abundant. Research in
obstetrics and gynaecology has almost eliminated infant
mortality and the hazards of childbirth. Research and skill in
surgery have achieved undreamed-of victories over disease

and accident. The discovery of antibiotics in recent years has removed the fears of sundry ills that in earlier times carried away their victims. Researches in the field of mental health have resulted in the virtual conquest of certain of the most serious types of mental disorders when discovered early.

These are but a few of the major advances achieved in recent decades. The result has been an increase in the average length of life in the United States from forty-eight years in 1901 to seventy years in 1958, practically a doubling of the working lifetime of those living in countries which have had the benefit of these developments in the medical field. Though most of these discoveries have been made by research scientists rather than practitioners, they are members of the medical education team and would have little outlet for their findings except through the profession.

New Zealand holds the record for longevity. The United States, Britain, South Africa and Australia (white population) are not far behind. Not all, but many, of the discoveries and advances in knowledge and skill which have resulted in the progressive lengthening of life throughout this century have been achieved by the English-speaking peoples.

In the light of these facts it is little wonder that the prestige of medicine as a profession is so high and that it has attracted so many talented youth. In addition to the prestige, the fact that the compensation of the rank and file of the medical profession is the highest of all the professions in most countries is also a factor in encouraging men and women who are talented and farsighted to be willing to spend the long years of training which medicine exacts of its practitioners. There is great variety and marked differences in the medical education programs in the various countries.

In the first place, in Commonwealth countries, except Canada, training begins at the end of the secondary school. There is no period of general education required for admission to the Medical Faculty as is true in Canada and the United States. Instruction in the basic sciences is provided by the

Medical Faculty. Clinical work absorbs the time of the student during the last three to four years. Non-professional courses are not generally provided the medical student in the Commonwealth countries.

The degrees awarded in these countries (Canada excepted) are usually Bachelor of Medicine and Bachelor of Surgery (B.M. and B.Ch.). The Bachelor of Science degree in medicine is found in Canada and India. The M.D. (Doctor of Medicine) is a graduate degree of interest chiefly to those who are seeking a career in academic medicine. In the United States and Canada the mode is four years of college plus four years of medical training, in addition to internship. This is not true of all, but of the majority of the Medical Faculties in Canada.

In Britain the outlook for the medical man is more limited than in other countries. A former Vice-Chancellor of Oxford observed in 1957 that medicine is no longer as popular as it used to be. It has yielded first place to science and technology in recent years in the talent which it attracts. This is also true in the United States. Engineering attracts substantially more than its nearest competitor—the Faculty of Commerce. Medicine occupies third place in popularity with students.

The cost of medical education in the countries under review is a matter of interest. In almost all of them it is higher than that of any other profession. Tuition fees in the United States are more than ten times greater on the average than in India, six times greater than in Australia and three times greater than in the United Kingdom. The costs in Canada are the highest in the Commonwealth, only a little lower than in the United States.

A brief review of medical education in the various countries may help to visualize its place in the university curriculum.

GREAT BRITAIN

In Britain the degrees of Bachelor of Medicine and Bachelor of Surgery are awarded in all universities except Exeter, Hull,

Leicester, Nottingham, Reading and Southampton. Cambridge University provides only pre-clinical instruction. The attendance required for the medical course is a minimum of five, and usually six, years from matriculation in the university.

Oxford and Cambridge require a minimum of three years' residence, since their students are allowed to take the clinical work at an approved hospital which requires three additional years. Both require a candidate to have a first degree before being admitted to clinical instruction.

The M.D. degree (D.M. at Oxford) is given by all universities except Bristol and Birmingham. The usual time required before admission to this degree is two years after the Bachelor of Medicine, or Bachelor of Surgery. If the candidate seeks the degree by examination rather than thesis, five years is the usual requirement.

CANADA

There are twelve Medical Faculties in the universities of Canada, distributed as follows: three in the Province of Quebec, four in Ontario, and one each in Alberta, British Columbia, Nova Scotia, Manitoba and Saskatchewan. There was talk in 1958 of establishing two more Medical Faculties. Three provinces are without medical schools, New Brunswick, Prince Edward Island and Newfoundland. The Medical Faculties at Halifax and Quebec take most of the students from these provinces.

There is no uniformity in the admission requirements of these several Medical Faculties. For example, Alberta and Saskatchewan admit students after two years in a College of Arts and Science. Others require three, and some, four years. The French universities require the classical college B.A. After admission to the Medical Faculty there is variation in the time required for graduation. Usually a four-year course beyond two, three or four years of college is the requirement. Laval and Montreal require five years after the classical college B.A.

Toronto and Western Ontario follow the British pattern, requiring six years from senior matriculation, which represents thirteen years of schooling.

In most of the Faculties of Medicine in Canada, as in the United States, the degree awarded is Doctor of Medicine. The B.Sc. in Medicine is also popular there. Alberta, Manitoba, Ottawa, Saskatchewan, Toronto and Western Ontario are among the institutions that grant this degree. The Master of Surgery (C.M.) is found in Dalhousie, McGill and Queen's. This apparently corresponds to the M.D. in Medicine and requires the same length of time. The Toronto Faculty of Medicine awards a Master of Surgery (M.S.) for two years' work beyond the M.D. degree.

AUSTRALIA

There are five universities with Faculties of Medicine in Australia. In 1953 there were only two full-time professors on their staffs. Since that time progress has been rapid. By 1957 the University of Sydney had seven full-time men in its Medical Faculty, involving the Departments of Medicine, Surgery, Obstetrics and Gynaecology, Pediatrics, Psychiatry, Tropical Medicine and Public Health. The University of Melbourne had two full-time men in internal medicine, one in surgery and one in obstetrics and gynaecology. Adelaide had one full time medical professor and provision for two others.

In the University of Western Australia there were four full-time men, one each in medicine, surgery, obstetrics and gynaecology and pediatrics. Brisbane had one in medicine, and two part-time in surgery and obstetrics. Table 13 presents the picture in Australia and New Zealand, as of 1957.

The Adelaide University Faculty of Medicine illustrates the growth in medical education. In 1939 it had a total enrollment of 180, and in 1957, 528.

A unique feature of this Faculty is its provision for a professor of humanities. This new staff member had not been

TABLE 13   STATUS OF FULL-TIME TEACHING STAFF IN MEDICAL
SCHOOLS IN AUSTRALIA AND NEW ZEALAND[3]

Subject	Sydney	Melbourne	Brisbane	Perth	Otago	Adelaide
Medicine	D	2D	D	D	D	D
Pediatrics	D	p.t.	p.t.	D	p.t.	p.t.
Social Medicine	D	p.t.	p.t.	p.t.	D	p.t.
Forensic Medicine	d	d	p.t.	d	D	p.t.
Psychiatry	D	p.t.	D	p.t.	p.t.	p.t.
Tropical Medicine	D	—	D	—	—	—
Surgery	D	D	D	D	D	p.t.
Obstetrics and Gynaecology	D	D	D	D	D	d
TOTAL	7½	4½	5	4½	5	1½

D.—Full teaching department—Professorial status
d.—Full time head—non-professorial status
p.t.—Part time honorary teaching only
Source: Courtesy of Dr. Robson, University of Adelaide.

selected in 1957; neither was it clear just what he would be
expected to teach. Another special feature of the Adelaide
Faculty is the plan of having the student begin contacts with
patients in his fourth year. In most institutions this experience
is not provided before the fifth or sixth year.

There are no chairs of social medicine in Australia as in the
United Kingdom. Perhaps the nearest approach is the Department of Child Life and Health at Sydney. Considerable
research in pathology, bacteriology, radio therapy and cancer
is conducted at the universities and associated research institutes in Adelaide, Melbourne and Sydney. An especially active
research program was in progress in 1957 in the John Curtin
School of Medical Research of Australian National University.

NEW ZEALAND

Otago is the only university providing medical instruction
in New Zealand. The cost of the medical program is £235 as
against £55 for the Bachelor of Arts. This medical school

provides training for the Bachelor of Medicine, Bachelor of Surgery, Master of Surgery, Bachelor of Medical Science and Doctor of Medicine. It graduates, in the several degree courses, approximately 130 students per year.

SOUTH AFRICA

South Africa has five Medical Faculties, Cape Town, Natal, Pretoria, Stellenbosch and Witwatersrand. The University of Natal Faculty is the only one that trains exclusively non-Europeans. It was caught up in the Apartheid struggle and was greatly disturbed in 1957 by the government's desire to transfer its control from the University of Natal to the University of South Africa.

The pattern of development of medical education in South Africa differs little from that found in Australia. It offers the same degrees, and has similar admission and time requirements for the completion of work for the degree.

INDIA AND PAKISTAN

There are forty-odd Faculties of Modern Medicine in the universities of India. Some have more than one college devoted to the training of doctors. For example, Calcutta has four; Agra, three; Madras, two. All six of the universities in Pakistan have Medical Faculties. In addition to modern medicine there are twelve ayurvedic, six unani and three homeopathic schools. Ayurvedic and unani systems are taught in the same schools in Madras, Jaipur and Delhi. In other places they are taught in different institutions.[4]

The program of study in the medical colleges of India is prescribed by the All-India Council for Medical Education, not by the universities. While the university has supervision over the work of the colleges, it does not set the curricula. The Council, which controls in these matters, is made up mostly of medical men. The M.B. and B.Sc. degree courses require five years after the intermediate examination at the universities of Agra, Bombay, Delhi, Gujarat, Lucknow, Madras, Nagpur, Osmania, Panjab, Rajasthan, Travancore and Utkal. At Andhra, Calcutta, Gauhati and Mysore the course is of five and a half to six years' duration. Aligarh University has a course in Unani which requires five years, while Banaras has a course in Ayurvedic medicine requiring six years. The numbers applying for admission to medicine far exceeds the places available, as much as ten to one in some instances.

A report of a Conference on Medical Education held in India in November 1955 throws light on some of the problems encountered there. Among its recommendations were the following:

1. That the medical curriculum should require 5,100 hours, 1,500 of which would be devoted to pre-clinical subjects and 3,600 to clinical subjects.

2. That each college should have a department of preventive and social medicine, which would be integrated with the teaching of all other departments, and be associated with the rural and urban health centers.

3. That there should be a separate department of pediatrics which would require at least three months of the students' time.

4. That there should be seventy-four systematic lectures and lecture-demonstrations in psychological medicine.

5. That teachers of embryology and physiology should emphasize the influence of function on structure and of stress and anxiety on conditions associated with homeostasis.

6. That psychological and sociological influences in illness should be emphasized by the professors of medicine, surgery, obstetrics and gynaecology, and pediatrics.

Special attention was called to the need for instruction in the history of medicine, important there because the patients' description of ailments are frequently in terms of the indigenous systems of medicine prevalent in India.

Great discontent was expressed over the methods of teaching

and assessment of results. The conference concluded that fewer hours should be devoted to didactic lectures and more to demonstration. While internship was not a requirement for the practice of medicine in India, in 1955 the Conference urged that at least six months, and preferably a year, of experience should be the goal. By 1958 all universities, except Agra and Mysore, required internship of six months to a year.

In medical education, as in all other phases of university work, the examination system came in for criticism. The Conference concluded that the present methods of examinations are unsatisfactory, and should be modified, that greater importance should be given to day-to-day assessment of the student's work, and that faculties should be allowed freedom to experiment where there is a willingness to undertake it.

While headway in carrying out the recommendations made by the Conference had been slight by 1957, they have served as a useful guide to the medical colleges in their efforts to improve the programs of instruction in their institutions.

THE UNITED STATES

The advances in medical education in the United States since 1910 have been greater than in any other professional field. While the number of approved medical schools have shown only a gradual increase from sixty-six in 1910 to eighty-two in 1955, the quality of students, of faculty, of instruction and of research has been transformed. The deplorable state of medical education in 1910 was revealed by Abraham Flexner, who conducted a study of all medical schools in the country, under the auspices of the Carnegie Foundation. As a result of the highly critical report which issued from that study, the American Medical Association and the public as well were stirred to action.

The Association classified the schools into A, B and C groups, according to the quality of their work. Within a decade approximately one-half of all the schools operating in 1910 had been closed, and by 1928 all B and C grade institutions were eliminated. Philanthropic foundations, state legislatures and individuals increased manyfold their support of the remaining schools, with the result that medical education in the United States became the most generously supported division of the universities.

In 1910 the enrollment in 66 schools was 12,530, of whom 3,165 graduated; in 1955 82 schools enrolled 28,583, of whom 6,977 were graduated. Six of the 82 schools had two-year and 76, full four-year programs. In the 1955–1956 year the estimated funds available for medical schools included $98,012,621 budgeted funds, $54,470,989 for research and $7,035,905 from outside agencies, for the improvement of the teaching program—a total of $159,519,415.

In addition to the services listed above, the medical schools play a significant part in other programs which concern the Council on Medical Education and Hospitals. Its staff is responsible for evaluating and approving 11,040 internship programs in 848 hospitals. Along with the specialty boards it also assists in the evaluation of 24,741 residencies and fellowships in the 1,186 hospitals which are approved for graduate training. A growing interest has been manifested since 1950 in postgraduate continuation education for practicing physicians.

In addition to teaching medical undergraduates, the Medical Faculties give instruction to dental, pharmacy, nursing and technical students and to graduate students in the medical sciences. The volume of this load is indicated by enrollments in 1953–1954 for which figures are available. That year the medical undergraduates numbered 28,227, while the medical schools reported teaching 59,430 students enrolled in other disciplines.[5]

Despite the vast sums budgeted for teaching and research in Medical Schools in the United States, they face critical financial problems. The cost of equipment, of maintaining full-time faculties in a wide variety of specialized fields and of conducting needed research in every area of the medical sciences has exceeded the support provided. The higher the caliber of students and faculties the greater are the needs for research facilities and staff. Thus the excellence of the medical program made possible by the funds available for its support calls for still further sums to utilize to the fullest the capacities of the scientists which constitute the faculties, and of the graduate student body.

To meet this need, the American Medical Education Foundation, supported by the American Medical Association, and the National Fund for Medical Education, supported by industry, have been established since 1950. Both organizations have made substantial contributions to the Medical Schools of the country, but more still is needed to stabilize medical education.

In 1955–1956 four new Medical Schools were developing four-year curricula, and a fifth, the University of California at Los Angeles, graduated its first degree class in 1955. In addition, three of the former two-year schools were being expanded to include four-year programs. These were the University of Mississippi, 1957; the University of Missouri, 1957–1958; and West Virginia University in 1958. It is estimated that by 1960 more than 8,000 first-year medical students will gain admission to Medical Schools in the United States, and that these institutions will be graduating more than 7,500 physicians annually.

SUMMARY

In each country under review medical education is undergoing serious scrutiny. Admission requirements, methods of selecting students, means of financing, integration of the curriculum and the length of the medical education program are among the topics of lively interest in the several countries. The variation in quality of medical education and research is probably greater than in other fields. Certainly the concerns and problems in Medical Schools appear more acute than in other professional schools.

In McGill University (Canada) the entire curriculum was being studied with a view to far-reaching changes. In Johns Hopkins (United States) a new program was initiated in 1957 looking to a substantial reduction in the time requirement. In Western Reserve (United States) a radical reform of curriculum and methods has been under way for more than five years. In Birmingham (England) efforts at a better integration of the curriculum have been fruitful. There is concern there, too, over the narrowness of the curriculum. In all the Medical Schools of Australia remarkable progress has been made in the past five years in increasing their full-time staffs. In Melbourne new requirements for admission to the Medical School were announced in 1957. In Adelaide a professor of humanities has been provided for, and in several American schools, social scientists have been added to the staffs. In Natal (South Africa) the status of the Medical School for non-whites was a burning issue in 1957. In India the problem of harmonizing three different systems—modern medicine, ayurvedic and unani—is extremely complex and difficult. Provision for adequate internships is still lacking, and relatively little vital research is being conducted. Perhaps the basic difficulty is inadequate financing, which results in poorly-equipped faculties and laboratories.

The programs of studies in the several countries cover essentially the same fields, though the amount of time devoted to each subject varies. Better integration of the several elements in the instructional program is a matter of universal concern in both the Commonwealth countries and the United States.

X

Professional Education — Teaching

❖❖❖❖❖❖❖❖❖❖❖❖❖❖❖❖❖❖❖❖❖❖❖❖❖❖❖❖❖❖❖❖

The background of the teaching profession has no parallel in other professional fields. Its origin and slow development as a respected calling is in sharp contrast with the learned professions of theology, law and medicine. They were prestige professions from the beginning. While the university professor, as a member of the Guild of Learned Men, had status in the Middle Ages, the teachers of children and youth were considered an underprivileged group. Theirs was a lowly occupation for centuries, and emerged from that status only in relatively recent times.

Professor Kneller suggested that in Greek and Roman times slaves were teachers; that celibates taught in the early Christian period; that in Medieval England the teacher had the rank of a stable boy; and that in Napoleon's time he was a servant of the state.[1] Caricatures of the teacher observed in modern times reflect the public attitude toward the profession in earlier periods. Centuries passed before teaching reached the status of a profession.*

The Commonwealth Countries

The story of its development in England dates from the early nineteenth century, when the National Society for Pro-

---

* What is said here about the status of teaching does not apply to Asian countries. There the teacher had a high status since teaching was linked with religion. In India, for example, the religious preceptors taught secular sub-

moting the Education of the Poor in the Principles of the Church of England and its nonconformist rival, the British and Foreign Schools Society, first attacked the problem of elementary education on a national scale. In both Societies, the monitorial system was used, providing for the selection of older pupils who would learn their lessons from the adult teacher and then teach them to the younger children. The need for training these youngsters for their role as teachers was realized early, and training schools were established to provide it. The Borough Road Training College, which originated under this system, is still in existence.

In about 1840 James Kay (later Sir James Kay-Shuttleworth) began the movement to replace the monitors with "pupil teachers." Under this system boys and girls were apprenticed for a period of five years from the age of thirteen and thus learned the art of teaching while continuing their education under the head teacher of the elementary school. This new scheme also involved training colleges where the professional and academic education of the best "pupil teachers" could be developed after their apprenticeship was completed. Kay, himself, founded a training college known as St. John's College, Battersea, London, which was taken over by the National Society and used as a model for others.[2]

It was not long before the church set up training colleges in many dioceses. Others were founded by nonconformist bodies. Through Kay's efforts the government began to take an interest in the colleges, providing financial assistance, both for building and for maintenance. As a condition of receiving this financial aid the government determined the courses of study to be followed, required inspections, and conducted the examinations, on the basis of which the successful candidates received certificates to teach in the elementary school.

---

jects. In Islamic countries most schools were located in mosques and the priest was the teacher. Mr. Humayun Kabir, Minister of Scientific Research and Cultural Affairs in India, notes that "In Asia, lowering of the status of teachers started only during the last fifty or, at the most, during the last hundred years."

The voluntary training colleges developed in this period became an important factor in the school system of England. By the end of the first quarter of the twentieth century approximately fifty schools were in operation, supplying about half the trained teachers for elementary school service. The training period became standardized at two years early in the twentieth century.

Regulations adopted in 1893 made it possible for the universities and university colleges to establish grant-aided departments for the training of elementary school teachers. These institutions were quick to take advantage of the opportunity which these new regulations afforded. Twenty-two had established such training arrangements by the end of the first quarter of the twentieth century.

The Education Act of 1902 empowered local education authorities to establish and maintain training colleges. About twenty of these had been established by 1926. They differed from the voluntary colleges in that they had no religious affiliation and were usually without residential accommodations.

The Act of 1902 made other important contributions to the system of elementary teacher education. Under it the local authorities were empowered to establish secondary schools. This in turn enabled the board of education to require those who entered training colleges to have a four-year secondary school course. The effect of this change on the teacher who had previously spent his life within the elementary school system proved beneficial in many ways. Indeed, it led to the gradual disappearance of the pupil-teacher system.

In 1955 there were 154 training colleges and twenty-three university departments of education in England and Wales. In Scotland there were four general training centers, two denominational colleges and a college for women teachers of physical education. In Northern Ireland there were two general training colleges for teachers. One was non-denominational and under the Ministry of Education; the other was under the sponsorship of the Catholic church. In addition to the general training colleges there are colleges for teachers of art and domestic science which are conducted by the Belfast Education Committee; and there is also a training college for women teachers of physical education under the Ministry of Education.

At the close of World War II a great shortage of teachers developed. As a result the government became concerned about the quality of the training programs, and the means of supplying the demand. The number of children between the ages of five and fifteen in the United Kingdom increased by over a million between 1948 and 1954, and the minimum age for leaving school was raised by a year in Britain in 1947. A committee was appointed by the government to study the problem of teacher education and the ways of meeting the needs in view of the birth rate increase and the new school-leaving regulations. The chairman of the committee was Sir Arnold McNair, now Lord McNair.

This committee, in addition to providing for more training colleges, sought ways of improving the quality of work done by these institutions. To this end it recommended that each training college should be affiliated with a university through an Institute of Education. The Committee felt that the interchange of ideas between faculty members in the colleges on the one hand, and in the universities on the other, would strengthen the colleges, and at the same time acquaint the universities with some of the more practical problems of teacher education. It was thought, too, that such a relationship would broaden the vision and stimulate the interest of the training college faculties through their association with the university faculty members.

Approval was given the recommendations of the McNair Committee; the Institutes of Education were established by the universities, and by 1957 all training colleges were affiliated to universities. Under the plan the head of the Department of Education may also serve as Director of the Institute, or the

Director of the Institute may be a full-time officer. If there is a Director of the Institute in addition to the head of the Department of Education, the two officers shall be considered of equal rank and be rewarded with equal pay, based on their training and experience. Whether or not the head of the Department of Education should serve also as Director of the Institute was left to the discretion of the university.

Each of the universities in England now has an Institute of Education; each has affiliated training colleges; and the head of the Education Department is, in some instances, also Director of the Institute. The London University Institute, with thirty-five affiliated training colleges, was directed by the head of the Education Department as late as the spring of 1957. The trend, however, is toward providing a full-time Director of the Institute.

The training colleges, as has been previously noted, have from the beginning required two years. At first only an elementary school certificate was necessary for admission, but this was soon changed to graduation from the secondary school. According to plans announced in 1957, three years instead of two will be required in training colleges after 1960. For some years all the universities have provided courses leading to the diploma or certificate in education. They have traditionally offered this training for the secondary school teacher. At the University College of North Staffordshire educational training is incorporated within the four-year B.A. course and a diploma in education is awarded along with the degree.

The Scottish universities offer a one-year postgraduate course leading to a diploma in education. It is the first year of a two-year course leading to a Bachelor of Education degree. In the Scottish universities a diploma examination is open only to graduates who have already had professional training for a period of time at a recognized training college, or approved teaching experience normally of at least three years' duration.

In Wales (Aberystwyth, Bangor, Cardiff, Swansea) a B.A.

degree with honors is awarded in education. At Aberdeen a one-year course in education is offered in the ordinary M.A. degree program. The Master of Education degree is conferred by Durham, Hull, Leeds, Manchester, Nottingham; and the Master of Arts in Education at Southampton. Education may be offered as a subject for the degree of Master of Arts at Birmingham, Bristol, Liverpool, London and Reading, and for the M.Sc. at Sheffield, Aberdeen, Edinburgh, Glasgow and St. Andrews. Belfast awards the degree of Bachelor of Education, honors standard, for two years of postgraduate work.

The Universities of Birmingham, Cambridge, Durham, Exeter, Bristol, Liverpool and Manchester provide diplomas in education. The Institute of Education of Leeds offers courses leading to diplomas in primary education, secondary education, education of backward children, religious education, physical education and educational administration. The University of Reading Institute of Education provides a diploma course in rural education.

Briefly, the United Kingdom, with its 154 training colleges, its four centers for teacher education in Scotland and two in Northern Ireland, in addition to the twenty-three universities that provide teacher education, is well supplied with facilities for the training of teachers. Improvement should be marked when the program of the training colleges is lengthened to three years. The specialized postgraduate courses in various fields allied to the training of teachers in the universities round out the program. The one weakness in the system is the lack of special provisions for training technical college faculties.

McGill University in Canada has provided teacher education for more than 100 years. The McGill Normal School was founded in 1857 by an agreement between the provincial government and the university. In 1907 it became an integral part of McDonald College. The system of training colleges found in the United Kingdom does not prevail in Canada. The

Canadian system follows more nearly that of the United States. Twenty-three of the degree-granting institutions have teacher education departments or schools of education. Many of them award undergraduate and graduate degrees in the field and provide also diploma courses.

The University of Alberta in 1944 assumed responsibility for all teacher training in that province, and on April 1, 1945, took over the provincial normal schools and their staffs. The Calgary Normal School, which was housed in the building of the Provincial Institute of Technology and Art, became the Calgary branch of the University. More recently the University of British Columbia has also taken over the responsibility for the training of teachers in that province.

Australia has followed the pattern of the United Kingdom in caring for its teacher education. State colleges for the training of teachers, taking the place of the training colleges in England, are found in each of the states except Tasmania. Two are in operation in New South Wales, and a total of six in the Commonwealth. In addition, all the universities provide teacher education, including diploma and degree courses.

Two universities, Melbourne and Queensland, have Faculties of Education and award the degrees of Bachelor and Master of Education. In each of these faculties the State Department of Education has representatives. Since 1948 the University of Tasmania has borne the full burden of training teachers for the state education department through its Faculty of Education. Graduates of the University may receive a diploma of education; non-graduates, a certificate. Western Australia also has a Faculty of Education, offering both the Bachelor's and Master's degree in Education. In the other universities the courses in education are under the Faculty of Arts. In most cases the professors of education in these institutions are associated with the state training colleges. University graduates may obtain special diplomas in education in Sydney, Melbourne, Adelaide, Queensland and Western Australia.

In New Zealand there are six training colleges located at Auckland, Ardmore, Palmerston, North, Wellington, Christchurch and Dunedin. Hostel accommodations are provided at all these institutions, but only Ardmore provides sufficient accommodations to care for all its students.

The boarding allowance of A£55 is paid to all non-graduate students who are required to live away from home. One free return travel warrant is also allowed to each student living away from home. These training colleges provide not only theoretical courses, but an opportunity for observation and practice teaching.

Two types of students are trained: (1) graduates of the secondary schools who enter upon training immediately for a two-year course followed by a further year of training, either as a probationary assistant or as a specialist; and (2) mature people twenty-one to forty years of age who take a twelve months' course and serve as a probationary assistant for one year, at the end of which the candidates are qualified to receive the teacher's certificate if their work has been satisfactory. The latter is considered a temporary measure designed to help meet the teacher shortage.

In both Australia and New Zealand the universities carry the burden of training secondary school teachers. While some education for elementary teachers is also provided by the universities, the state colleges in Australia and the training colleges in New Zealand play the major role in the preparation of elementary teachers.

The South African program of teacher education is similar to that of Australia. There are thirteen training colleges in the Union, seven in Cape Province, four in Transvaal, one each in Orange Free State and Natal. The matriculation examination (university entrance) is not required for admission to the training colleges, only the school-leaving certificate. All these train only primary teachers. The course is three years in length. It leads to a certificate and not to a degree. The Faculties of

Education in the universities also train for primary, as well as secondary, school teaching. However, to transfer to a university from a training college means loss of credits for all the work taken in the training college. The English courses, for example, are not even considered of sufficient quality to warrant university recognition. The psychology course is non-transferable.

The training colleges, along with the primary and secondary schools, are under the control of the provinces, and supported solely by them, while the universities receive no help from the provinces, only from the central government. A province may contract with a university to perform a particular service. Witwatersrand, for example, had a contract with Pretoria for training speech and hearing clinic specialists. The universities receive financial assistance from the provinces only for specific services rendered.

Training for secondary school teaching requires four years, one year beyond the B.A. or B.Sc. degree. If one wishes to secure the B.Ed. he must complete two years beyond the first degree. Thus, five years are required for full qualification for secondary school teaching.

Successful teachers with five years experience may take the Bachelor of Education degree in one year instead of two. Those who wish to take courses while teaching may do so and may secure degrees for not less than two years' part-time work. One may proceed in the same way to the Master's and Doctor's degrees. The universities give the Master's and Doctor's degree in Education.

In 1954 there were fifty-seven training colleges in India and in 1955 sixty-eight. They are all affiliated to universities, and in this respect differ from those in South Africa. In 1954 twenty-five universities had one or more affiliated training colleges. The University of Madras had six such colleges among its affiliated institutions.

In India all the universities except three, Andhra, Roorkee

and Utkal, have Faculties or Departments of Education, though Utkal has one and Andhra four training colleges. The Bachelor of Teaching, or Bachelor of Education is a postgraduate degree requiring one year's work beyond the arts or science degree. The universities also provide Master's degrees and diploma courses one year in length. A few universities grant the Ph.D. degree. All six of the universities in Pakistan have Departments of Education and provide all teacher education.

Interest in improving teacher education has been expressed in a number of ways. Since 1950 representatives of the training colleges have been meeting annually to consider their common problems. The amount of graduate work in teacher education has increased steadily since Indian independence. The training colleges have been engaged in a variety of experiments looking to the improvement of their programs. Summer schools have been held for prospective teachers, including instructors in colleges. Perhaps the most significant steps taken to improve the quality and status of the teachers are the organization of headmasters' seminars on an all-India or state basis and the provision of extension courses in the training colleges.

The United States

Teacher training in the United States as in Britain began with the monitorial schools. The system was introduced into New York in 1806 and spread rapidly to other cities, but it was short lived. By 1830 monitorial schools were dying out. The second type of teacher training institution was the academy, the first of which was established in 1823. The New York legislature in 1834 recognized training classes in selected academies and authorized the Regents to subsidize them. This was probably the first state law on the training of teachers. The academies continued for some time to train teachers after state normal schools began to take over that function.

Massachusetts established the first normal school in 1839

and later added three more due to the insistence of Horace Mann. Before 1860 eight states had established such institutions and by 1900 practically every state had one or more.

Most of the training of elementary teachers was performed by two-year normal schools in 1900. These schools frequently did not insist upon graduation from the secondary school. The university degree without special professional training was sufficient for those who wished to teach in the secondary school. Indeed, there were many without degrees who taught in the high schools.

Gradually the normal schools extended their offerings to three and then to four years, at which time their names were changed to "Teachers Colleges." The change from the normal school to collegiate status began about the beginning of the third decade; in some sections of the country earlier, in others later. Within the past twenty years more than one-third of the teachers' colleges have dropped the word "teachers" from their title and are known as "State Colleges." The trend has been toward more emphasis on basic subjects, with less time devoted to methods. Also, in some cases, the purposes of the institutions have been extended to include pre-professional courses for law, medicine, engineering, etc. Many of these institutions have added a fifth year leading to the Master's degree in Arts or Education.

The present trend is in the direction of requiring a four-year pre-service collegiate training for both elementary and secondary school teachers, with a fifth year to be completed while in service, or after a minimum of one year's teaching experience.

The problem of formal education for teachers began to receive serious attention from institutions of higher education about 1900. Great expansion in this area has occurred since then. Very few secondary school teachers were prepared by the teachers' colleges before 1920 when they began to be degree-granting institutions. Since that time most of them have prepared as many secondary as elementary teachers. It was the universities, however, that first gave specific attention to the preparation of teachers for the high schools. Lectures on teaching were given at Brown University as early as 1850 and at the University of Michigan in 1860, but both these programs were discontinued. It is not clear which of the universities first offered regular courses in pedagogy. It is known that the state universities of Iowa, Michigan and Wisconsin established professorships in education between 1873 and 1881. From this beginning interest grew rapidly. By 1892 more than thirty universities had established chairs of education which were sometimes called didactics. By 1950 most four-year colleges and universities had departments or schools of education.

The present program of elementary education requires the prospective teacher to devote roughly one fourth of her four years' study to learning about children, the role of the school in the community and materials of instruction. On the other hand, requirements for the secondary school teacher ordinarily involve giving less than one-fifth the student's time to these considerations. Those preparing to become secondary school teachers usually include a major in one subject and one or more related minors, in order to be prepared to teach at least two subjects. Those preparing for elementary teaching seldom have a subject-matter major in the course of their preparation. Instead, they take work in several fields, devoting usually one-third to one-half their time to the study of liberal arts courses.

A great variety of institutions participate in preparing for the profession of teaching: the teachers' colleges, public and private colleges and universities, professional and technical schools, and even junior colleges.

Table 14 shows the distribution of teachers in preparation in 1949, by type of institution.

The departments of education reported in 1953 a total of about 1,200 colleges and universities that were engaged in the training of teachers. More than 300 of these have no accredita-

TABLE 14

TYPE OF INSTITUTION	NUMBER OF TEACHERS PREPARED			PER CENT OF TEACHERS PREPARED		
	Elementary	*High School*	*Total*	*Elementary*	*High School*	*Total*
Teachers colleges	12,475	14,489	26,964	33.6	16.9	21.9
Public colleges and universities	11,592	34,548	46,140	31.1	40.2	37.4
Private colleges and universities	10,510	33,533	44,043	28.3	38.9	35.8
Professional and technical schools	72	3,354	3,426	.2	3.9	2.8
Junior colleges	2,522	123	2,645	6.8	.1	2.1
Total	37,171	86,047	123,218	100.0	100.0	100.0

Source: *The Journal of Teacher Education,* "Accreditation and the Professionalization of Teaching," by T. M. Stinnett, March 1952, p. 34.

tion except that which comes with the approval of their respective state departments of education. All except nine of the forty-eight states grant authority to institutions to prepare teachers. Such authority is usually granted on the recommendation of a visiting team. Institutions in the nine states are not required to have the approval of any agency. They simply offer courses required for certification by the state department if they wish to prepare teachers. More than 800 institutions are approved by their respective regional accrediting associations. Only 285 are approved by the National Council for Accreditation of Teacher Education. This means that only about 23 per cent of the total number of institutions preparing teachers have been specifically approved by the National Council. This 23 per cent, however, prepares approximately one-half of the teachers who enter the profession each year.

In the Commonwealth countries, except Canada, the major burden of preparing teachers for the elementary schools is borne by the training colleges, or state colleges, as they are called in Australia. In all the countries, however, universities take some part in the program. The pattern generally is three years for graduation from the university and an additional year for the diploma, or if one is seeking the Bachelor of Education degree, two years beyond the first degree, a total of five years.

In Australia the state colleges provide for all types of teachers, those in the sub-primary, primary and secondary schools, and for teachers of special subjects, such as music, art, handicrafts, etc. The universities there take a less active part than do universities in the other countries. The training colleges in England and Wales are more numerous than in any other section of the Commonwealth, and bear the major responsibility for the training of elementary teachers. They do not, however, prepare for secondary school teaching.

In South Africa the training colleges, which operate under the Ministry of Education, have little cooperation from the universities, which do not accept work done at the colleges as of university grade.

In Canada, as in the United States, the degree-granting institutions, colleges and universities, play a more important role in teacher education than those in other Commonwealth countries.

In India the education for the profession of teaching is provided by university faculties or departments or in colleges which are affiliated to them. Only one university, Roorkee, has neither a Faculty or Department of Education nor an affiliated training college.

Teacher Shortage

The teaching profession at mid-century is experiencing one of the most critical periods of its history. It is failing to attract an adequate number of qualified practitioners; the shortcomings of the public schools are being attributed to it; the public is not supporting it with the same generosity as the other professions; and while the numbers to be taught are being doubled and trebled, those seeking teacher education are declining relatively in numbers.

The experience of every country included in this study has one element in common—an inadequate supply of qualified teachers.

In the United Kingdom the Ministry of Education in 1957 announced plans to extend the program of the training colleges from two to three years. This will doubtless be followed by South Africa, Australia and New Zealand as early as it is feasible to do so. Shortage of teachers at all levels has characterized the post-independence period in India and Pakistan.

In the United States only 37,922 who were specifically prepared for teaching in the elementary schools were graduated in 1956–1957, yet that year school boards employed 78,938 new elementary teachers. The high schools in that year employed 5,000 new mathematics teachers, though only 2,500 college graduates of that year were qualified to teach these subjects, and of these only 1,700 actually entered teaching. Four thousand, three hundred and twenty science teachers were graduated in that same year, yet the high schools employed 5,500 new science teachers.[3]

Staffing the colleges and universities presents an equally difficult problem. The universities in the English-speaking countries are preparing barely enough to replace those who retire each year, or leave the profession for other reasons, and a large proportion of those trained for teaching, especially in science and technology, enter business or industry where monetary rewards are greater. Thus the supply of teachers diminishes as the demands of the classroom increase.

Figures presented in the report of the President's Committee on Education Beyond the High School, which appeared in 1957, presents graphically the situation in the United States. It is estimated that 15,000 to 22,500 teachers will be required annually during the next ten to twelve years. Currently the universities are awarding approximately 9,000 Doctor of Philosophy degrees annually, and of those receiving them only about 5,000 actually enter the profession, less than one-third the number required. The cumulative deficit, if heroic measures are not taken to check it, could prove disastrous.

The problem of replacing the present teaching staff, more than 35 per cent of whom are forty-five or older, further complicates the situation. The group twenty-four to forty-five years of age in the United States, already small due to the low birth rate of the depression years, will be relatively smaller during the decade ahead when college and university enrollments are reaching new heights. In other words, when the student population will be climbing from 3,000,000 to an estimated 6,0000,000 the loss of teachers through death and retirement will be accelerating.

Canada employed 6000 college and university teachers in 1957. In ten years, estimates indicate, 10,000 will be needed and in twenty-five years, 30,000. Similar prospects face other Commonwealth countries. In 1958 India reported a shortage of 2,000 scientists and technologists in its universities.

Shortages in any other profession affect only one aspect of community welfare and progress, whereas failure to attract, educate and hold an adequate supply of teachers at all levels affects the entire community. Not only the general level of culture but the progress of all other professions depends upon the effectiveness of the teacher, for the doctor, lawyer, preacher or engineer owes much of his knowledge, skill and professional outlook to his teachers in the medical, law, theological or engineering school.

Just as teaching is the most basic of all the professions, so its effectiveness is most dependent upon the community's attitude toward it. The esteem in which the teacher is held, the willingness of the public to reward his services and to encourage his efforts will determine the success of the profession in meeting society's needs. Colleges and universities have an important role to play, but in the final analysis public understanding and support will be essential to the solution of the teacher-shortage problem.

Requirements of the Profession

The army of men and women in teaching determine the quality of the educational program. More than that, they influence the lives of all young people, their ideals and motivations, as well as their mental development. They have the responsibility of discovering talent and developing it; if it is undiscovered and wasted they must share the blame for it. In the United States, more than half of the secondary school graduates who are in the upper ten per cent scholastically never go on to college. This represents a loss to the nation that cannot be estimated. If the situation is to be rectified, it will be largely through the efforts of elementary and high school teachers. The premium on talent is so high in these times that few really gifted graduates, if highly motivated, would fail to find a way to go to college.

Of course, dull and uninspired teaching is not always responsible for lack of motivation, but it is more often than we would like to think. Capacity for faith in one's students is the mark of a great teacher. Nothing inspires maximum achievement like the confidence and interest of one's teacher. But more than personality is required. Sound learning and an inquiring mind are the essential sparks for igniting the tinder of young minds. Knowledge and the love of learning are contagious.

The effective teacher must first of all know his subject. The debate on this issue which sometimes occurs between the scholars and school men is fruitless. Obviously knowledge of the principles of teaching and acquisition of skills in imparting knowledge are important but they cannot make up for lack of scholarship. Understanding the psychology of youth is also essential to maximum results. But all of these will avail little if the teacher is without a genuine interest in youth. This quality needs emphasis in the selection and training of prospective teachers.

As long as the teaching profession attracts too few candidates discrimination in their selection will be limited. Somehow the profession must be made more attractive. Greater financial rewards would help, but this alone will not solve the problem. Other satisfactions are as important as financial returns in attracting and holding gifted teachers. Their standing in the community, the considerations of the board of education, conditions of employment, appreciation of students and parents are among them. The universities cannot control these matters, but they can assist in developing proper attitudes by encouraging a healthy climate of opinion in the communities to which they send teachers. Through departments and schools of education the picture of the satisfactions, the rewards, and the opportunities for service which the teacher has can be presented more effectively by universities than by any other agency. Thus, their responsibilities do not end with providing courses for the training of teachers; they include also the task of promoting an interest in the profession through all the resources at their command.

Encouragement of gifted students by professors in the college and university could be highly effective in recruiting for the profession. This suggests one of the values of university affiliation of the training colleges. To deprive gifted students of contact with university professors could affect definitely the quality of those attracted to the profession.

The relationship of the university to the training of teachers is a matter which needs examination and study. The potential influence of universities on the educational system has never been fully realized. If they should devote as much energy to teaching as to engineering, the status of the profession might be substantially improved.

Progress in Teacher Education

In the United Kingdom, as already indicated, a significant step was taken in affiliating training colleges with universities. Through this affiliation the university professors are able to exert a greater influence on the profession as a whole. It should be helpful, too, to the universities by increasing their understanding of what takes place in the elementary and secondary schools which prepare the future university students. They will have an opportunity to understand more fully the problems of the school system as a whole, of the secondary schools, and particularly of the training colleges.

The association of the teachers in the training colleges with university staffs should also lift their sights. The prestige of their university connection tends to dignify and exalt the profession, thus enabling the colleges to attract men and women of higher caliber. All elements of the educational system should profit from the change.

In both Australia and South Africa the teacher training institutions are closely tied to the ministry or departments of education. The vision which the universities might provide through closer contact with these institutions, if the McNair plan were adopted, should result in helpful stimulation of the staffs of the training colleges and of the ministry or departments under which they work. Any efforts which make for closer collaboration between the training colleges, the ministry of education departments, and the universities should strengthen the profession.

The extension of the program of the training colleges in England from two to three years, thus giving teachers the same length of training as university graduates, should elevate the status of the teacher in the minds of the public. It is a step toward giving the training colleges degree-granting powers, which will doubtless come in time though present sentiment does not favor it.

In the United States, as well as in England, efforts are being made to strengthen the teacher education program. As suggested earlier in this chapter, the teachers' colleges in the United States have added graduate departments and are devoting more time to basic subjects. The object is to provide better teachers and more effective instruction.

Some teachers' colleges are seeking to attract able graduates of liberal arts colleges and to provide special professional programs for them. The Master of Arts in Teaching has been established in some institutions to cater to these students. The George Peabody College for Teachers has for several years provided substantial scholarships for outstanding liberal arts college graduates, who, after twelve months of training, receive the M.A. degree and a teacher's certificate.

The American Association of Universities some years ago raised a large sum with which to establish the Woodrow Wilson Fellowship Fund. This fund provides fellowships to able young people to attract them to graduate schools for at least one year, in the hope that many who have one year of graduate work may be led to continue to the Ph.D. degree, and ultimately to enter the university teaching field. The experience of this plan has been gratifyingly successful.

In Canada, as in the United States, the training of teachers is shared by a large number of institutions—more than two-thirds of all its colleges and universities. Canada has neither the training college system of the United Kingdom, South Africa, Australia and New Zealand nor the large number of Teachers Colleges such as are found in the United States. Its degree-granting institutions bear the major share of the burden of teacher education.

In India and Pakistan practically all the universities provide teacher education and many have training colleges among their affiliated units. Teacher education is more nearly on a par with the education of engineers, doctors and lawyers in India than in most other Commonwealth countries.

Conclusion

In all the countries under review the outlook for teacher education is encouraging. The reforms already adopted in England—the affiliation of training colleges and lengthening their programs—may have quite profound effects on the future school system through providing better educated teachers. In the United States the great variety of efforts already referred to, designed to strengthen teacher education, also gives promise of producing useful results. A clearer recognition of the central importance of the teacher in all countries has resulted from the critical shortage experienced in recent years. While these developments indicate progress, the provision of an adequate supply of qualified teachers remains the most critical of all the problems confronting the educational systems of the English-speaking countries.

XI

Professional Education — Science and Technology

Long before universities had generally accepted engineering and allied subjects as worthy of recognition, other institutions were providing technical training in Britain.

The Mechanics Institutes, designed to instruct workingmen "in the scientific principles of Arts and Manufacture," began as early as 1824 with the founding of Birkbeck College and expanded rapidly. By 1841 there were more than 200, and by 1860, 750 such institutes. These were the forerunners of what are known today as the technical colleges, the first of which was the Regent Street Polytechnic established in 1880. This institution marked the beginning of technical education in its modern form. Early instruction was elementary in character, involving courses for tradesmen, craftsmen, operators, process workers, laboratory assistants, in short, for those concerned with essentially practical processes of production, manufacture and design. It was geared to the needs of the men already employed in industry, who for the most part could take it only on a part-time basis.

In the curricula of higher education science and technology are relative newcomers. The University of London was a pioneer in these areas. Its King's College created a chair of engineering in 1838[1] and its University College established a chair of civil engineering in 1841 and of mechanical engineering in 1846.[2] It also granted a first degree in science in

1859, in advance of other British universities.

Cambridge began science instruction in 1851 but not at the first degree level. The science honors degree program was introduced some years later. It was still later when engineering was added to the curriculum.

Some of the civic universities either began as science or technical schools or incorporated them as constituent units. For example, Mason Science College was the forerunner of the University of Birmingham; Durham College of Physical Science became a part of Durham University; Yorkshire College of Science, a part of the University of Leeds; and the Sheffield Technical School, a part of the University of Sheffield.

To understand the status of science and technology in British universities, it is necessary to look briefly at non-university programs which have played so important a role in the development of the applied sciences.

Technical Colleges

The activities of the technical colleges range all the way from craft courses to the newly-created Diploma in Technology, which has the rank of an honors degree course in the university. These courses are given on both a part-time and a full-time basis. They undertake to provide the technical training and education required by industry and commerce. In recognition of their value, in the case of boys and girls under eighteen years of age, industry has provided day-time release for attending the courses. The scope of this program is indicated by the numbers served: 41,000 in 1938; 167,000 in 1953; and 355,000 in 1955. By 1960–1961 it is proposed to double the 1955 figure.

The system of technical colleges in England and Wales comprises more than 500 institutions. Three hundred of these provide for full-time, as well as part-time, students; 250 take part-time students only. The work of the part-time institutions is usually of elementary grade. Most of the colleges offering advanced work give some elementary work also. As the colleges expand and raise their standards the elementary courses will be relegated more and more to those institutions not qualified for advanced work.

The ordinary national certificate, for which the technical colleges give training, requires three years of part-time work. The higher national certificate requires two additional years. The latter certificate is considered of approximately first degree standard in the subjects taken, though the course is narrower in scope.

Some British specialists visited the United States in 1951 to examine its program of technical training. They concluded that the higher national certificates are as advanced as the first degrees in the American universities, or the standard reached in the British universities by the end of the second year.

There are three types of technical colleges based upon the areas served: (1) the local college; (2) the area college; and (3) the national college. In the main the local colleges provide training for the ordinary national certificate; the area institutions for the higher national certificate; and the national colleges provide training for special types of industries which cannot be maintained profitably on a local basis because of the small number of students desiring the work.

The national colleges have been established since World War II. The following were in operation in 1957: The College of Aeronautics; the Royal College of Art; National Foundry College; National Colleges of Food Technology, of Horology and of Rubber Technology; National College for Heating, Ventilating, Refrigeration and Fan Engineering; National Leather Sellers College; and the Scottish Woollen Technical College. As the listing indicates, they are highly specialized in character, and relatively few technologists in these fields are required by industry.

The technical college system in Scotland began with several

central institutions. Later smaller local institutions were developed to supply the needs of outlying areas.

The chief central institutions in Scotland are Royal College of Science and Technology, Glasgow; Heriot-Watt College, Edinburgh; Robert Gordon's Technical College, Aberdeen; Dundee Technical College; Paisley Technical College; Scottish Woollen Technical College at Galashiels (a national college); and Leith Nautical College. These institutions serve both full-time and part-time students. In 1954–1955 there were 1,822 full-time and 11,951 part-time students enrolled in them.

The specialization in the technical colleges of England, Wales and Scotland reflects the industrial patterns of their localities. For example, courses relating to the cotton industry are found in Lancashire at the Bolton Technical College; woollen textiles in Yorkshire at Bradford, Halifax and Huddersfield; hosiery at Leicester and Nottingham; and the silk industry at Coventry and Macclesfield. Likewise, in the heavy industry field, foundry work and metallurgy are found in Middlesborough; chemical technology at Cheshire and Merseyside, which are chemical manufacturing cities; and marine engineering and naval architecture at Cardiff, Plymouth and other port cities. The Hatfield Technical College opened in 1952 to serve the aeronautical engineering needs of students from the De Haviland Aircraft Company. The Rugby Technical College, noted for its electrical laboratories, was equipped by a company with large local electrical works.

There are four types of technical colleges, based upon the character of the work performed: part-time local institutions providing mainly craft courses and elementary work; regional colleges giving the ordinary and higher national certificate courses, and serving an area involving several towns; some twenty-five colleges (to be increased to thirty) devoted chiefly to advanced work for which the government provides 75 per cent of the cost, rather than the 60 per cent which is available to the local and regional colleges; and colleges of advanced technology. The last category will give only advanced work, and award the Diploma in Technology. It is designed to serve those who wish work beyond that required for the higher national certificate. Its courses in technology are of university quality and its staff conducts research programs.

In 1957 the location of eight of ten projected Colleges of Advanced Technology had been selected: Birmingham College of Technology; Bradford Technical College; Cardiff College of Technology and Commerce; Loughborough College of Technology; Royal Technical College, Salford; and, in London, the Battersea, Chelsea and Northampton Polytechnics. In addition Bristol College of Technology was selected as a potential institution for advanced work. A tenth college was to be chosen from among those on the northeast coast of England.

Of the 300 local colleges providing the ordinary national certificate, 175 provide also one or more technologies at the advanced or higher national certificate level. A few of the technical colleges operate in close association with universities. For example, five of the eight polytechnics in London have teachers recognized by the university. This means that their students may come up for the internal University of London degrees. The Sunderland Technical College has a similar arrangement with the University of Durham. The Manchester College of Science and Technology incorporates within it the Faculty of Technology of the University of Manchester.

A vast teaching staff is required for the technical colleges. As indicated in an earlier chapter, the training of technical college staffs is less adequate than that of other types of teachers. In 1957 there were 11,000 full-time and 40,000 part-time teachers in the technical colleges of the United Kingdom. Two-thirds of the teaching work is done by the full-time staff. Sixty per cent of the full-time staff have university degrees, or their equivalent. Just over half teach science and technology. Only one-third have received professional training as teachers, but most of them are teachers of subjects other than technology.

About one-quarter of the part-time teachers in the technical colleges are full-time teachers in the schools and other educational institutions who teach in the colleges in the evenings. Over half of the technical college staffs are engaged in industry, commerce or the professions.

Certain special developments in the technical colleges have already been mentioned, such as the Diploma in Technology. Emphasis on research also has characterized these colleges since 1946. The White Paper on Technical Education states that the colleges of advanced technology are expected "to develop a substantial amount of research, particularly research sponsored by industry. . . . They should also encourage their staffs to undertake a reasonable amount of consulting work."[3]

The scope of research suggested is not limited to pure and applied physical science. Research on management problems in industry is needed and is expected of these institutions. While the major research expected is confined to the colleges of advanced technology and those receiving the 75 per cent grant, it is expected that the smaller colleges also will undertake limited investigations. This new emphasis upon research in the technical colleges of all types is a post-war development of considerable significance.

The most recent addition to the technical college programs is that of management studies as a separate discipline. The definition of management in terms of scientific method is only a little more than a half-century old. The Institute of Industrial Administration worked out a syllabus for Management Studies in the 1920s which, since 1946, has been used as the basis of management education in the technical colleges, some of which have established separate departments. Some have also developed short full-time courses which are designed to serve the needs of various grades of management and deal with special aspects of the subject.

Some universities have set up postgraduate courses in management and related subjects. The Administrative Staff College at Henley and other independent bodies are also providing courses of an advanced nature in this field. The development of management studies has not been without its problems. Due to the novelty of the program it has met with both external and internal skepticism, based partly on its own shortcomings and partly on misapprehension as to the nature and purpose of management education.

It is clear from this description of technical colleges that the scope of work undertaken by them is expanding rapidly. They have been handicapped by lack of equipment. To supply this need, the government has announced its intention of making a substantial grant for equipment in the quinquennium ending in 1961, though the major responsibility for providing this equipment remains that of the local education authorities.

The technical programs in Northern Ireland, Australia, New Zealand, Canada, South Africa and India follow the same general pattern as those of England, Wales and Scotland. Recent figures on the number of students attending these technical colleges are not available, but in some Commonwealth countries they outnumber the students attending the universities. These agencies have provided a major portion of the technical education required in most Commonwealth countries. While many of the curricula in these institutions are elementary in character, the work in some fields is of university standard. For example, when the diploma in technology was established in 1951 it was designed to provide instruction of as high standard as the honors degree work at the university. It would not be surprising if the colleges of advanced technology in time develop into universities of technology along the lines of Massachusetts Institute of Technology, California Institute of Technology and other such institutions in the United States.

In some of the Commonwealth countries the technical colleges provide a large proportion of the technology training. For example, in New South Wales, Australia, Professor Brown points out that more professional engineers have been trained through part-time technological courses in the technical colleges than through full-time courses in the universities. Indeed, he asserts that about one-half the professional engineers in that Commonwealth have neither a university degree nor a technical college diploma. Table 15 indicates the variety of the backgrounds of 3,303 engineers in Australia.

TABLE 15   NEW SOUTH WALES
MISCELLANEOUS PROFESSIONAL ENGINEERS[4]

Technical College Certificates (any)	70
Technical College Trades Courses	319
Technical College—individual subjects	747
Special departmental or industrial training courses (e.g. P.M.G.)	110
Miscellaneous Certificates (non-college)	279
Miscellaneous Certificates and Diplomas (Colleges other than recognized Technical Colleges or Schools of Mines, e.g., I.C.S., Australian Radio College)	101
Private Study (including I.C.S., etc., incomplete)	152
Statutory Certificates (e.g., Local Government Engineers)	265
Marine Certificates (e.g., B.O.T.)	651
Industry	609
Total	3,303

The above discussion of technical colleges may suffice to give a general picture of the non-university programs of science and technological training in the United Kingdom and other Commonwealth countries. Since the United States has no agencies corresponding to the technical colleges, this section has dealt only with Commonwealth countries. It now remains to trace developments of science and technology in the universities of the countries under review and picture their present status and outlook. This will be dealt with in three sections: Science and Technology in (1) British Universities; (2) Commonwealth Universities; and (3) the American Universities.

British Universities

The industrial revolution antedated the scientific and technological age. In this early period Britain was the pioneer. There are several reasons for its leadership. It had favorable political institutions, and free trade. It had the advantages of good climate, geographical location and special connections with the New World. Moreover, it was experienced in foreign trading and had an abundance of coal.

The iron industry developed after coal displaced charcoal in the blast furnaces. The heavy industries were slow to develop in countries such as the United States and Continental Europe before the time of the railroads, because transportation is an important factor for their success. In Great Britain there were canals and roads, but, above all, there was proximity to the sea. Britain was therefore in a better position than the other countries to take the leadership in the early decades of industrial development.

The perfection of the steam engine by Watt made possible machines for the production of other machines. The machinery for manufacturing steam engines at the time railways were developing gave England a great advantage over other countries. Mechanical engineering became important there as early as 1821. Thus Britain was a half-century ahead of Germany and the United States by the middle of the nineteenth century.

Despite these industrial advances, British universities were slow to recognize technological education. The development of the technical colleges described in the preceding section was the result. There was little basic science required in this period, but it was accepted as a worthy university subject earlier than technology in the ancient universities. Technical education throughout the early period was the responsibility of the Ministry of Education, which still supports the technical colleges. Until 1919 it provided university funds for technological instruction. The University Grants Committee, on its inauguration, assumed the responsibility for aiding science and technology in the universities.

There was little progress made toward providing courses in science and its application before 1840. Five university schools of engineering, however, were established in Britain by 1851. Two of these were located in London and one each in Glasgow, Belfast and Dublin. Between 1851 and 1878 four new schools were established, Manchester, Newcastle, Cambridge and Edinburgh. Between 1878 and 1900, nine additional university chairs were founded mainly through the efforts of local benefactors. Thus, by the beginning of the twentieth century there were eighteen engineering faculties in British universities.

University technology up to 1919 was fostered largely by private enterprise, though some support was received from the Ministry of Education, as already noted. In the twenty-year period 1919–1939 government grants for university support rose from £900,000 to £2,224,000. The University Grants Committee in the beginning allocated funds to the university for support of its program. The purposes for which funds were to be used were determined by the universities. The growth of support was gradual, as indicated by the fact that an increase of only £1,249,000 had been made during the first twenty-year period.

As a result of the needs revealed by the war, and the slow progress being made toward meeting them, great discontent developed throughout Britain with scientific and technological progress. Lord Ernest Simon of Wythenshaw gave figures to show why the United States was so far outstripping Britain in its industrial and scientific development. He compared the university income in the two countries for the period 1937–1938 and found the following: income from fees, U.S.A. £34 million—Great Britain £2 million; grants from government authorities, U.S.A. £32 million—Britain £3 million; endowment income, gifts, etc., U.S.A. £31 million—Britain £1.5

million; or a total of £97 millions in the United States and £6.5 millions for Great Britain. He pointed out that the total expenditure on American universities was fifteen times that in Great Britain, and that when one allowed for a population ratio of three to one, the rate of expenditure per capita of population was still five to one. While the United States had more than one million students in degree-granting institutions in 1938, Britain had approximately fifty thousand.[5]

A British Parliamentary and scientific committee report described as urgent the demand for doubling the number of scientists and technologists. It said:

If we are to maintain our position in the world and restore and improve our standard of living, we have no alternative but to strive for that scientific achievement without which our trade will wither, our Colonial empire remain undeveloped, and our lives and freedom will be at the mercy of the potential aggressor. Doubling the number of scientists and technologists is a matter of the utmost concern. This task will fall upon the universities and major technical colleges.[6]

Sir Henry Tizard, Chairman of the United Kingdom Defense Research Policy Committee, the United Kingdom Advisory Council on Scientific Policy, and the United Kingdom Committee on Industrial Production, had this to say in 1948:

All social progress, such as spread of education, promotion of health, opportunities for leisure and health recreation, must depend on the power of science and technology to increase the productivity of industry.

All really new developments of industry are the product of the work of very few men. In general, knowledge in the physical sciences now accumulates at a rate much faster than it is, or possibly than it can be, applied in industry. There is a vast amount of knowledge waiting to be used. No new discovery in any field is likely to have so quick and beneficial an effect on British industry as the application of what is already known.[7]

The concern expressed by these leaders was shared also by

the rank and file of British industries. At the Federation Conference of British industries in 1946 a series of resolutions was passed which ended with the following:

This Conference urges the full collaboration of the Government in giving the highest priority to the provision of the essential buildings and personnel for research on the condition precedent to securing that increase in the volume of production on which the economic recovery of this country depends.[8]

These extracts from the literature of the period indicate the recognition of the significant role of science and technology and the deep concern of industry over its advancement. Industry not only expressed its views, but played an active part in encouraging technological education. University chairs were founded at several universities with funds which it raised. Gifts of equipment were also made to the universities. Industrial corporations provided an increasing number of scholarships for study and research in science and technology. In turn, the universities developed new postgraduate courses designed to meet special local industrial requirements.

The University Grants Committee responded to the universal demand for support of science and technology. It increased substantially support to the universities during the quinquennium 1952–1956. In addition large sums for buildings and equipment were provided in the fields of science and technology.

In 1957 plans for the second quinquennium, 1957–1962, were announced, including grants for buildings and equipment, and increases in maintenance support. The overall increase in maintenance recommended by the Committee and approved by the treasury contemplated annual expenditures ranging from £30.6 million in the first year to £39.5 million in 1961–1962. These grants do not include the cost of the new rates of salaries for the teaching staff, which in 1957–1958 amounted to £3.5 million. At the time of this writing, the amounts for subsequent years had not been assessed.

In addition to the recurrent grants, the following grants for buildings, exclusive of sites, fees and equipment, were authorized:

1957	£10.4 million each year
1958–1959	£12.0 " " "
1960–1963	£15.0 " " "

The program of the later years is provisional and subject to review if the economic situation should change substantially.[9]

These plans also called for increasing the student population by approximately 40 per cent, with the understanding that two-thirds of this increase should be enrolled in science and technology. The additional allotments for buildings, as well as for recurrent grants, were to be devoted largely to science and technology, particularly in the earlier years.

Eighteen of the twenty-one universities now in Britain have Faculties of Civil, Mechanical and Electrical Engineering. Chemical and aeronautical engineering departments have also developed within recent years. Customarily universities in the industrial centers have developed studies related to the needs of local industries. For example, Faculties of Metallurgy are found at Birmingham, Sheffield, Swansea (Wales) and other centers of the steel industry; Naval Architecture and Marine Engineering at Glasgow, Liverpool, Belfast, Durham and Southampton. Since Manchester is in the textile area it offers courses in textile chemistry and engineering, while Leeds has specialized programs in wool textiles, including color chemistry and dyeing. The only university in Britain to offer courses in the chemistry of leather manufacture is Leeds; in paper technology, Manchester; in glass technology, Sheffield. The Sheffield Department of Glass Technology was the pioneer of all such departments in the world. Nine universities have mining departments, Edinburgh, Glasgow, London (Imperial

College), Leeds, Nottingham, Durham, Birmingham, Wales, Cardiff and Sheffield.

A significant post-war development has been the establishment of postgraduate courses in various branches of technology at several universities, including Birmingham, London and Edinburgh. Vast expansion has taken place at the Manchester College of Science and Technology and at Imperial College of Science and Technology in London. In the latter institution, for example, plans called for increasing the student population from 1,650 to 3,000. Buildings to care for this increase were under construction in 1957. Outside London there are projects in chemistry at Birmingham, Leeds, Newcastle, Sheffield; in chemical engineering at Birmingham, Cambridge and Manchester; engineering at Bristol, Glasgow, Manchester, Newcastle and Southampton; fluid mechanics at Cambridge; fuel technology at Leeds and Sheffield; mining engineering at Sheffield, and physics at Birmingham and Leeds.

As a result of these developments, by 1955–1956 the number of full-time students of science and technology reached a peak of 29,013, which was 124 per cent more than the 1938–1939 figure and 34½ per cent of the entire university student population. Plans call for increasing the number to 55,000 by 1962.

The general conclusion in 1956 was that in order to produce an annual rate of 4 per cent growth in industrial output it would be necessary to increase the number of qualified scientists and engineers from 135,000 to approximately 200,000 by 1966, an increase of somewhat more than 60 per cent. It was estimated that more technologists will be required than scientists. For example, the need for engineers was estimated at about 70 per cent increase between 1956 and 1966, while the demand for scientists was expected to rise only about 50 per cent over the same period. In the light of this projection the number of people qualifying each year in science and engineering should increase from 10,000 in 1954–1955 to 20,000 in 1970.

In addition to the output of the universities, it was planned to increase substantially those completing advanced courses in the technical colleges in England and Wales. In 1956 approximately 9,500 graduated from advanced courses in technical colleges, one-half of whom would ultimately become qualified technologists eligible for membership in a professional institution. It was the government's declared intention to raise the capacity of the technical colleges in advanced courses as soon as possible to 15,000 per year. Thus, with more than 50 per cent increase in scientists and technologists from the technical colleges, and 100 per cent increase from the universities, it was hoped that the needs of qualified scientists and technologists would be fairly well met.

The length of the engineering course at British universities is three to four years full-time study. In the technological faculties of most universities this leads to a Bachelor of Science degree, but at Oxford and Cambridge it is a Bachelor of Arts degree. In some universities the degree is named after the branch of study, B.Eng. (Bachelor of Engineering), B.Met. (Bachelor of Metallurgy), and so forth.

Commonwealth Countries

The British Commonwealth countries have in general followed the pattern set by the United Kingdom in its training and research activities in the fields of science and technology. Hence there will be no need for a detailed description of the technical colleges. The general framework of their development has been similar to that of Britain. The sections, therefore, dealing with the separate Commonwealth countries will be brief.

There are three types of organizations active in the fields

of science and technology: (1) the technical colleges; (2) industrial research organizations; (3) the universities.

In general, technical colleges are less highly developed in the Commonwealth countries than in the United Kingdom. They train craftsmen, technicians and some technologists, but the advanced work in the Commonwealth institutions is less than in the mother country. These institutions do not provide advanced courses such as are found in the colleges of advanced technology.

In their respective countries, the Councils or Departments of Scientific and Industrial Research have established laboratories or institutes for carrying on the industrial research of interest to the major industries of the countries. For example, India had eighteen such laboratories in 1957, twenty-one in 1958 and was expecting to establish another in 1959. South Africa has five well-developed institutes, but industries there have been slow in coming to the aid of this development. In Australia the laboratories operated under the direction of the Commonwealth Scientific and Industrial Research Organization conduct researches on a wide variety of industrial problems. In England and Canada the D.S.I.R. is apparently a less significant factor in technological research than in the other Commonwealth countries.

Research rather than training is the purpose of these units, yet in some countries they constitute an asset to the universities by providing graduate students job opportunities enabling them to pursue graduate study while employed in the laboratory. They also furnish scholarships to graduate students and in other ways aid the universities directly.

The chief agency for the development of scientists and technologists is, of course, the university. Each of the Commonwealth countries has well-developed programs in science and engineering in most of their universities and in some of their colleges.

Table 16 indicates the extent to which the various phases

of engineering have been developed in the several Commonwealth countries.

TABLE 16   BRANCHES OF ENGINEERING OFFERED IN INSTITUTIONS
OF THE COMMONWEALTH EXCEPT INDIA AND PAKISTAN[10]

Branch	United Kingdom	Austra- lia	New Zealand	South Africa	Can- ada	Total	% of Total
Chemical	5	4	1	2	10	22	12
Civil	11	6	1	4	11	33	18
Electrical	12	6	1	4	12	35	19
Mining	6	5	1	1	8	21	11.4
Metallurgy	5	4	1	1	8	19	10.3
Mechanical	11	4	1	4	10	30	16
Aeronautical	3	1				4	2.18
Engineering Production	1				1	2	1.09
Industrial Fermentation	1					1	.54
Marine	2					2	1.09
Naval Architecture	1					1	.54
Fuel Technology	1					1	.54
Glass Technology	1					1	.54
Municipal	2					2	1.09
Mining Geology	2	1		1		4	2.18
Surveying		2		2		4	2.18
Agricultural	1			2		3	1.63

AUSTRALIA

All six state universities in Australia, in addition to the NSW University of Technology, have Faculties of Engineering. Their offerings are varied. The smallest is the University of Tasmania which, in 1956–1957, had only two departments, Civil and Mechanical Engineering, and fifty students. Melbourne has the most complete program. It offers sixteen different degrees in engineering: Bachelor's and Master's in

Civil, Mechanical, Electrical, Mining, Metallurgical and Chemical Engineering; Bachelor's and Master's degree in Surveying; a Bachelor's degree in Agricultural Engineering; a Master's degree in Engineering Science; and the Doctorate in Engineering.

A number of the technical colleges in Australia have aspirations to become degree-granting institutions. The Royal Melbourne Technical College, with a total of 18,000 students, would like to be given the title "Institute of Science and Technology," and the power to grant degrees of university standard. The Perth Technical College has requested the University of Western Australia to recognize its three-year diploma course as being of degree standard. Some in the University favor the establishment of a Bachelor of Technology degree of the type given at Adelaide University.

The Murray Committee warned against such changes in its report.

There is grave danger in most countries that a technical college or other institution of similar type which is performing excellently its proper function of producing the technicians and craftsmen for whom there is urgent national need, may be led by a false sense of values to try its hand at producing another type of professional engineer or technologist and to lessen its effectiveness for its own particular task.[11]

The Committee expressed disapproval of institutions that seek to serve a dual purpose in the training of technicians and technologists.

The University of Adelaide has developed a new program jointly with the South Australian School of Mines and Industries, leading to the degree of Bachelor of Technology. It has organized courses in nine subjects leading to the degree. Much of the teaching is done by the staff of the South Australia School of Mines.

There is a great shortage of men trained in science and

engineering in Australia. For example, in Victoria the estimated need in 1956 was for 1,083 in science and engineering. The total number of graduates turned out by Melbourne in that year was 323. While figures are not available for all the institutions, the Vice-Chancellor's Committee on Australian Universities suggests that the situation in Victoria would not be far different from that found in other states.

NEW ZEALAND

The University of New Zealand has four constituent universities in addition to two agricultural colleges. Three of the four universities have some phase of engineering. Through these programs the university provides instruction in mechanical, electrical, civil, chemical, mining and metallurgical engineering.

The degree of Bachelor of Engineering may be awarded with honors or without. The candidate who has met the requirements may be recommended by the professorial board of his college for admission to the degree with first or second class honors.

CANADA

Applied science and engineering have been provided by Canadian universities since 1856, when McGill University included them in its Faculty of Arts. L'Ecole Polytechnique, founded in Montreal in 1873, was the first French school of applied science and arts. Dalhousie University, in the Maritime Provinces, established a Faculty of Science in 1877. This was reorganized in 1906 in such way as to include pure science in the Faculty of Arts and Science. The applied sciences were taught by the Faculty of Engineering. This Faculty was discontinued when the Nova Scotia Technical College was organized. The University of New Brunswick established lecture courses in physics and in civil and electrical engineering in 1899. A school of practical science was established in Toronto in 1877.

This later became the Faculty of Applied Science and Engineering of the University of Toronto. In 1893 a School of Mining was established in Kingston and associated closely with Queen's University. It was assimilated by Queen's in 1916 as the Faculty of Applied Science.

The provincial universities of Western Canada, which were established later, provided for instruction in applied science and engineering from the beginning. Recently the University of Ottawa has organized a Faculty of Applied Science. The engineering program covers four years from senior matriculation, or five years from junior matriculation in the English-language universities. In the French-speaking universities, Montreal and Quebec, the Baccalaureate in Arts is required for admission. Under both systems courses in basic scientific principles, in cultural subjects and in technical training are followed by two years of specialization. The specialized courses in Canada include aeronautical, agricultural, ceramic, civil, electrical, geological, mechanical, metallurgical and mining engineering, as well as engineering physics.

In 1955–1956 10,500 students, or one-sixth of the entire Canadian university student population, enrolled in engineering and applied science.

Table 17 presents a picture of engineering programs in Canadian universities.

In addition to the above listings, the University of Western Ontario opened an engineering science program in 1954. Its first class graduated in 1958. It is not listed in Table 17, since it had not granted a degree before 1956. The new engineering science building of the University of Western Ontario will provide for an enrollment of 500 students. It will combine engineering, humanities and social sciences.

The University of Western Ontario has a strong science background. Though it has only 4 per cent of the Canadian university population, it graduates 15 per cent of its honors students in chemistry, 50 per cent in physics, 20 per cent in geology, 13 per cent in biology and 18 per cent in mathematics

TABLE 17

	Alberta	British Columbia	Dalhousie	Laval	Manitoba	McGill	Montreal	New Brunswick	Nova Scotia Tech.	Ottawa	Queen's	Saskatchewan	Toronto
Agricultural		X										X	
Chemical	X	X		X		X	X		X	X	X	X	X
Civil	X	X		X	X	X	X	X	X		X	X	X
Electrical	X	X		X	X	X	X	X	X	X	X	X	X
Engineering & Business													X
Engineering Physics	X	X	X			X	X					X	X
Forest		X		X									
Geological	X	X		X	X						X	X	X
Irrigation	X												
Mechanical		X		X	X	X	X	X	X		X	X	X
Metallurgical	X	X		X		X	X		X		X		X
Mining	X	X		X		X	X		X		X		X
Petroleum											X		

Source: *Canadian Universities and Colleges*, 1956.[12]

and physics. With this background it is well-equipped to develop a program in the applied sciences.

In addition to those universities and colleges which provide the degree course in engineering, a total of eleven others provide one or more years of engineering work which is accepted on transfer by degree-granting institutions. Those institutions are: Acadia, three years; Assumption, two years; Carleton, two years; McMaster, one year; Memorial, three years; Mount Allison, three years; Royal Military College of Canada, four years; St. Dunstan's, three years; St. Francis Xavier, three years; St. Mary's, three years. Sherbrooke, a new institution, will provide a diploma in engineering after five years of work.

The universities of Canada have more adequate equipment than the universities of other Commonwealth countries, excluding the United Kingdom. For example, McMaster and the University of Toronto have reactors for nuclear research; McGill, a cyclotron; and British Columbia and Toronto have computing centers. Funds for the computing centers came from the National Research Council and the Defense Board.

There are some unusual features in Canadian engineering programs. The University of Montreal, for example, requires all students in engineering to take two years of philosophy, or eight semester hours, during their four-year period. In the Polytechnic Institute, which is affiliated with the University of Montreal, the philosophy requirement in the science and engineering curricula is a three-hour course during the first year (six semester hours).

Bishop's University requires all students majoring in science to take two courses in religion. They must also take a course in the classics in English translation if they have not had Latin. If they have had Latin in the secondary school they may continue it or take the classics course.

SOUTH AFRICA

South Africa has both university programs in technology and technical colleges. One may become an engineer either by taking the degree course at a university or by apprenticeship, with study in a technical college. This study may be pursued while holding a full-time job, by attending one or two classes each week, or through the "sandwich" system, whereby the student works half time and studies half time in the technical college.

There are four universities that have engineering programs, the Universities of Cape Town, Stellenbosch, Natal and Witwatershed. Pretoria University founded a Faculty of Engi-

neering in 1957, dedicating a new building in which to house
it in April of that year.

There are nine departments in which engineering instruction
is given in the universities: civil, electrical, mechanical, chemical, metallurgical, aeronautical, agricultural, land surveying
and naval architecture. Four universities have civil, electrical
and mechanical engineering; two have chemical and agricultural engineering and land surveying; one has mining engineering; and one, metallurgy.

Usually the matriculation examination which admits one to
the university will also admit him to the Engineering Faculty.
However, some institutions have special requirements. For
example, Witwatersrand insists upon mathematics and physical
science, English and Afrikaans in the secondary school record.
The length of course is usually four years. One year is actually
pre-engineering, the three remaining being devoted to the
major.

The need for engineers in South Africa is greater than the
supply. Professor Bozzoli estimated that while the universities
and technical colleges provide approximately 300 per year,
500 are needed.

INDIA

In 1954, according to *Engineering Research,* a bulletin published by the Council of Scientific and Industrial Research,
there were forty-five colleges, universities and institutes,
including those under formation, offering courses in various
branches of engineering. Six of these provided postgraduate
level courses; sixteen had limited facilities for research in one
or two fields; the remaining twenty-three had no facilities for
research.[13]

No discussion of science and technology in India would be
complete without reference to the work of the C.S.I.R. and its
contribution to the field. According to Professor M. S. Thacker,
the Director, the function of this organization is threefold: "the

promotion, guidance and coordination of scientific and industrial research in India, including the institution and financing of specific researches" and "the establishment and award of research studentships and fellowships." It also "encourages research in universities and other research institutions through a system of grants-in-aid." [13] In this respect the C.S.I.R. performs something of the same functions as the National Science Foundation in the United States. The Council cooperates in other ways with the colleges and universities. It takes able young men from the university, pays them well to assist in various types of research and, after a few years, returns them to the universities as teachers and researchers. Thus the Council provides a kind of training ground for those with special talents. In addition, the Council encourages research in the university by supporting worthy projects. It does industry-sponsored research in its laboratories. Thus, it serves in some respects the function of research institutes in the United States.

The Council has a total of 21 laboratories. Its president is the Prime Minister. The Vice-President, the Minister of Scientific Research and Cultural Affairs, Humayun Kabir, is the executive head of the organization, to whom the Director-General reports. These laboratories have been built with the help of industry, individuals and state governments. For example, the House of Tata donated Rs.12 lakhs for the establishment of the National Metallurgical Laboratory. The Indian Steel Wire Products added one lakh and the Metallurgical Association Rs.10,000. The Tata Laboratories, Ltd., also placed at the disposal of the Council eight acres of land for laboratory space and eighteen acres for staff quarters. This laboratory was opened in 1950.

The Government of Mysore offered to place the Cheluvamba Mansion in the City of Mysore, together with the attached buildings, gardens, parks and grounds, covering about 150 acres, at the disposal of the Council for the location of the Central Foods and Technological Research Institute. For the Central Research Institute, the Government of Madras made a gift of a site of eighty-four acres and in addition provided 3.07 lakhs of rupees for reclaiming the site and diverting the road which ran through it. For the establishment of the Central Electro-Chemical Research Institute at Karaikudi, Dr. R. A. Chettiar donated 15 lakhs of rupees and spacious grounds comprising 300 acres. This Institute was opened in January 1953.

In addition to instituting and supervising the work of the twenty-one research laboratories, the C.S.I.R. sponsored the first atomic reactor designed and built by Indian scientists and engineers. That reactor has been in operation since August 1956.

The Government of India has expressed great interest in the promotion of science and technology. It appointed a committee to survey the field of technical education and to make recommendations. In its report, submitted in 1946, the committee recommended the setting up of four higher technological institutes on the lines of the Massachusetts Institute of Technology in the United States. It recommended also that the first in the chain of these four higher technical institutes should be set up in the East. The result of this recommendation was the establishment of the Indian Institute of Technology in 1951.

This Institute offers first degree courses in civil, mechanical, electrical, metallurgical, and agricultural, engineering, naval architecture and marine engineering, geology and geophysics, architecture and mining engineering. These courses, which lead to a Bachelor's degree, are three to five years in length, depending on the field of study.

The undergraduate program provides for a thorough study of (1) basic sciences like mathematics, physics and chemistry; (2) humanities; (3) engineering sciences; and (4) technologies. Attention should be called to the fact that the humanities program is included along with the sciences and technologies. This follows the pattern of Canada and the United States.

In 1956 this Institute enrolled about 1,400 students, including both undergraduates and graduates. Its teaching staff of 192 included many distinguished foreign experts, who were loaned to the Institute by international agencies of UNESCO.

In 1956 an act was passed conferring upon the Institute degree-granting powers. It was not constituted as a university, "because the normal university type of organization set up is cumbersome and will not do for an institute that has to respond quickly to the swiftly changing needs of modern technology." [13]

Kharagpur Institute is a residential institution with a capacity for 1,500 students. It was designed to serve as a model for technological education in India.

It was announced in 1957 that the University Grants Commission was making available the sum of five hundred million rupees for strengthening science and technology. It was first proposed that a large number of new institutions should be established. This plan was later modified to provide for enlarging existing institutions and adding only three new ones. The Kharagpur Institute was the first of four technological institutes planned by the central government.

Twenty-two of the thirty-eight universities in India and Pakistan provided degree courses in engineering in 1957; nineteen of the thirty-two in India and three of the six in Pakistan also granted them.

The several institutions vary in the time requirement for the engineering degree. The universities in Pakistan (Dacca, Panjab and Peshawar) and one in India (Roorkee) require three years beyond the intermediate examination; four require three and one-half years; ten require four; and four require five years.

A large proportion of the government grant for buildings and equipment referred to above will be devoted to strengthening university programs. These, along with the research institutes, are laying the foundations for a strong program in science and technology. The full potential of these institutions will not be realized for a decade or more, but substantial progress is under way.

One of the problems which disturbs those concerned with technological education is the difficulty of finding adequate staff. In 1958 Kabir reported a shortage of 2,000 in science and technology. Plans were under way in 1957 to provide government funds with which to increase the pay of teachers in the technical field to the point where the universities could compete with government for the services of scientists and technologists.

The United States

In the American colonies no industries except agriculture and the production of raw materials were developed prior to 1776. Other industries were repressed by the British Parliament. It was not until after the War for Independence that industrial development began. Societies for the promotion of the useful arts were formed, and prizes were offered for improvements. Trained artisans were recruited from abroad. The notion that the sciences, through a new kind of education, could aid the industries seems to have been expressed first by Benjamin Hale at Bowdoin College (Maine) in 1822. Though this program survived only a decade, its purpose, scope and plans bore fruit in the modern engineering school.

The United States Military Academy at West Point began engineering instruction in 1817. It was modeled on the European military engineering pattern of that day, particularly that of the Ecole Polytechnique in Paris. The first civilian school of technology was established in 1824 by Stephen Van Rensselaer at Troy, New York, and was called the Rensselaer Polytechnic Institute. In the beginning it was a school for teaching "the sons and daughters of farmers and mechanics the application of science to agriculture, domestic economy, the arts and manufactures." [14] The depletion of the soil in an agricultural society led to an early emphasis on agricultural problems, but in 1829 civil engineering was inaugurated. The first degree in this field was conferred in 1835. Here again the French influence made itself felt. The program of studies in this institution was re-constituted in 1849 on the pattern of the Ecole Centrale of Paris and required three years' work.

Thus the Rensselaer Polytechnic Institute and the Military Academy at West Point were for many years the only schools affording technological training in the United States. Their graduates played a leading role in the building of highways, bridges, canals and railroads, which were involved in the early development of the country. Through the years the Rensselaer Polytechnic graduates have given leadership to scientific and engineering activities and to engineering education.

Harvard and Yale, both in the year 1847, established scientific schools: the Lawrence Scientific School at Harvard and the Sheffield Scientific School at Yale. In 1853 the University of Michigan offered a course in civil engineering. This was one of the earliest engineering courses to be offered by a state institution.

In 1862 Congress passed the Morrill Act, establishing the land-grant colleges of agriculture and mechanic arts. As indicated earlier, this gave great impetus to the development of engineering education. The number of schools had increased from six in 1862 to seventeen by 1870 and eighty-five by 1880. About half of these newly-established programs were in land-grant colleges. This rapid development was in response to industrial trends. Between 1820 and 1870 the proportion of the country's working population engaged in manufacture, trade, transportation and professional service increased about threefold.

Originally all engineering was called civil engineering. It was some forty years after the founding of Rensselaer Poly-technic Institute that courses in mining and mechanical engineering appeared in the curriculum. These three departments dealt with such problems as have been experienced by man over many generations. Then new departments began to appear: electrical engineering in the 1880s and chemical engineering a decade later. As industry expanded and scientific and technical knowledge increased, further differentiation and subdivision emerged. Forty or more engineering curricula, which

TABLE 18   ENGINEERING DEPARTMENTS IN THE
UNITED STATES

Program	Number of Departments	Percentage Relationship
Electrical	131	19%
Civil	129	18%
Mechanical	125	18%
Chemical	84	12.1%
Metallurgical	44	6.3%
Aeronautical	33	4.7%
Industrial	29	4.2%
Mining	29	4.2%
Agricultural	23	3.3%
Architectural	18	2.6%
Geological	14	2.03%
Petroleum	14	2.03%
Ceramic	12	1.7%
Marine	3	.4%
Business and Engineering Administration	1	.014%

Source: *American Universities and Colleges,* Seventh Edition, 1956.[15]

are essentially offshoots of the initial civil engineering, appear now in university catalogs. Table 18 indicates the main divisions and the percentage of student enrollment in each.

The engineering curriculum, following four years of secondary school work, contains three groups of subjects: (1) scientific (mathematics, physics and chemistry); (2) technical (specialized courses in a variety of engineering fields); and (3) non-technical (history, philosophy, social science, etc.). The scientific and non-technical courses are essentially similar in the several engineering curricula. Differentiation takes place in the technical content of the later undergraduate years. The degree conferred is usually Bachelor of Science, with or without specification as to the particular branch, conferred after four years of study. The professional degree, on the other hand, such as Bachelor of Civil Engineering, is normally reserved for graduate work.

Though engineering education began in the 1820s, it was a long while before it was given full recognition as a university subject. Even scientific training was viewed with reservations by the traditional college and university. In some instances the scientific and technological curricula, which were organized within established colleges and universities, were kept separate from the regular classical or traditional courses. It is of interest to note in this connection that engineering education in America had its beginnings under the auspices of educational institutions with scientists and professional educators taking the lead, rather than professional engineers or government bureaus as in Europe.

By 1942, when the United States entered the Second World War, there were about 36,000 men entering engineering colleges each year. This dropped during the war but rose again rapidly. A total of 90,000 freshmen entered engineering colleges in 1947. The post-war low in number of graduates in engineering was in 1955 when there were 22,589 degrees awarded. Since 1954 the freshman classes have been increasing. Seventy-eight thousand entered engineering in 1956. It is estimated that by 1960 there will be 43,000 engineering graduates and by 1965 a total of 56,000 graduating. Even with this expansion an annual deficit in the number of trained engineers of 8,000 is anticipated.

A discussion of American science and technology would not be complete without reference to the National Science Foundation, which was established by an Act of Congress in 1950. The purposes of this government agency, as set out in the Act, are to: (1) develop and encourage the pursuit of a national policy for basic research and education in the sciences; (2) initiate and support basic scientific research in the mathematical, physical, medical, biological, engineering and other sciences by making contracts or other arrangements (including grants, loans and other forms of assistance) for the conduct of such research; (3) by similar means (after consultation with the Secretary of Defense) initiate and support scientific research on matters relating to the national defense; (4) grant scholarships and graduate fellowships in the mathematical, physical, medical, biological, engineering and other sciences; (5) foster the international exchange of scientific information; (6) correlate the Foundation's programs with those undertaken by individuals and by public and private research groups; and (7) establish special commissions as it may deem necessary. The Foundation shall endeavor to strengthen the work throughout the United States and avoid undue concentration.

Grants in support of the Foundation have grown steadily since its establishment. Congress appropriated the sum of $40,000,000 for the fiscal year 1958 for "support of basic research in the mathematical, physical, engineering, biological and medical sciences; for fellowships and research education in the sciences, for improvement of science teaching through special institutes, for the exchange of scientific information, for support of the International Geophysical Year, and other purposes related to its basic mission." For 1959 the appropriation was increased 225 per cent to $130,000,000.

As evidence of the interest in science and technology in the United States a bill was introduced in the National Congress in 1958 calling for the creation of "a Department of Science and Technology headed by a secretary with Cabinet rank." The objective is stated in the following language:

The proposal to create a Department of Science and Technology has as its main objective the coordination and centralization of certain federal civilian science functions now vested in agencies which carry on science activities and which have some general relationship, and should, therefore, be brought into closer cooperation with other similar or related activities of all Federal agencies operating in various fields of Science and Technology.

Many independent agencies such as the Atomic Energy Commission, the National Advisory Committee for Aeronautics and the National Science Foundation conduct major programs in the field of science. Components of other departments such as the National Bureau of Standards, the Office of Technical Services and the Patent Office also support such programs. Some thirty components of executive departments and independent agencies engage in science activities. Though this bill had not passed at the time this book was written, its introduction and approval by many American leaders emphasize the great concern in America over the advancement of science and technology.

Conclusion

From this review of developments in the Commonwealth and the United States, it is obvious that a special emphasis in higher education, in this mid-century decade, is on science and technology. They absorb the lion's share of the expansion in budgets and are attracting an increasing proportion of youth in all English-speaking countries. This is the most striking phenomenon of the post-war years. It is a common feature in all the countries under review.

Undergraduate programs in science and engineering embrace the same scientific, technical subject matter with minor variations. There is, however, a marked difference in the non-scientific courses required in the universities of the several countries. In Britain the science and technology students devote their entire time to these subjects. In Australia the

New South Wales University of Technology requires courses in the humanities and social sciences. In India, Canada and the United States, humanistic-social studies are required subjects in all engineering curricula.

The philosophy prevailing in Canada was set forth in the report of the *Royal Commission on National Development in the Arts, Letters and Science,* in the following statement:

Humanistic studies do not belong only to the Faculty of Liberal Arts, but should pervade the professional schools as well. They should permeate the entire university. One of the functions of the university is to train persons for the liberal professions, but a liberal profession is liberal only because it includes education in the Liberal Arts. A professional school without the humanities is little more than a technical institute.[16]

Canadian universities vary in their methods of fulfilling the requirement and in the amount of work stipulated, but all engineering programs incorporate some humanistic-social studies. In the Schools of Engineering in the United States, from 15 per cent to 30 per cent of the requirements for the degree are in the humanities and social sciences. In the Higher Technological Institutes of India study of humanities is compulsory for all students.

The Massachusetts Institute, one of the strongest and most respected of American institutions, in a recent bulletin, sets forth its purposes in the following language:

In attaining its present position, the Institute has constantly kept before it three objectives—the education of men, the advancement of knowledge and the rendering of service to industry and the nation. It aims to give its students such a combination of humanistic, scientific, and professional training as will fit them to take leading positions in a world in which science, engineering and architecture are of basic importance. This training is especially planned to prepare students, according to their desires and aptitudes, to become practicing engineers or architects, investigators, business executives or teachers. The useful knowledge and mental discipline gained in this training are, however, so broad and fundamental as to constitute an excellent general preparation for other courses.

In most American universities dissatisfaction with the engineering curriculum prevails. The content of the liberal arts segment needs to be reconstituted, and in many institutions the administration feels that it should be expanded. Much thought has been given to this problem and considerable experimentation has been conducted in several of the stronger technological institutions in the United States, including M.I.T.

Sir Eric Ashby, Vice-Chancellor of Queen's University (Belfast), after declaring that, "the prime purpose of studies in humanities for technologists should be to remedy" their deficiencies in "arts subjects necessary for an understanding of contemporary society," suggested the criteria for selecting the subjects which should be made an integral part of higher technological education. He said:

First, they should not include subjects which can and ought to be taught at school. Second, they should be taught as genuine humanities, that is to say, they should deal with the creative and social acts of man, and particularly with value-judgments: ideas of right and wrong, of good and evil, of justice, freedom and government. Third, they should be taught in such a way as to be relevant to the contemporary world and to technology. . . . Fourth, humanities at this level of teaching should be instruments to enhance the individuality of students to resist that levelling of differences in taste and personality, that tendency to increase social entropy, which is a melancholy consequence of the modern techniques of mass communication.[17]

This highly perceptive analysis is a valuable contribution to contemporary thought on a subject of central importance and, at the same time, indicates the concern over this matter in the United Kingdom.

XII

Extension and Extra-Mural Studies

The first university extension lectures were given by Cambridge in 1873. Oxford and London followed the lead shortly afterwards, and within a decade the other universities and university colleges were providing them. By 1900 there was a wide variety of lecture courses being given.

This development in England excited the interest of American institutions to the extent that between 1880 and 1900 many universities inaugurated extension lectures similar to those that had thrived in England. Some of the oldest and best-known American universities participated in the program and, for a brief time, it received substantial support, particularly in the cities of the Middle Atlantic states and as far West as St. Louis. In 1892 a national congress of those interested in the movement was convened, and it was reported there that within the preceding four years twenty-eight states had organized extension lecture courses.

For several reasons the plan did not prosper long. By 1900 interest had waned to such an extent that it was practically abandoned. Lack of sufficient financing, the scarcity of suitable lecturers, the difficulty which the university staff had in understanding the interests and capacities of adults and its inability to develop a new set of educational standards for adults were some of the reasons assigned. The rapid increase in campus enrollments which absorbed the full time of faculties may have been a determining influence in the decline of the movement.

While England and the United States followed the same pattern in the beginning of their extra-mural efforts, they did not continue parallel programs after 1900. The British maintained interest in extension lectures and gradually added "tutorial classes." Instead of giving single lectures, or two or three in a series, classes were established and instruction on a more sustained basis was given. Early in the century the universities joined forces with the Worker's Education Association, which has been an outstanding factor in the development of the tutorial classes. This Association, founded in 1903, established relations first with Oxford University in 1907. This proved to be of such mutual interest to the University and the Association that other institutions soon followed the lead of Oxford. Within a short period the Association had established working relations with all the universities and university colleges of Great Britain.

There are now joint committees, composed of representatives of the universities, local education authorities, and the W.E.A., which promote sessional classes or three-year tutorial classes. Elementary and advanced tutorial classes and vocational courses have been developed by these committees. The Ministry of Education early recognized the work of the W.E.A. and provided financial support for both its independent classes and those sponsored jointly with the universities.

In the United States there was no W.E.A.; the state departments of education did not generally provide financial support for adult education and the extension lectures were discontinued. Description of the American development will be given in a later section, but it may be well to note that a basic difference between the American and Commonwealth off-campus programs is this. The American colleges and universities accept some extra-mural courses for credit toward a degree, while the Commonwealth institutions (except those in Canada) do not.

The universities in Commonwealth countries have followed

the pattern of the United Kingdom in developing extension lectures and tutorial classes. For example, in Australia extension lectures were begun at Sydney in 1886, and at Melbourne in 1891. The W.E.A. was formed there in 1913. In all the states, except Western Australia, this organization early established relations with the universities. The same type of development was followed in New Zealand and in South Africa. A somewhat different plan developed in Canada. While extramural work there began with university extension lectures and was followed by tutorial classes, the universities did not develop the relationship with the Worker's Education Association as in Great Britain.

The third step in the development of off-campus instruction in Britain was that of extra-mural or adult education departments. In 1926 the Universities' Extra-Mural Consultative Committee was formed to give attention to all aspects of extra-mural work and to assist in the development of a uniform policy. This Committee was reconstituted in 1946 as the Universities Council for Adult Education. In the extra-mural program courses are planned and conducted by the universities without the aid of the Worker's Educational Association and frequently provide a content different from that of the tutorial classes.

Since 1946 there has been rapid development of extra-mural studies. Before 1939 most adult education was sponsored jointly by the W.E.A. and the universities, but since the war, the universities have been so active in the field as to prompt the conviction that the main burden, henceforth, for liberal adult education in England will be borne by the universities. The expansion of the extra-mural studies has caused some to feel that the universities are trespassing on the preserves of the W.E.A. This problem will be discussed in a later section.

The organization of university programs in Britain differs from that found in the United States. For example, in some of the universities of the United Kingdom there are Extra-

Mural Boards of Studies composed of staff members from the various faculties. In the United States, in the larger universities particularly, extension is a regular division of the university organization, with a dean in charge who reports directly to the president, as do other deans of the university.

The Commonwealth countries, except Canada, have in general followed the lead of Britain in the organization and development of extra-mural programs. Canada has tended to follow the United States both in organization and in the nature and purposes of extension programs.

With the above general description of extension and extra-mural studies in the Commonwealth and the United States, it is appropriate to consider developments in each of the countries and to give in more detail the nature of the off-campus programs provided.

The United Kingdom

Universities and university colleges in England and Wales have geographical areas in which they are responsible for adult education in collaboration with the W.E.A. and the local education authorities. The extra-mural departments of the universities arrange for lectures and give courses in local centers. The lecture courses have developed differently in different localities. In some instances they have cooperated with public libraries and less frequently with vocational groups. These courses rarely lead to the award of a diploma or a certificate.

A more intensive method of study is represented by the tutorial class, which requires the student who wishes to be admitted to attend twenty-four classes in each of the three winter sessions. He also obligates himself to do reading and written work under the guidance of the tutor. The size of the classes is limited. The students have the privilege of sharing in the choice of the subject and the tutor. Part-time students may attend evening institutes, which make available both vocational and recreational classes in a wide variety of fields. Many of these institutes are quartered in day school buildings.

The Ministry of Education plays a significant part in adult education. Indeed, its assistance is essential to its success. Before World War II the Board of Education made grants to six residential colleges, which provided up to one-year courses for adults. Since the war more than twenty additional residential colleges have been established. These are either maintained or assisted by local education authorities. In these institutions adults may take short courses lasting from a few days to a few weeks.

The variety and extent of the program is indicated by tables. Table 19 shows the number of subjects offered through the extra-mural program in each of the universities in 1955–1956, and the totals for the two preceding years.

It will be noted that the basic subjects found in the Arts Faculty predominate, though new courses involving vocational and professional training are being introduced.

The Universities Council for Adult Education in 1954–1955 estimated that, excluding the Scottish universities, 93 per cent of the tutorial classes and 62 per cent of the sessional classes were still provided in cooperation with the W.E.A. In 1955–1956, however, a detailed study of these courses was made which revealed a different picture. While there was some difficulty in distinguishing between the two types of courses because of the close interlocking of the extra-mural and the W.E.A. machinery, the figures produced were regarded as reasonably accurate. They showed that for all British universities, including those in Scotland, W.E.A. was partner in providing 1832 courses in 1955–1956, or 41 per cent of the total. It included 677 tutorial classes, 635 sessional classes, 455 non-residential shorter courses, and sixty-one residential courses. These figures are incorporated in Table 20.

TABLE 19   SUBJECTS OF STUDY[1]

H—History	PH—Philosophy	BSC—Biological Sciences
IA—International	PSY—Psychology	G—Geography
Affairs	R—Religion	L—Language and Literature
GOV—Government	PSC—Physical	A—The Arts
SS—Social Studies	Sciences	CS—Combined Subjects

University	H	IA	GOV	SS	PH	PSY	R	PSC	BSC	G	L	A	CS
Belfast	11	8	7	7	5	2	3	3	17	14	28	22	2
Birmingham	107	8	15	30	18	14	21	25	21	21	71	93	15
Bristol	58	10	8	25	6	9	15	27	23	3	32	29	2
Cambridge	53	27	4	9	9	5	3	7	10	1	24	23	4
Durham:													
Durham	21	14	4	10	5	5	13	3	4		13	19	4
Newcastle	11	13	6	20	7	6	6	23	14	2	20	36	9
Edinburgh	20	18		11	4	7	2	11	22	3	25	37	
Exeter	44	9	3	6	3	7	7	5	10	2	18	21	
Glasgow	28	11	4	19	12	7	12	20	13	4	36	18	3
Hull	28	9	2	19	7	6	17	8	1		49	23	2
Leeds	21	9	10	30	4	8	2	4	5		24	12	3
Leicester	15	1	8	17	3	9	10	3	2	5	18	18	1
Liverpool	24	7	10	17	6	7	1	18	11	10	32	24	2
London	90	27	5	92	26	45	30	25	34	25	73	129	5
Manchester	22	10	1	81	13	15	14	21	15	13	45	51	5
Nottingham	64	34	19	24	15	10	15	14	15	15	41	39	5
Oxford	49	10	5	41	11	5	3	13	11	2	42	44	6
Reading	1			1		1				1	1	3	
Sheffield	28	2	3	33	4	6	2	18	4	4	8	8	4
Southampton	32	8	2	12	6	3	4	1	3	1	14	24	1
Wales	80	43	12	79	16	5	42	18	17	5	61	23	9
TOTALS	807	278	128	583	180	182	222	267	252	131	675	696	82
Totals, 1954–1955	769	351	96	554	210	176	211	238	258	72	685	682	
Totals, 1953–1954	684	313	139	500	192	184	180	189	245	80	636	652	

Source: Report of the Universities Council for Adult Education, Year 1955–56.

TABLE 20 GENERAL SUMMARY OF COURSES[2]

University	NON-RESIDENTIAL						RESIDENTIAL					TOTAL OF ALL COURSES	
			Other Courses										
	Tutorial Classes	*Sessional Classes*	*13–19 meetings*	*10–12 meetings*	*3–9 meetings*	*Total*	*Up to 3 days*	*4–7 days*	*8–14 days*	*Over 14 days*	*Total*	*1955–56*	*1954–55*
Belfast	15	25	7	56	20	123	6				6	129	142
Birmingham	19	143	16	141	104	423	20	5	8	3	36	459	467
Bristol	47	77	6	69	42	241	1	3	2		6	247	224
Cambridge	32	42	3	45	27	149	7	14	6	3	30	179	146
Durham:													
Durham	52	27	1	11	20	111	2	2			4	115	125
Newcastle	45	35	4	30	52	166	2	2	3		7	173	150
Edinburgh	18	36	1	101	4	160						160	149
Exeter	3	40		57	22	122		3	10		13	135	169
Glasgow	22	102	13	24	24	185			2		2	187	162
Hull	40	44	12	18	39	153	12	3	2	1	18	171	166
Leeds	96	16	2	4	4	122	5	3	2		10	132	121
Leicester	2	31	9	47	20	109				1	1	110	100
Liverpool	32	34		49	38	153	9	7			16	169	150
London	141	283	2	77	48	551	37	2	12	4	55	606	589
Manchester	67	78	4	35	47	231	26	38	7	4	75	306	311
Nottingham	46	112	15	58	64	295	6	5	4		15	310	277
Oxford	69	58	2	49	46	224	8	2	3	5	18	242	224
Reading	7	1				8						8	7
Sheffield	26	37	4	29	16	112	4	6	2		12	124	112
Southampton	35	52	2	14	6	109	1	1			2	111	111
Wales	145	96	16	76	71	404	3	3			6	410	400
Totals	959	1369	119	990	714	4151	149	99	63	21	332	4483	4302

Source: Report of the Universities Council for Adult Education, Year 1955–56.

Of the 4,483 courses given, 59 per cent were given by the universities without the aid of the W.E.A. The number of students enrolled in the W.E.A. classes was 29,799, or 31 per cent of the total. While the relative proportion of work being done in collaboration with the W.E.A. is declining, from these figures it is obvious that it still plays an important role.

There are those who question the advisability of the universities' taking on so large a share of the adult education program. The matter of changing the type of courses given is also a subject of debate. In an article entitled "The Great Tradition" published in *Adult Education,* Mr. H. C. Wiltshire, Director of the Extra-Mural Studies of Nottingham University, viewed with some alarm the trends such as the instituting of extra-mural examinations and the relating of courses of study to student's occupational interests. He feared that "the great tradition in English university adult education of special concern for non-vocational study, by adults of all classes, of the humanities and those subjects which bear on the understanding of man's life in society might be jeopardized."[3]

On the other hand, in a lecture before the Scottish Institute of Adult Education, Sir Eric Ashby suggested that "an approach to humanism through technology can and should be one of the growing points of adult education." He proposed that "classes should be deliberately organized on a vocational basis and that vocational interests should be used as a starting point for teaching designed to lead to the study of scientific ideas, society and ethics, literature and art."[4]

The two fears that disturb the workers in the adult education field are: (1) that much will be lost if the W.E.A. gives up active cooperation, since it has been highly important in the development of tutorial classes in the past; and (2) that the traditional type of course which was fostered by the W.E.A., namely the non-vocational liberal arts, may be abandoned in favor of more utilitarian vocational courses.

The 1955–1956 annual report of the Department of Adult

Education and Extra-Mural Studies at the University of Leeds sums up certain of the problems and concerns of the adult education leaders:

From this brief review, certain trends are apparent. A regrettable one is the reduction in the amount of work done in association with the W.E.A. As already stated, this was neither intended nor foreseen, and it is hoped that in this respect the current trend will be reversed, or at least arrested. In the new work, apart from that done in Services' education and the research into aspects of Adult Education, which do not appear to call for further comment here, the chief points to which attention may be drawn are the increasing volume of teaching in technology and subjects other than the humanities and social studies; the rapidly-growing proportion of students who have already received a good school, and often additional full-time, education; the provision of courses of special interest to members of particular occupations and professions; the institution of extra-mural examinations and qualifications; and the activity of the department as an agency for assisting other departments of the university to undertake extra-mural teaching. Similar developments have occurred in other universities, and they are especially referred to here because they are giving rise to a considerable amount of discussion and some criticism.

This summary of developments and comments suggests some of the changes taking place in the adult education program in Britain and the reactions to them.

In concluding a description of the overall program in Britain, it is appropriate to present a picture of the extra-mural teaching staff. In Table 21 the number of lecturers and tutors employed is indicated. In brief, there are 273 full-time staff tutors, 1,461 part-time university staff tutors and 1,683 part-time tutors from outside the university. Thus, the total of non-university staff members serving on a part-time basis approximately equals the total university staff, including full- and part-time members.

There has been a substantial increase in the number of adults

TABLE 21   LECTURERS AND TUTORS EMPLOYED[5]

UNIVERSITY	STAFF TUTORS		PART-TIME TUTORS	
	For Civilian Work	For Forces' Work	University Staff	Others
Belfast	6		51	40
Birmingham	24	2	84	152
Bristol	16	2	83	104
Cambridge	12		44	46
Durham:				
Durham	5		45	57
Newcastle	8[1,2]	3[1]	58	51
Edinburgh		1	126	58
Exeter	9	1	24	26
Glasgow	8		54	61
Hull	14[2,3]	3	33	62
Leeds	22[4]	7	31	39
Leicester	2		26	30
Liverpool	8	1	104	52
London	13		230	372
Manchester	13		129	48
Nottingham	16	1	35	137
Oxford	32[1,2]		128	81
Reading			3	5
Sheffield	10	1[2]	61	21
Southampton	6	5	12	37
Wales	22		100	204
Totals	246	27	1461	1683

Notes:
1. Includes 1 half-time tutor.
2. Includes 1 full-time non-staff tutor.
3. Includes 2 half-time tutors.
4. Includes 1 tutor working jointly with an internal Department.

Source: Universities Council for Adult Education, Great Britain, Report on the Year 1955–56.

desiring courses of various kinds since the end of World War II. Indeed, the enrollment in extra-mural and extension courses has increased more rapidly than that of full-time students in the universities. The curve of expansion has flattened out in the past three or four years, though the new types of extra-mural courses being introduced may prolong the growth when they have been generally accepted. The grant-aid to extra-mural work is now strictly limited and this in itself may slow down, or even prevent, further expansion.

Two types of programs in the United Kingdom universities deserve special mention, since they are not found in other countries under review: (1) the summer schools offered under a joint program at Oxford, Stratford-on-Avon and in the two capitol cities of London and Edinburgh; and (2) the archeological field courses which are conducted by the Departments of Extra-Mural Studies at the Universities of London, Birmingham, Nottingham, Hull and Leicester.

In 1957 the joint summer school program offered a choice of subjects and periods that might appropriately be studied at the universities concerned. The program at Stratford-on-Avon was on Shakespeare and Elizabethan Drama. It was planned and carried out under the joint auspices of the Shakespeare Institute and the Department of Extra-Mural Studies of the University of Birmingham. The program at Oxford included literature, politics and the arts in Seventeenth Century England. According to the announcement of the course,

the Seventeenth Century offers the opportunity of studying English politics, literature and the arts in one of their most formative phases. The Seventeenth Century was a period of political experiment and of political theorizing; in literature it was the century in which the modern prose style was evolved, but it included also the poetry of Milton, and it saw the beginnings of present-day attitudes towards the natural sciences; its architecture was rich and varied, and it was the golden age of English music.

Lectures were given on all these aspects of Seventeenth Century England, mostly by the professors and lecturers of Oxford University. The University of London had two programs:

(1) English Law and Jurisprudence, a Study of Modern Tendencies; and (2) Literature and Art in Georgian England (1740–1830). The program of the Edinburgh summer school, which was arranged jointly by the Scottish universities, dealt with European inheritance, providing an opportunity for special study of history, literature and philosophy.

These programs, planned cooperatively by the several universities, were designed primarily to meet the needs of postgraduate students from the universities of America, Europe and the British Commonwealth. Approximately two-thirds of the students came from the United States. There have been from twelve to twenty nationalities usually represented at each of the summer courses. All of these programs were developed by the Departments of Extra-Mural Studies of the Universities of Birmingham, Oxford, London and Edinburgh.

The second type of program of special interest embraces the archeological courses organized by the Departments of Extra-Mural Studies in five civic universities. For some years the University of Birmingham has conducted summer courses in archeological excavation at Wroxeter. Because of the demand, in 1957 the University developed programs on three levels, for elementary, intermediate and advanced students.

The chief center of the excavations, as announced, was the Romano-British city of Viroconium, the Cantonal capitol of the Conovii and the fourth largest town in Roman Britain. Its defenses encompassed an area of more than 170 acres.

In addition to the summer programs the Extra-Mural Department conducts regular courses during the school year. The Field Studies Council has recently established a center at Preston-Montford, and, through an arrangement with the Council, the Department of Extra-Mural studies is using Preston-Montford as a center for many of its own field courses, particularly those in archeology.

London also has a well-developed program in this field. It established a Diploma in Archeology, which requires four weeks of field courses during the four years of part-time study. Other extra-mural programs in archeology are found at Nottingham, Hull and Leicester.

Overseas Commonwealth Countries

CANADA

Extension services in the Dominion of Canada have shown marked increase in popularity in the past few years. In the larger cities universities offer a variety of evening courses for academic credit. The Sir George Williams College in Montreal enrolls the majority of its students in evening classes. While the extra-mural credit courses are comparatively limited in scope, the adult education classes and special lectures are becoming increasingly popular though they provide no academic credit.

Seventeen colleges and universities in Canada, more than one-half the total number, provide extension courses to a greater or less extent. British Columbia provides the following: extension lectures at various places throughout the province, evening classes, discussion groups, dramatics, agriculture, short courses carrying academic credit, visual instruction through lantern and film slide services, moving picture services, radio broadcasts and library assistance to those who wish to do systematic reading, art and music courses, public relations, educational programs for British Columbia fishermen, correspondence courses, extra-sessional courses for academic credit, home economics, arts and crafts, parent education, family life education, and group development courses. A substantial number of correspondence, as well as other types of extension courses, carry credit toward a degree.

McGill University provides courses in some seventy-five subjects through afternoon and evening classes for residents of Montreal and vicinity. Some of these prepare for special examinations such as those required by accountancy associations and the intermediate and final examination of the Chartered Institute of Secretaries. A few of them may be counted for the degree of Master of Engineering. Rural extension work is developed through McDonald College. Manitoba, Queen's, Saskatchewan, Western Ontario, and Toronto all have elaborate programs of extension which provide both credit and non-credit courses.

The program at the University of Western Ontario may be considered typical of Canadian institutions. It provides four types of work: (1) lecture courses, given by members of the university faculty in numerous centers in southwestern Ontario, attendance on which satisfies part of the residence requirement for the degree; (2) tutorial courses, given in several centers in northern Ontario, where they are planned and supervised by members of the university faculty, but taught by local tutors who are college graduates; (3) correspondence courses, provided in a limited number of subjects (examinations are provided in these courses and papers are marked by members of the University staff); and (4) summer school courses, six weeks in length, beginning the first week in July.

Among the special extension features is the British Columbia program in the field of drama. It employs a full-time worker who usually spends a week, and sometimes as much as a month, in a single community. He may have two or three groups working in each. In the course of the year, through his lectures as well as his work with play groups, he reaches some seventy communities. The fine arts program which has developed on the campus of the University grew out of the work which began as an extension course.

The University of Saskatchewan is particularly strong in the field of agricultural extension. It has a Commission on Agricultural and Rural Life which established a center for community studies: (1) to train community workers; (2) to do research in rural life; and (3) to serve as a consulting bureau.

A special extension program in the fine arts, held at Banff each year, has attained great popularity. A general managers' school is conducted also at Banff by four universities, Manitoba, Alberta, Saskatchewan and British Columbia. The course is six weeks in length. In 1952 it attracted twenty-two students; in 1957, 2,822.

AUSTRALIA

The background of university extension in Australia has been sketched briefly earlier in this chapter. The state grants made in support of adult education have grown rapidly in recent years.

In Victoria there is a statutory Council of Adult Education, which works in liaison with the extension committee of the university. The Board of Adult Education activities in Queensland has developed a Correspondence Study Department. In Western Australia adult education is under the control of a board which is representative of the university and other interests. It acts under the university senate and has charge of all adult education.

The University of Sydney has developed what is known as the "Kits" system—courses for groups covering arts and social science fields. It also has library facilities for tutors and, through the adult education section of the public library of New South Wales, for the students in extension classes and groups. It issues fortnightly a current affairs bulletin and other adult education publications, which circulate throughout Australia and to the armed services.

The "Kits" scheme is designed for groups of all kinds, and for any organization which is looking for suggestions as to what can be planned for meetings. It suggests activities in which anyone can join, and arranges these activities in a plan which, step by step, opens up new ideas and new ways of doing as well as of learning. According to the Sydney catalogue, it "is an educational service intended for the use of groups planning their programs and wanting to enjoy a subject by doing as well as by reading and talking."

In Western Australia the adult education board has theater, ballet, opera, music and films for the city and for some sixty country towns. It also conducts a summer school in Perth called "The Perth Festival." It has classes in the arts, social sciences and applied art subjects and also provides library facilities for town and country students. In New England University the Department of Adult Education provides classes in arts and social science fields for towns throughout the region. It has short residential courses in animal husbandry and a few courses in the applied arts field. It also has student library facilities.

The Workers' Educational Association of New South Wales and South Australia provide classes for their respective universities, and some classes of their own in arts and social science fields. It also makes provision for various student clubs and organizations, making books available through a central reference lending library.

The largest of the extension programs in Australia is that conducted by Sydney University. Its 1956 report showed total class enrollments of 3792, an increase of about 500 over the preceding year. There was also an increase in the number of discussion groups, from 124 to 138, and in the number of courses offered. The combined figures for tutorial classes, discussion and "Kits" groups showed that the Department conducted 345 classes and groups, with a total enrollment of 7228. Of these classes and groups, 162 were provided outside the metropolitan area.

In Tasmania adult education is sponsored by a statutory board which is headed by a director. The university is represented on this board. Canberra University College provides a program through which any person, whether matriculated or not, may attend lectures in most of the subjects taught for degrees by paying the usual fee. This does not, however, entitle students to present themselves for university examination.

The New South Wales University of Technology has extension courses in scientific and technological subjects designed to keep practicing scientists and technologists abreast of recent developments in their respective fields.

The volume of adult education activity has been steadily expanding since 1946 in every one of the Australian states. It is supported by a variety of organizations. Unfortunately little information on its program has been made available in published form, with the exception of the reports issued annually by the agencies engaged in adult education work.

NEW ZEALAND

Adult education in its modern form came into being in New Zealand when the Workers' Education Association was established in 1915. As noted, it was developed in England twelve years earlier and serves as a coordinating federation of working class and educational interests. It seeks to promote the higher education of working men and women by arousing their interest and directing their attention to the facilities available. It also calls the attention of boards of education and of educational institutions to the need for providing facilities for study, either in conjunction with educational bodies or otherwise.

Support in the amount of £500 was provided by the Dominion Council for Adult Education as early as 1922. Through the University Act of 1919 a permanent annual grant of £2,000 for tutorial classes was divided equally among the four colleges. In 1925 this was raised to three thousand. The period 1920 to 1930 witnessed remarkable growth, both in the kinds of work attempted and in the number of people attracted by it. There was a fivefold increase in enrollments from 1,496 to 7,355. However, during the period following 1930, due to the financial depression, the adult education movement was seriously jeopardized. Except for a grant from the Carnegie

Corporation, which was made in support of an experimental scheme in the South Island, it might not have survived. The project was known as the Canterbury Adult Rural Library Scheme, which was centered in Canterbury University College, and provided a van and a tutor-driver to carry collections of books to country areas. Another Carnegie grant to Otago University supported home science extension work projected by the university college and aided by women's organizations. In 1935 the two schemes were combined under the title of The Association for Country Education, and operated both in Canterbury and Otago.

Because of the scarcity of funds, some institutions in New Zealand have been inclined to view the grants for adult education as taking from their intra-mural work. A second objection raised is that the university which engages in adult education work may be devoting energies that should be concentrated on its primary academic function to fields which are not its special responsibility. The teaching staffs especially seem to feel that their first obligation is to develop the academic program of the college. As a result only Otago and Canterbury Universities now have active adult education programs. The constituent universities work with the regional councils for adult education and play some part in the activities of the W.E.A. For this latter service they receive special grants from the National Council for Adult Education.

SOUTH AFRICA

The extra-mural program of South African universities is not as advanced as that of Australia. The University of Cape Town has developed a variety of programs. The Board of Extra-Mural Studies there is responsible for organizing vacation courses, week-end conferences and tutorial courses. It also provides courses on citizenship and current topics. Orange Free State has extra-mural work in the Faculties of Arts and Law; Rhodes University staff provides extension lectures in the larger towns of the Eastern province; and Witwatersrand University has public lectures under the auspices of university departments, student's societies and a Student's Visiting Lecturers Trust Fund. It provides also courses for part-time students in the fields of commerce and law.

The University of Pretoria provides lectures for public servants, articled clerks, business men and teachers. More than one thousand students were enrolled in 1956 under this program. Practically all of these were studying for the degree. These courses provided credits toward the following degrees: B.A., B.A. in Law, LL.B., Bachelor of Commerce, Bachelor of Administration and Master's degrees. The fact that Pretoria is one of the three capitols of the Union accounts for the large number interested in regular courses.

In addition to these offerings for business and government workers, the Faculties of Agriculture and Veterinary Science collaborate with the Union Department of Agriculture in developing extension training services. Public lectures are also provided in Pretoria and nearby districts.

INDIA

A variety of extra-mural programs are developing in India, where the University Grants Commission has offered financial assistance for extension courses to those universities prepared to undertake them. A brief description of a few of them may suffice to indicate the progress being made there.

The Board of Extra-Mural Studies of the University of Poona has sixty-five extra-mural centers in which some 600 lectures were given in 1956. It also has summer and autumn schools, chiefly for school teachers, at a few extra-mural centers. The University of Mysore has a committee on extension lectures which arranges an annual program. Lectures are delivered in different parts of the state under the auspices of the University Teachers' Association. Extension lecture camps are arranged each year in the interior of the state. Panjab University provides extension lectures, using specialists to address the students in the various colleges. The lectures are of a general nature. It has also established a camp college, which provides educational facilities for employed students. Bombay University has recently begun adult education classes in Hindi and Marathi for workers in mills and factories and in English for office employees. In Rajasthan University there is an arrangement for enabling candidates in the service to undertake higher education as external students. These candidates enroll in evening classes which are conducted by certain of the colleges. This plan enables some who are gainfully employed and cannot enter college as regular students to prepare for the university examinations. The staff of the university also provides extension lectures at various centers, which are published in both English and Hindi. The Thackersey Women's University also has an arrangement whereby those who do part-time work may be admitted to the university examinations as external students. In 1958 it was decided to organize a number of evening colleges under Delhi University for part-time students.

The Ministry of Education in India, with the assistance of the Ford Foundation, has initiated an extension service scheme for teachers in the secondary schools. This scheme was already in operation in 1957 in twenty-four out of the sixty-eight training colleges in the country. Aligarh University, one of the participating institutions, has been conducting courses in librarianship through which it is developing teacher-librarians. The University has also sought to stimulate interest in new teaching materials. To that end it has provided exhibitions of professional literature, school textbooks and audio-visual aids at a number of other places. It includes a speaker to explain their purpose and demonstrate the way in which the materials may be used.

In addition to these activities, other extension services are conducted by the Education Department of the University. Among these are: (1) short-term courses on content and methodology of selected school subjects; (2) periodical meetings, lectures, discussion symposia, one-day conferences and week-end conferences; (3) on-the-spot study and discussion of local problems and of special problems confronting individual teachers and schools; (4) discussions of problems connected with curricula, methods, organization and discipline; (5) the planning of school programs; (6) selection and use of test materials; (7) curriculum development and textbooks, cooperating with teachers for developing teaching units in selected subjects, particularly in the new areas of social studies, general science, language and art teaching; and (8) counseling and student personnel problems.

University Extension in the United States

In the Commonwealth off-campus activities of universities are called extension lectures, tutorial classes and extra-mural studies. In the United States these activities go under the single title, extension, derived from the "extension" lectures which developed in Britain and the United States in the last quarter of the nineteenth century.

As in Britain, a number of agencies participate in adult education. There local groups have organized it, the Ministry of Education has supported it, the Workers' Educational Association, the universities and numerous other organizations have fostered its development. In the United States universities and colleges, including junior colleges, have borne the major share of the burden of adult education, though foundations have supported it and the Adult Education Association has promoted it.

This section will deal only with the university and college programs. The first extension course was given by Queen's College, now Rutgers University, when a professor gave public lectures on chemical philosophy in 1816. A total of eighteen universities were providing some kind of extension work prior to 1900. Harvard University began in 1840; Michigan State

College in 1855; Kansas State College in 1868; the University of Minnesota in 1881; and the University of Wisconsin in 1885. The other twelve institutions began their programs of off-campus activities in the 1890s: the Universities of Kentucky, Oklahoma, Kansas, Chicago, Nebraska, Indiana, California, Oregon, and Wyoming, also Pennsylvania and Iowa State Universities. Extension is now a vast enterprise involving a budget of $112,224,547 in 1953–1954, approximately 5 per cent of the total expenditures for educational and general purposes that year.

While lectures, correspondence work and college credit courses were the earliest forms of off-campus university activities, other kinds of service were emerging during the first quarter of the present century. As a background for discussing the extension movement in the United States, it will be useful to list the different types of activities encompassed by it. They fall into five broad classifications:

1. The programs of study for in-service rather than pre-service people, dealing with such topics as marital and parental adjustment; current events and foreign affairs; and other problems affecting the total population, such as public health, gerontology, community planning, etc.

2. Specialists in various fields are sent into communities to assist individuals and groups in a variety of projects and programs. This is best illustrated by the farm demonstration and home demonstration agents of the land-grant colleges. They work with the farmers and their wives on conservation, production, marketing, budgeting and management problems.

3. Special advisers on community organization, education, group programming, theater production and other types of activities are made available to communities. Materials have been provided to meet special needs, such as books, pamphlets, phonograph records, audio-visual aids, plays and other items, along with the services of the advisers.

4. Short courses of various kinds are organized offering

opportunities for specialized learning. Such courses usually involve occupational groups, voluntary organizations, or other associations of people with common interests.

5. Extension divisions have experimented with new media of communication. Several universities have radio stations which have had a long experience of successful operation. Others have recently acquired television channels which have enabled them to reach a large proportion of the population of a state or region. Television courses of study which one can pursue at home have been provided by several institutions.

State universities now have general education extension divisions, while the land-grant colleges generally have specialized agricultural and home economics programs. Most state university departments participate to some extent in adult education activities. Professional schools have been particularly active in recent years. The largest single program is agricultural extension, which is supported by the federal government. Its first grant was made in 1914. Supplementary legislation in subsequent years had increased this support until by 1955 approximately $40,000,000 was appropriated exclusively for agriculture and home economics annually. The major portion of these funds is used to support the county agricultural, home demonstration and Four-H Club agents.

The origins of the various types of programs and services provided by the extension divisions of universities were based upon demands. Professor Morton, author of a volume on university extension in the United States (1953), cites a series of examples of ways in which various programs began:[6]

A professor of secondary education suggested to the principals of some secondary schools, which lacked adequate library facilities, that they borrow from the university library. The university librarian, interested in serving a community larger than the campus, cooperated readily with the principals in working out a relationship of mutual advantage. A group of public school teachers petitioned a university to make arrange-

ments for courses at times and places which would enable
them to continue their professional training on year-round
schedules; a local board of education wanted programs of
study for their school faculties; owners of a machine shop
requested engineering courses at night for their employees; a
wholesale grocery chain asked for courses in business management for their employees, agreeing to pay all tuition costs;
and a group of community leaders sought expert advice on
planning for the growth of their small town faced with sudden
industrial expansion.

Universities respond to a wide variety of calls from business
and professional groups, corporations and communities for help
in securing educational services. In addition, the extension
faculties take the initiative in suggesting programs to meet
group and community needs. In these ways extension divisions
of universities have contributed substantially to the cultural
and economic progress of American life.

The examples cited illustrate the way in which university
extension is geared to the interests and needs of individuals
and communities. The vitality of the movement has stemmed
largely from the close relationship to the people, which has
characterized it from the beginning. It should be remembered,
however, that special services to groups and communities are
by no means the central task of university extension. Its major
business is the regular university degree-credit programs.
Though complaints have been registered against the quality
of these programs, and the appropriateness of undertaking to
give credit for work done away from the campus, the responsible institutions, in the main, provide work of university grade.
While British universities do not allow credit for extra-mural
courses, they do award the external degree to students who
may have had no university courses.

The American extension and British extra-mural studies
differ in their character and purposes. Those tutorial classes
offered in collaboration with the W.E.A. in Britain were origi-

nally provided by the Arts Faculties, technical and professional courses being a recent development. On the other hand, in the United States some of the earliest programs were in applied science and professional fields. This is indicated in Table 22.

The first university extension courses included engineering sciences, teacher education and general education.

Developments in the land-grant colleges, which stressed both research and extension, affected the university extension movement in a variety of ways. Legislation providing federal funds for agricultural experiment stations and extension services made it possible for universities to demonstrate that research and extension can promote the general welfare when applied to industrial and community problems. The emphasis upon scientific experimentation and the practical use of the findings have affected other types of extension. The land-grant college was concerned with the "mechanic arts" as well as with agriculture. Under this heading it stimulated significantly the development of engineering schools and was responsible largely for the fact that engineering sciences have long been popular subjects in American extension.

A war-time development which gave great impetus to the extension movement was the program styled ESMWT ("Engineering, Science, Management, War Training") sponsored by the federal government. Its purpose was to assist industry in achieving maximum production during the war. It demonstrated the effectiveness of education and training as a means of accelerating production.

In the period 1945 to 1952 some 10 million war veterans receiving educational assistance from the federal government utilized the educational services of American universities and colleges. Of this number almost 20 per cent enrolled in university extension classes or short courses. The number enrolled in the ESMWT program was 1,794,058. The experience of these ex-service men and women with university programs during

TABLE 22   DATES OF INITIATION OF INSTRUCTION IN VARIOUS
SUBJECT-MATTER FIELDS BY UNIVERSITY EXTENSION
ORGANIZATIONS IN FIFTY-TWO UNIVERSITIES[6]

Date	A	B	C	D	E	F	G	H	Total
1881						1			1
1886–1890		1						1	2
1891–1895		4						5	9
1896–1900									
1901–1905						1	1		2
1906–1910	1	4	1	1		5	1	6	19
1911–1915		9	3	7	2	4	6	9	40
1916–1920	4	12	1	5	4	5	4	6	41
1921–1925	1	7		9	1	4	4	6	32
1926–1930	4	2		5	2	6	1	3	23
1931–1935		1		1		1	3	2	8
1936–1940		5	1	3	3	2	2	3	19
1941–1945	1		1	2	5	4	1	3	17
1946–1950	4	2	3	5	9	3	3	2	31
1951–1952	1			1	2	2	1	1	8
Unknown						1	1		2
Total	16	47	10	39	29	38	28	47	254

Key:
    A—Medical science
    B—Teacher education
    C—Law
    D—Business administration
    E—Nursing
    F—Engineering
    G—Home economics
    H—General education

Source: John R. Morton, *University Extension in the United States.*

the war doubtless had much to do with their enrolling in extension after the war.

The enrollment of veterans in such large numbers not only
stimulated public interest but strengthened the financial base
of extension organizations, enabling them to make needed additions to buildings, equipment and staff. The net result was that
they commanded greater consideration and respect after the

war than they had ever enjoyed before.

American university extension has developed three kinds of programs: extension classes, resident centers and correspondence courses. Extension classes are conducted by the university staff or part-time instructors appointed by the university. In resident centers there is a small full-time resident staff and part-time instructors. Correspondence courses are usually conducted by the extension staff, though sometimes by campus instructors. More than 60 per cent of all the offerings in the resident centers and in the correspondence division are in the arts and sciences, according to Professor Morton's study of thirty-three universities. In the extension classes slightly less than 50 per cent are in these fields. In the resident centers more courses in English language and literature are offered than in any other single field. Mathematics, other languages, art and economics, follow in that order in popularity with the students.

The National University Extension Association had a membership of seventy-six institutions which enrolled more than 500,000 full-time students on their campuses in 1951–1952. During this same period more than a million and a half participated in organized and continuing instructional programs under the auspices of their extension divisions. For example, 133,000 persons were enrolled in correspondence courses offered by 44 institutions; 325,000 were in extension classes conducted by 57 institutions; 480,000 engaged in resident center activities in 23 institutions; 305,000 were served through library extension services in 17 institutions; and 403,000 participated in conference activities conducted by 38 institutions. In addition, millions made use of audio-visual aid services provided by these institutions. Even more were served by radio and television broadcasts from forty of these institutions.

Many faculties believe that strict limitation should be placed on the amount of degree credits allowed extension courses. Some institutions accept 25 per cent, others 50 per cent and a few place no limit, though one year's residence instruction is usually the minimum requirement for a degree, regardless of the source or amount of credits previously acquired. In cases where the university maintains a strong resident center, with a good library, the accrediting associations are less inclined to insist upon limitation of credits. Resident centers are called branches, evening colleges or university colleges. In rare instances these centers provide full four-year programs leading to a Bachelor's degree, and occasionally to an advanced degree.

Twenty-three members of the National University Extension Association in 1951–1952 operated ninety-four centers, serving some 480,000 students. A third of these were within fifty miles, and one-half within 100 miles, of the parent institution. More than one-fifth were from 200 to 700 miles away; one of every three centers was found in a population area of less than 100,000 and the same proportion in areas having more than 300,000 population.

Professor Morton reported that less than 10 per cent of the total correspondence offerings were non-credit courses and 10 per cent graduate extension courses. In the resident centers slightly more than half the offerings were in the lower division; 15 per cent in the upper division, and 13 per cent in graduate work. Seventy-three per cent of students enrolled in the resident center activities were seeking degree credit for their work. Only 24 per cent were not interested in credits of any kind. Six institutions reported groups of correspondence course offerings leading to certificates of various types, the largest number being in the engineering fields. Offerings in the arts and sciences and in business administration followed in that order as the next largest groups.

The relationship of the extension division to the central administration follows no set pattern. In the stronger universities, it is presided over by a dean who reports directly to the president. In other institutions extension has no full-time staff.

Programs are set up within schools or colleges of the university and operated informally. In some cases extension organizations have departmental status. One large organization reported that each undergraduate school of the university had a director of extension, with a staff; that these several staffs were coordinated by the general extension office; and that policies were formulated by a council on extension composed of school directors, the directors of general extension, and representatives from the offices of the deans of admissions and graduate schools. This arrangement is similar to the Board of Extra-Mural Studies found in Commonwealth countries.

Other variations appear. Some state systems of higher education operate under the jurisdiction of a single board of trustees and have a central university extension organization. In one instance the extension organization is administratively coordinate with the various institutions that make up the state's system; in another, extension is a subordinate department, though responsible directly to the board of trustees and charged with specific functions. One university is reported to have an arrangement whereby each of the ten colleges making up the institution has a separate extension organization in addition to its evening college.

The extension organizations have influenced the development of universities in many ways. As indicated earlier, summer schools have in some cases originated in extension activities. The publication of pamphlets, monographs and books, usually written by staff members, began to appear in the last quarter of the nineteenth century. This led to the development of the university press. Professional training programs in the field of business administration were inaugurated by extension divisions and later incorporated in the university curriculum. Programs for teachers in service, given on the campus of the universities by the extension division, have influenced significantly the school of education offerings in the field of teacher education. Extension divisions have been useful in helping the public to understand the function of the university.

The American universities have generally accepted the responsibility for advancing adult education. High schools are not adapted to serve this purpose; the junior colleges can render only a limited service in this field; and the regular university programs are too inflexible and specialized to meet the needs of adults. Extension programs have been the answer.

Three of every four persons served by extension classes, resident center programs and correspondence instruction are seeking college credit, according to recent studies. More than 80 per cent of those enrolled in non-credit courses are motivated by the desire to improve their incomes or their vocational efficiency; while only 19 per cent have general education, recreational or avocational objectives.

Radio and television broadcasting services are recent developments which have enlarged the area of influence of the extension divisions. University broadcasting began in cooperation with commercial stations. Some institutions have only studios in which radio-television programs are prepared for broadcast from stations which are operated by other agencies. Others supply occasional programs. University professors frequently give lecture series of interest to the general public. Credit courses are provided by some universities.

Within the past few years rapid progress has been made in the field of educational television. Several states have statewide networks and are operating through their own stations, providing exclusively educational programs. Alabama, North Carolina and Oklahoma have been leaders in this activity.

College credit courses have been conducted with marked success by a number of universities. One institution solved its problem of inadequate staff and classrooms by providing a substantial proportion of its instruction to resident students through telecasts. One of the foundations has televised a full year's instruction in physics and recorded it on films. These films have been purchased by industrial companies and educational institutions for use with industrial workers and college freshmen. This experiment proved so successful that the foundation is producing films in other areas designed for use in the classroom.

There is little doubt that television intelligently employed can be a real factor in meeting the critical shortage of staff and classrooms which is already acute but will become more severe in the decade ahead. The extension divisions in the universities that have already had considerable experience with instruction by television have their greatest challenge in this critical period. Their flexibility, knowledge of telecasting and experience in producing educational programs make them the logical agencies for promoting education by television. Once again they have an opportunity to make a major contribution to their parent universities.

Summary

Extension and extra-mural studies divisions have a history of distinguished service. They reach more individuals through their services than any other division of the universities, though they represent a relatively new phase of university activity. The development in its present form is the product of the twentieth century. Though extra-mural enrollment has grown more rapidly than intra-mural instruction since the Second World War, the expansion which lies ahead will be even greater if recent trends continue.

In Britain, where until recently only liberal education courses have been provided, a beginning has been made with programs in science and technology. While the technical colleges offer instruction on a part-time basis for workers in industry and have been highly successful in up-grading them, a similar service has not been generally available to technologists and the managerial staff. The development of such courses by universities through extra-mural programs might render a new service of great promise.

Programs for professional workers—doctors, dentists, lawyers and business executives—have been established in the United States. As science advances and society becomes more complex, it is increasingly difficult to keep abreast of new developments and social changes which may affect professional practice. It is the professor in the professional school who must of necessity keep current with advances in his field. He is therefore in a unique position to assist the busy practitioner in keeping up with the latest research findings, theories, methods and practices. Through extension and extra-mural programs the professors in the universities can pass on promptly to men in the field the latest discoveries and thus add to their effectiveness. The University of California has developed an extensive program of service to medical, legal and other professional groups. In light of developments in California and elsewhere, it would appear that a large proportion of professional men and women may in time be enrolled in extension or extra-mural programs.

The average citizen, as a member of his community, has need of help in understanding the changes taking place in his society. Adjustment to changes imposed by science and technology is a major problem of modern man. Like Alice in Wonderland he has to run as fast as he can to stand still, so swiftly moving are the changes taking place around him. It is the historian, sociologist, economist or psychologist on the university staff who is in the best position to be helpful. Through extension lectures, television discussions and organized classes, professors of the colleges and universities can make real contributions to community stability and progress by helping the average citizen to understand what is occurring.

Since 1945 the new responsibilities of English-speaking peoples in the world community, as exponents of western ideals, require new emphasis upon international understanding and international relations. The universities have not yet met their responsibilities in this area. Through extra-mural programs they have an opportunity to render a unique service to modern society. Small beginnings have been made by institutions in some of the countries under review. Much more needs to be done. This is an area in which great expansion may be expected.

XIII

Problems and Prospects of Higher Education

❖❖❖❖❖❖❖❖❖❖❖❖❖❖❖❖❖❖❖❖❖❖❖❖❖❖❖❖❖❖❖❖❖❖

The contemporary college and university scene presents a variety of issues. My purpose here is to identify some of the major ones, to analyze them and to comment on their implications. Certain of these prevail in all the countries included in this study; others are unique to particular areas.

An expanding demand for higher education is a marked characteristic of this period; it is more pronounced in some areas than in others. Australia expects an increase of 120 per cent in its university population in the next decade, while South Africa is planning on no more than 40 to 50 per cent growth. India and Pakistan had the most rapid growth of all, from 250,000 students in 1947–1948 to almost 800,000 in 1958. The other countries under review expect at least a doubling of their present numbers in the next fifteen years. This poses a variety of problems. Housing, equipping, staffing and financing an enterprise serving twice as many in 1973 as in 1958 is an enormous undertaking.

The rapidity of growth since World War II has already produced a series of difficulties. Attempts to meet the needs of students have resulted in a bewildering number of courses, in lack of educational focus and in confusion as to aims and purposes. The situation will worsen with the further growth of student numbers unless vigorous measures are employed to correct it. The conservatism of colleges and universities in undertaking basic curriculum reforms is notorious. They will add courses too readily but are slow to drop old ones. As a result the curriculum is often a hodge-podge that makes little sense. Clarification of objectives and realistic revision of curricula and methods are long overdue. Prompt steps in that direction should be taken if higher education is to fulfill its mission. This looms as a major issue in all English-speaking universities.

Another need, deriving partly from increasing enrollments, is provision for the gifted student. As student bodies grow it is more difficult to give adequate attention to the few with greatest potentialities. British universities have been more successful in attracting and catering to the needs of the able student than their American counterparts. Honors courses and the tutorial system are more common there. They serve as aids in identifying talent and in developing it, but they are less suited to the needs of students in the fields of applied science and technology, where laboratory work is of central importance. Both the Commonwealth countries and the United States lack an adequate plan for identifying the talented and calling forth their best efforts. For many years educators on both sides of the Atlantic have expressed concern about it, but little has been done to correct it. As the search for talent is intensified and the importance of the gifted individual to society becomes more apparent in a highly competitive era, the need to identify him early and to develop his latent powers will be more and more urgent.

The story of women and higher education as sketched in Chapter VIII is a record of great progress. The recognition of women's rights to higher education, of their capacity to profit from it and of their intellectual abilities and interests has genuine significance for the future. It was only eighty years ago that women were first admitted to a Commonwealth university; now they are admitted with full privileges to all Commonwealth universities. In the light of that progress it is conceivable that the changes witnessed in the past century will be rivaled by those of the next. In some institutions women's potentials have not been recognized; in others curricula have been built around them. An issue of growing importance yet to be resolved is that of providing more adequately for the distaff segment of the university population.

These then are some of the problems common to all countries under review: (1) housing, equipping, staffing and financing an enterprise double its present size; (2) reform of the university curriculum and clarification of its objectives; (3) identification and attraction of the gifted, and a more effective program for insuring their maximum development; and (4) recognition of the value of the educated woman through equal treatment and the development of more realistic curricula.

The section which follows will deal in some detail with the character and scope of the issues briefly sketched above. There will be no attempt to suggest answers to questions raised. They must evolve through the collective efforts of boards of control, administrations and faculties.

Some Common Problems

HOUSING

In the majority of the universities in the Commonwealth and the United States temporary housing constructed to care for the returning veterans of World War II still mars the campus scene. This emergency housing, having already served beyond its allotted time, is still required to meet the shortage, not only to house the overflowing student body but to provide classrooms and laboratories. On a medium-sized American campus it was estimated in 1957 that $6 million would be required to replace the temporary buildings in use before adding new buildings. In South Africa, Australia, New Zealand, Canada and the United Kingdom the situation is much the same. More outmoded temporary and dilapidated buildings housed university students and instructional activities in 1957–1958 than in any previous period, yet most of the institutions anticipated a doubling of numbers within ten to fifteen years.

Buildings were under construction on every campus, and in many cases they were imposing. At Wellington, New Zealand, for example, a seven-story classroom and laboratory building was nearing completion. Buildings for science and technology, medical and other professional faculties, hospitals for medical instruction, libraries, student unions and residence halls were in various stages of development. Banaras Hindu University had a variety of new buildings, and others under construction, on a new campus of 1,500 acres. A long row of hostels for about 7,500 students, three-fourths of those in residence, and faculty housing were among the newly erected buildings at Banaras.

Despite the all-out concentration on new construction, it was everywhere obvious that when all were completed they would not be adequate to serve the increasing enrollments. The phase of the university program that was faring best in the matter of capital improvement was science and technology. The new structures in London, Sheffield, Cambridge and other university communities, either completed or under way, were impressive. The current five-year plan calls for vast additions to these facilities through government grants. In India the University Grants Commission announced a program calling for the expenditure of Rs.500,000,000 ($100,000,000) during the current quinquennium for buildings and equipment in the same fields. Previously the U.G.C. had offered up to Rs.1,000,000 per institution for libraries, and the technological institutions have been offered grants or loans for the construction of hostels.

Australia, stimulated by the Murray Committee report, contemplates major additions to university physical plants. As of January 1958, every Canadian university either seemed to be planning a campaign for funds or had one under way. They ranged from $3 million in a small university to some $55 million in one of the largest. The United States in 1958 had on the drawing boards, or in progress, building programs involving an outlay of more than $1 billion.

This vast program is remarkable for its broad base of support. Individuals, business corporations and government at local, state and national levels are contributing. The citizens of New York state, in November 1957, voted the authorization of a $250 million bond issue for its state university.

The shortage in hostel accommodations is acute. Less than half the students live in residence halls at present in the United Kingdom. Oxford and Cambridge in 1958 could accommodate only 52.5 per cent of their students in the colleges. When enrollments are doubled, the term "residential university" may become obsolete. Communities and governments are helping in this emergency. Manchester University raised £800,000 locally for this purpose in 1956. The United States Federal Government has loaned vast sums to institutions to build dormitories. In some areas state governments provide one-third to one-half the cost of student housing, requiring the balance to be amortized through room rent charges.

Lack of residential accommodations in some communities will limit student numbers if drastic steps are not taken to provide them. In Australia 9 per cent lived in colleges or halls, 17 per cent in lodgings and 74 per cent at home, in 1958. Figures showed in South Africa a variation from 10.7 per cent in university housing at Pretoria to 90 per cent at Rhodes, with an overall distribution as follows: in halls of residence, 31.8 per cent; in lodgings, 12.6 per cent; and in other (mainly at home), 55.6 per cent. In India and Pakistan university housing was provided for 10 per cent to 20 per cent of the student enrollment.[1]

STAFFING

In the chapter on the Teaching Profession the problem of staffing higher education was dealt with at some length. It remains here to suggest that it is common to all the countries under review; more critical in some than in others, and more desperate in some areas of study than in others. The shortage of mathematics and science teachers is the most critical at both the secondary school and university levels.

Three major factors operate to produce the alarming situation. First of all, the rapid increase in school and college attendance results in a natural shortage. In a period of expansion the ratio of qualified teachers to the numbers to be taught is bound to be low. This factor is sufficient to produce a major problem because of unprecedented enrollment increases at all levels due to birth-rate growth and greater public interest in education.

In an expanding economy there is a natural manpower shortage, which means that the competition of the various occupations for workers is keener, especially for those who have superior training. Since teachers are in this class they have a much wider choice of occupations than in a static economy.

Finally, in a time of rising prices and pay scales the teachers have traditionally been the last group to receive compensation commensurate with rising living costs. This means that the teaching profession is at a disadvantage in competing with other vocations for manpower. This is particularly true in the fields of science and technology in a scientific and technological age. The undue competitive advantage of business and industry is likely to continue until such time as society reappraises the importance of the teacher and provides compensation accordingly. This appears to have happened in Russia in the university field, a fact which should be a matter for sober reflection and a stimulus to positive action in other countries.

Considerable progress has been made in English-speaking countries during the past ten years. Compensation of teachers has been increased substantially and one senses that the university professor has an appreciably higher status than before World War II, but the battle is far from won. The critical shortages of teachers now prevailing and the desperate situation confronting universities in the next decade, in view of mounting enrollments, are convincing evidence.

CURRICULUM REFORM

In both Britain and the United States the multiplicity of courses and the consequent overloading of curricula are common concerns. A distinguished university administrator in the United States put the matter bluntly: "American school and college students are in critical danger of being intellectually smothered in a sea of irrelevant and obsolete subject-matter, courses and teaching methods." In England the Goodenough Report on medical education urged the essential importance of lightening the curriculum by eliminating material that belongs to the province of the specialist or is redundant, and of shortening the time requirement. It pressed the matter: "This reform is so urgent that its accomplishment might well be a condition to be satisfied before any increase is made in Exchequer grants in aid of undergraduate medical education." It is reported that no university refused the grant, though few made any serious attempt to follow the recommendation. Indeed, additions to, rather than subtraction from, the curriculum have occurred since the Goodenough Report was issued. New subjects have been added and the length of the course has not been reduced.

In engineering education the problem is equally acute. New courses are being developed and professors in one department no longer know what others are requiring, due to the rapid expansion of applied science and technology faculties. The result is an exaggerated case of overloading the students. An obvious remedy would be to extend the course to four years, as has been suggested, but it does not seem feasible from the standpoint of either the student or the national need. Elimination of courses, the only other alternative, is rarely achieved. This is a particularly sensitive issue at this time when the expansion of science and technology is at its peak.

In the consideration of this subject, whether in the area of general studies or in professional education, the main issue is ignored. The chaos in the curriculum may derive in part from the growth of knowledge, but curricula have always represented selection. At no time in the history of universities have they attempted to cover all fields of knowledge. They have selected those subjects designed to achieve a particular purpose. The real difficulty in modern higher education is the lack of clearly-formulated objectives.

The classical curriculum was designed to prepare a small group for the learned professions and for leadership in public affairs, but the modern university no longer serves only a few. It trains millions for a host of occupations and professions. The chaos in the curriculum arises more from the number and variety of its students and their demands than from the expansion of knowledge. Institutions have never adjusted fully to their multi-purpose functions.

In the United States the general education movement was designed to find the content and methods best suited to provide the fundamentals of university education as it relates to non-professional studies. Some progress has been made but no consensus has been reached. In North Staffordshire University College and in Canadian and Indian institutions concern for a well-rounded program of basic studies is manifested, but in other Commonwealth universities the curricula do not exhibit such concern. The science major studies science, and the humanities major, the humanities. Neither is given a chance to become acquainted with the field of the other. The general assumption is that the preparatory schools provide adequate basic education, but in fact they do not. The secondary school student makes his selection of science or humanities early in his school career and concentrates on his choice for the remainder of his school and college years.

The American objective in undergraduate education is to

provide some acquaintance with the broad fields of knowledge, the humanities, the social sciences and the natural sciences during the first two years, and an opportunity for a degree of concentration in the final two years. Breadth of background characterizes the first half and depth of scholarship the second half of the undergraduate program. While this purpose is generally accepted, no agreement as to the nature of the courses that should be developed within the three broad fields has been reached. Experiments with interdepartmental and general education courses have been conducted by many colleges and universities. No two are identical, though the basic objective is the same and the general areas covered are similar.

In the English universities, where honors courses may be pursued in one, two or three subjects, there is little evidence of concern over the matter of a balanced program. In the Scottish universities, where five subjects are pursued the first year, both natural science and humanities courses are required, but this requirement does not involve special science courses for the non-scientist or arts courses designed especially for the scientist.

In America universities are more subject to public pressures than in the Commonwealth countries. Demands for new curricula and activities have resulted in an undue proliferation of courses. In this respect the American institutions have erred more seriously than the British, but the listing of a school of malting and brewing in one of the civic university calendars suggests that pressures there, too, are not unknown.

In professional faculties the unhealthy growth of the curriculum is more marked than in the Arts and Science Faculties. In medicine, science and technology it is most in evidence. With the constant discovery of new knowledge, new techniques and new theories the temptation to expand the offerings and requirements is ever present. The needs of the doctor, the scientist or the engineer for the new course can be easily demonstrated. Thus new offerings and, in time, new requirements find their way into the curriculum.

Frequently there is lack of discrimination between the facts and skills which can be learned later on the job and those which are basic to an understanding of principles which must be learned in the university if they are to be learned at all. A clearer definition of the purpose of professional education, and a more careful scrutiny of what is required to achieve it would make possible the elimination of non-essential elements. The need for such a re-examination of program is found in most professional fields in every university. It will become more and more necessary to restrict instruction to basic principles, the fundamental concepts underlying processes, as professional theories and practices multiply. Only such skills as may be necessary to a complete understanding of the principles involved can be justified.

To state the case simply and in briefest terms, the university must fulfill three requirements, whether it be in the arts, science, technology, or the professions. 1. It must provide the general foundation for work in the field, in what someone has styled "the essence and method of the subject." 2. It must develop some degree of intellectual initiative and independence, the critical faculty, which is required of leadership, whatever the field of endeavor. 3. It must appraise the capacity, the potentialities—not simply the knowledge—of the student. His ability to build upon the foundations laid in the first, or first and second, undergraduate years is infinitely more important than the knowledge or skills acquired.[2] Such a pattern of purpose constantly borne in mind would affect the range and type of subject matter, the methods and aims of instruction and the nature and quality of the examination.

PROVISION FOR THE GIFTED STUDENT

Premium on talent was never so high as it is today. Sputnik excited the imagination and admiration of the world. This first invasion of outer space symbolized a new triumph of the mind and spirit of man. It was not achieved by the Western nations, but by their rival. Along with admiration came apprehension.

What could it mean in case of international conflict? It aroused the instinct of self-preservation, it stimulated a new interest in science and technology and a new appreciation of the possibilities of education and learning. It is probably the first time in history that men have begun to sense so vividly that success in the long run will be determined by the advances of the mind, that supremacy of intellect means ultimately supremacy in world affairs. This at least seems to be the net effect of recent developments. They have spurred the support of universities and intensified the search for talent. Scholarships and bursaries for the gifted are as old as universities themselves, but the national interest in, and support for, youth of superior ability is of recent origin.

In Britain economic barriers to higher education do not exist for the able student. Scholarships for his tuition and living expenses will be provided by the university or the government. More than 70 per cent of all university students in Britain have grants which provide a substantial part, or all, of the cost. No such generous provision is found in other Commonwealth countries or in the United States. Even in Britain it is not assumed that all able students are identified. Some are lost in the secondary schools, and often graduates are not interested in attending the university. The same is true in the United States. It is estimated that a large proportion of potentially able students do not finish high school, and that half of the upper 10 per cent of those who do, fail to enter college. Many able college students drop out before completing the course for lack of motivation, inadequate finances or other causes.

Waste of talent, resulting from the failure of youth to continue their education, is only one facet of the problem. If gifted young people go through secondary school and college without being challenged to maximum effort, the loss may be comparable to that suffered when they leave school or college prematurely. Identification and stimulation of the talented in school and college are central responsibilities of the educational system which have been emphasized far too little. An imaginative, systematic and persistent effort to identify the gifted and to nurture the fullest development of their potentialities is perhaps the greatest single educational need of our time.

An essential element in any program designed to stimulate maximum effort on the part of students is the institutional attitude toward academic excellence. This involves faculties, administrations and students. Where there is little premium on scholarship and much attention to social and recreational activities it is impossible to create and maintain a spirit conducive to the motivation of learning.

At a time when student demands are greater than facilities to accommodate them, standards for admission to colleges and universities could be raised. Reports from Russia indicate that in 1957 two million students applied for admission to universities and institutes where vacancies existed for only 420,000. Entrance examinations lasting more than a month were used in the selection of the top students. Where such competition exists, not only is the quality of students high but their motivation as well, lest they lose their places to others. To compete successfully with such an educational system will require greater seriousness of purpose than is found in the countries under review.

For years American educators have been concerned over the lack of intellectual effort required of students in the secondary schools and colleges, and the lax standards which prevail. When the brightest students in colleges and universities can make the highest records on two to three hours of study a day it means not only that institutions are not offering them a challenge, but that they are permitting them to develop working habits that will in later years be a detriment.

Tests are available that indicate fairly accurately the general and special abilities of youth. By use of these early in the school career the talented could be identified and encouraged to continue their education. By making special provision for this group in the university many who would otherwise drop out might be saved. This is a matter of interest to every division of the university. Aptitude tests in the fields of law, medicine and engineering have been used with marked success, in addition to the general scholastic tests which are better known.

WOMEN AND HIGHER EDUCATION

Chapter VIII dealt with this subject at some length. The purpose of this section is to analyze the nature of the problem which the current situation poses. The reader may wonder at finding it listed as a problem. More colleges and universities are open to women than to men at the present time in the English-speaking world. With few exceptions all Faculties within the universities freely admit women. This does not, however, mean that men and women are on an equal footing with respect to educational opportunities, as an examination of the facts will disclose.

In some institutions the quota for women students is one-fourth the total number, the ratio of one woman to three men. This is usually not an announced policy, but a working arrangement. The proportion of men to women in the ancient universities is seven to one. In the United States private universities in particular often limit the number of women students. Housing and scholarship funds for women are more restricted than for men, even in the state institutions. In professional schools frequently only a token number of women students is admitted, 5 per cent or less. This means that standards of admission for men and women are different. This is obviously unfair and unsound from the standpoint of society.

In most Commonwealth universities the admission of women is not reflected in the curriculum. In Canada there is considerable evidence of the presence of women students in the programs of home economics, nursing, library science and social work courses. This is also true in the United States, but in the other countries considered in this study there is little evidence in university curricula of the recognition of women students. The same realism applied to the inauguration of curricula for women as that employed in establishing engineering, applied science, veterinary medicine, commerce, etc. would prompt the addition of a variety of courses now rarely found in the offerings of the typical Commonwealth university programs.

The simplest means of picturing the inequities of higher education is to note the disparity in the number of men and women in the colleges and universities. In India and Pakistan the proportion of men to women is about ten to one; in other Commonwealth countries three to one; and in the United States, two to one. Early marriage, lack of incentive due to the absence of the economic motive, less interest on the part of parents in their daughters' education, and family tradition, all are cited as causes of the preponderance of men. But not all countries present this picture.

In Russia it is reported that in institutions of higher education as a whole 50 per cent of the population is women. In Russia's higher education system there are universities and institutes. The former are concerned with basic subjects, pure science, mathematics, philosophy, history, literature, etc., with a student population of 200,000; while the latter provide technical and professional courses with an enrollment of 1,800,000. Men predominate in the institutes of technology and agriculture, while women constitute the majority of those enrolled in medicine, pedagogy and foreign languages. Humanities in the university include law and journalism, in addition to the traditional humanistic subjects. In medicine 90 per cent of the students are women. Even the technical institutes attract a substantial number. In 1957 the Kharkov Polytechnic, for example, was reported to have 37 per cent women. In the universities the sexes are about evenly divided. Thus, where students are selected by examination and on merit without consideration of other factors, men do not outnumber the women.

This raises the basic question whether society can afford to neglect the education of its able women any more than its able men. At a time when there is a shortage of manpower and prospects for an even more acute deficit during the next twenty years, it is important that all resources be tapped and that all capable and qualified young people be given the education needed today and in the decades to come. No one will doubt that the proportion of gifted to the total number applies to women as well as to men. In Britain and in the United States women outnumber men in the total population. Why should they not at least equal the number of men in the college and university population? To achieve this it would be necessary to multiply by three the number of women now attending British universities and double the number in American institutions of higher education. This array of potential university students not in institutions of higher learning represents a vast pool of undeveloped talent that these countries can ill afford to ignore.

To put the matter briefly, there are two facets to the problem of women and higher education. On the one hand, the university curricula should reflect more adequately the interests of women by the addition of a variety of courses not now listed in university offerings. On the other hand, the existing curricula should in fact be open to men and women alike; equal residential accommodations should be provided for them; and inducements to develop their talents should be extended on equal terms to men and women. Intellectual ability is no respecter of the sexes, as a century of coeducation has amply demonstrated. It is found in men and women alike and should be developed wherever found. Only in this way can the full potential of the intellectual power of any country be realized.

Special Problems in Countries Under Review

In addition to problems that are common to all the countries dealt with in this study there are special issues in each of them that warrant review. It will suffice, for the purposes of this discussion, to select one or a limited number of characteristic areas of conflict and sketch briefly their nature and implications. If the issues are skillfully chosen and vividly described it may enable the reader to sense the quality, tone and atmosphere of university life in the several countries. Though the general pattern of university development in the Commonwealth countries is essentially the same, the variations in circumstances under which the institutions have sought to achieve their goals have resulted in differences in methods of approach. Moreover, the changes in university programs, in response to the demands of society, have been more difficult in some areas than in others. For example, adjustment to the emphasis on science and technology and on training for a variety of new professions has been more difficult for the older universities than for the newer ones where traditions are less binding.

In Australia and South Africa the difference in the relations of the native to the European population and the bilingualism in Africa accounts for differences in the problems encountered by higher education in the two countries. The presence in Canada of French-speaking as well as English-speaking universities means a variety of difficulties there which are not found in the United Kingdom. The large percentage of youth who attend college in the United States affects the variety and quality of the programs offered and produces difficulties not found in the Commonwealth, where the proportion of youth enrolled in the universities is much lower. The enormous growth in the number of universities and in enrollments in India and Pakistan—far greater than that experienced in any other country—has resulted in a series of difficulties unique to that area. Thus in each of the countries the problems of universities differ, though the basic goals are the same and the patterns of organization similar.

With this general background in mind, let us examine in more detail certain specific concerns of higher education in the various areas under review.

THE UNITED KINGDOM

For centuries the classical curriculum prevailed in the ancient universities of Britain. During this period the tutorial system was perfected to such an extent that there is perhaps no educational system that can rival it as a means of developing the intellectual powers and interests of youth. It is particularly well adapted to honors course work in history, philosophy, literature, ethics, law, etc. It is not so well suited to instruction in technology, which was introduced into the British curriculum in the latter half of the nineteenth century. For honors work in pure science it has been used with success, but in the applied sciences, such as clinical medicine, engineering or agriculture, another technique is needed. A basic problem in British universities today is the adjustment of curriculum and methods of instruction to the new program demands.

The special honors course, involving only one subject, is a popular feature of the civic universities as well as of Oxford and Cambridge. The ablest students are encouraged to take it, so accustomed is the staff to considering special honors as the only really satisfactory university program. Second- or third-rate men are encouraged to take general honors, involving two or three subjects, or the pass degree. Few are awarded first honors in the general course. In technological and applied science fields, where the student must take a wide range of subjects, adjustment to the situation is still more difficult.

Professor Coulson of Durham stated the case clearly at the 1956 Home Universities Conference. He said:

The staff of any one department must realize that in many ways they are acting as two distinct people. On the one hand they teach their own students their main subject, requiring full specialization, but they also act as a service department teaching a great many other students what their subject is about, but not in the sense of specialization. It is very difficult to persuade our own people to act as service departments.[3]

He suggested that students "who are compelled to study a wide range of subjects should study critically in one, or perhaps two subjects, but should be given a general education in the others."[4] The application of such a principle would have drawbacks. For instance, in medical education the student requires chemistry, physics, biology, anatomy, physiology, etc. He must not slight any one of them. Similarly, the engineering student must have a wide variety of subjects, no one of which he can neglect without jeopardizing his career.

The traditional system which involves specialization in one subject affects British higher education in a variety of ways. At Cambridge, for example, the different engineering specialties are not listed in the offerings. The graduate engineer has mastered the principles of engineering as a single subject. In the applied science and professional fields the tendency to emphasize depth is more likely to produce narrow theoretical specialists than broadly educated technologists or professional practitioners. A part of the problem of the overloaded curriculum stems from the tendency to teach all subjects as if the students were specialists in them. The failure of the curricula in science, technology and professional fields to provide humanistic-social studies appears to be derived from this same attitude. It is difficult to appreciate the logic of adding courses extraneous to the major objective of the curriculum if all subject matter is to be presented as if to specialists.

The adjustment in the Scottish institutions is not so difficult as in the English universities, since their undergraduate program requires instruction in several subjects, rather than in one, with specialization in a fourth year if the goal is an honors degree.

The tutorial system dating from the seventeenth century and the individualized instruction which it implies is not adapted to meet the demands of the modern university, particularly in the technological and professional fields. Re-orienting instruction and revising the curriculum to meet modern demands are basic needs of British universities, particularly those of England. Such adjustment will be difficult in view of the long-established tradition and success of the tutorial and special honors plan under which most British professors have been educated.

COMMONWEALTH COUNTRIES

In South Africa the Apartheid (segregation) issue overshadowed all others in 1957. The government proposed to close all universities to non-whites, and to establish separate university colleges for them. In some of the English-speaking institutions several hundred non-Europeans have been enrolled annually in recent years. These "open" universities were greatly disturbed by the government's proposal and held numerous protest meetings. Action on the bill was postponed but not abandoned.

The struggle was bitter. University autonomy was threatened. If government can prescribe who shall be taught, it may also determine what shall be taught and who shall teach. The opponents of the proposal contended that the life of their institutions was at stake and that the passage of the bill meant the end of true universities in the Union. Some members of the teaching staffs as well as the administrations were distraught. It was often the subject of conversation where university people gathered.

In Canada the French- and English-speaking universities have developed an excellent working relationship. Language is no barrier to cooperation between them. Government support is provided alike to both, whether it be the provincial or the

Dominion government. Collaboration in the consideration and solution of higher education's problems is not handicapped by differences in language and background. The University of Ottawa, in the capital city, is bilingual: all courses are given in both English and French. Examinations may be written in either language. Some differences in program derive from differences in background or outlook, but these do not detract from the cooperation between the two groups.

An example of the background affecting the program is found in the Province of Quebec. There the laws are based on the French Civil Code rather than on the English Common Law. Law schools in the province reflect this difference. Ottawa Law School teaches both systems. Legal practitioners trained in Quebec have difficulty transferring to other parts of Canada and vice versa.

Quebec has another difference in outlook which affects higher education. The government of the province is opposed to receiving university support from the Dominion treasury. Determined to treat all alike, the central government has deposited with the National Conference of Canadian Universities the sums allocated to the Quebec institutions. In January 1958 large sums allocated to Laval, McGill, Montreal and other institutions in the province were held in escrow by the Conference. The opposition of provincial authorities to the institutions' accepting these funds derived from the fear that it might result in loss of autonomy.

The National Conference of Canadian Universities, due largely to the cordial relations between the two groups of institutions, is an unusually effective organization. Its sessions held in 1956 and 1958, concerned with meeting the impending enrollment crisis and other problems, indicated rare foresight and wisdom. The present encouraging aspects of Canadian university development would not be possible except for the cooperative spirit which motivates both the English- and French-speaking institutions.

The Murray Committee on Australian Universities (1957)

styled the high failure rate of students "the most disturbing aspect" of university education. The records at six universities showed that only 35 per cent of the students who entered in 1951 graduated in the minimum time and only 58 per cent had graduated or were expected to graduate. After a careful study the Committee concluded that this situation derived from a variety of causes: "previous preparation of students, the gap between school and university, the pressure of curricula, teaching methods, inadequate staffing and the absence of student guidance."

The second area of concern to the Committee was the weakness of the honors work and of postgraduate training and research. It listed among the causes of these weaknesses the general acceptance of the pass degree as the normal objective of university education and the lack of contact between students and faculty early in their university careers. Financial stringency was considered the basic cause of these and other weaknesses.

Shortage of residential facilities is more marked in Australia than in any other English-speaking country. It is not lack of appreciation of their value educationally, but lack of funds that accounts for it. Classrooms, libraries and laboratories have first priority in expanding universities. Residential halls must take second place. So far the government has not sanctioned loans or bond issues, to be amortized by rentals, to provide such facilities.

The University of New Zealand is handicapped by lack of funds, its isolation and the geographical separation of its units. Buildings and equipment are limited, salaries of professors lower than in any other area except India and Pakistan; its closest neighbor is the University of Sydney, 1,200 miles away; and Auckland University on the North Island is some 600 miles distant from Otago on the South Island. The other units of the university lie in between. The difficulties in developing a strong university program when the units are so widely scattered are obvious. By the same token the relatively small size of each unit is a barrier to the development of quality and strength.

Despite the problems inherent in the situation, the university enrollment in New Zealand has grown more rapidly than in any other country under review except India and Pakistan, from 1,700 to 5,600 full-time students in the 1939–1958 period.

The enthusiasm for education in India and Pakistan, following independence in 1947, stimulated great growth, which in turn created a host of difficulties. The number of universities increased from eighteen in 1939 to thirty-eight in 1958, the enrollment from 130,000 to 710,000. Lack of organization, inadequate staffing, shortage of funds and weakness in student preparation for university studies, all contributed to the confusion and chaos that has characterized the post-war period. Over and above these is the language problem. English is the medium of instruction in most of the universities of India, but the Constitution provides that Hindi shall be the official language from 1965.

Student indiscipline throughout India and Pakistan occasioned much private and public discussion in 1957. Riots, strikes, ignoring of regulations and defiance of authority were among its manifestations. Banaras University was closed by the Executive Council in October 1958 in view of "acts of grave indiscipline and defiance of law, committed systematically and in an organized manner."[5] (*New York Times*, October 12, 1958.) A former secretary of the Ministry of Education, Mr. Humayun Kabir, wrote a brochure on the subject, in which he analyzed the problem and suggested remedies. He attributed it to four main causes: (1) loss of leadership by teachers; (2) growth of economic difficulties; (3) defects in the existing system of education; and (4) general loss of idealism.

The high rate of student failures is also a major issue. It is estimated that of a thousand matriculants, on the average only one hundred complete the course. The loss of 90 per cent of those matriculated represents a formidable waste, but the frustration of the failures is perhaps an even more serious aspect.[6]

Everyone agrees that it will be impossible to make Hindi the language of instruction by 1965 when it becomes the official language of the country. Many scientific terms do not exist in the language. A commission has been appointed to invent a Hindi vocabulary of scientific and technological terms, but this will not solve the problem. As Vice-Chancellor Sidhanta of the University of Calcutta pointed out at the Centennial Celebration in 1957, without a command of English the door would be closed to a vast storehouse of useful knowledge.

Though Indian leaders are unanimous in urging that the national language replace English as early as possible, they are fully aware of the need for learning English. For some years following independence (1947), there was a reaction against use of English, but that was short-lived. Recent reports indicate that English is becoming more popular, and that there is a revival of interest among Indian youth in achieving competence in the English language.

THE UNITED STATES

The inability of some state universities in the United States to care for the numbers seeking entrance has resulted in the adoption of new admission policies. California, North Carolina, Texas, Oklahoma and other states now require special entrance examination of high school graduates. Formerly a diploma from a standard secondary school was sufficient. This departure from tradition of a few state universities is likely to spread throughout the country as enrollment pressures increase. It is, therefore, a significant step.

Democracy in higher education has been a marked characteristic of the United States. What will be the effect of selective admissions on the democratic spirit of the institutions concerned? Other English-speaking countries are extending the opportunities for university education to a larger proportion of their youth than ever before, while the pioneer in tax-supported higher education, the United States, is beginning to restrict admissions to its state institutions. Does this represent a reactionary movement in American higher education?

I believe the answer is no. The vast network of junior and community colleges can now absorb large numbers who would have, in earlier decades, had no place to go except to the state universities. These institutions have flexible programs which are better adapted to meet the needs of the weaker high school graduates than those of the four-year college and university. In the light of these facts, selective admissions to state universities represent an adjustment within the system of higher education designed to serve better all youth who have the ability to profit from post-high school education.

The new plan should upgrade the universities concerned and the secondary schools from which their students come. When a high school diploma is not enough to insure admission to the university there is a natural emphasis on quality of work which the universities in turn can insist upon after the graduate matriculates. Thus, the change which has occurred is a forward rather than a backward step, though the adjustment to the change will constitute a real problem in some areas. The education of the public to the necessity and wisdom of the step will be important to its solution.

Racial Issue. The most publicized of all the issues in American higher education is that of the segregation of the races. It is a serious and difficult problem but it is restricted to a relatively small geographical area. All fifty states except four have already established the policy and practice of admitting students of all races to their colleges and universities. The Supreme Court has declared that educational institutions may not decline to admit students on account of race, color or creed.

It will be many years before this problem will be solved, but gradual progress is being made toward its solution. In those states which have not complied with the Supreme Court order there are colleges for negroes in operation and an increasing proportion of negro youth is being enrolled in them each year.

The segregation issue in the southern region of the United States has its counterpart in the Apartheid issue of the Union of South Africa, but the terms of reference differ. In the United States the federal government, through the Supreme Court, has forbidden the practice of segregation whereas in South Africa the central government is seeking to enforce it. The matter has thus become a political rather than an educational issue. Nevertheless, the governments' actions in both cases have posed real problems for the universities.

Contract Research. At the other end of the spectrum from university admissions to the undergraduate curriculum is the problem of contract research. Government and industry not only compete with universities for scientifically trained Ph.D.'s just out of graduate schools but seek the services of research professors on the campuses to conduct what is known as contract research. It may be some question that industry wants answered called "project" or "development" research, or it may be a long-range defense project which the government wants investigated.

Most institutions undertake to limit sponsored research to fields in which the staff is already interested, but it is not always feasible to do so. Even if a research proposal is in line with the professor's interest, it may involve an undue amount of his time and energy. In any case it means an educational distraction that often results in lowering his efficiency as a teacher because of a degree of pressure which always accompanies a contract program.

It is unfortunate that at a time when there is desperate need for the training of more science teachers some of the best professors are devoting half their time or more to investigations for outside agencies. In the long run both industry and government might be better served if instead of taking the time of professors for research they should seek to strengthen the science teaching staffs and encourage them to give the production of future science teachers top priority in their schedules.

A modest amount of contract research can probably be justified on several grounds, but for the next few years, at least until the shortage in science teachers can be met, the emphasis should be on producing the "seed corn" of future generations of scientists. Neglect in this area will be at the peril of basic advances in science and technology. This problem has not yet been faced realistically in the United States.

Other issues in American higher education were highlighted by President Eisenhower's message to Congress on January 27, 1958. A brief summary of his recommendations will indicate the range of problems that concern not only the colleges and universities but the government as well.

As in the Commonwealth countries, first in the list of needs came strengthening programs in science and technology. To that end the President proposed that the appropriations to the National Science Foundation be increased fivefold for a variety of purposes: (1) to sponsor institutes for supplementary training of science and mathematics teachers and to provide additional funds for teacher fellowships; (2) to stimulate improvement of the content of science courses at all levels; (3) to encourage able students to consider science as a career; (4) to increase graduate fellowships, to enable more men and women to prepare for productive and creative scientific effort; and (5) to initiate new programs which will provide fellowship support for secondary school science teachers during the summer, for graduate students who serve during the year as teaching assistants, and for individuals who may wish further education in preparation for becoming science and mathematics teachers.

In addition to the National Science Foundation program the

President recommended increased appropriations to the Department of Health, Education and Welfare for a four-year period only, to reduce the waste of talent, to strengthen the teaching of science and mathematics, to increase the supply of college teachers, to improve foreign-language teaching and to strengthen the Office of Education.

The alarming shortage of college teachers already referred to prompted the President to urge universities to expand graduate school facilities.

As a preamble to the proposal that grants be made for improving foreign-language teaching, the President said:

Knowledge of foreign languages is particularly important today in the light of America's responsibilities of leadership in the free world, and yet the American people generally are deficient in foreign languages, particularly those of the emerging nations in Asia, Africa and the Near East. It is important to our national security that such deficiencies be promptly overcome.

He recommended support for special centers in institutions of higher education where instruction would be provided in languages which are not now generally taught in the United States, and for institutes designed to help those already teaching foreign languages in schools and colleges to improve the quality and effectiveness of their work.

In suggesting funds for the strengthening of the Office of Education the President called attention to the need for more information, on a national basis, of the progress of education, and recommended federal grants to assist in the collection of the necessary statistical data.

In this array of proposals are mirrored some of the concerns of the government and of educators in the area of higher education.

XIV

Summary and Conclusions

Various aspects of university education in widely separated areas have now been considered in some detail. The object has been to identify characteristic features, to compare and to contrast developments in British universities and in their offspring in the Commonwealth countries and the United States. As this study has progressed, impressions have gradually crystallized respecting changes in university education which suggest some fundamental trends and issues that should not be overlooked. It will be our purpose here to highlight these impressions, to comment upon their meaning, and to suggest certain procedures that might prove useful if undertaken at this stage in the history of university education.

University Education a Public Enterprise

The mid-twentieth century decade witnessed a metamorphosis in higher education in both the United States and the Commonwealth. Treasury grants in the United Kingdom expanded from a fraction of the total support during the war to become the major source of income. In Canada and Australia the federal governments initiated support of colleges and universities. In South Africa, where the central rather than provincial governments have traditionally subsidized the universities, supporting funds were multiplied. When India gained independence and partition took place these political changes were accompanied by an amazing growth in the number of universities and in support from state and federal sources. Indeed the outburst of interest and enthusiasm for higher education on this subcontinent have resulted in one of the most significant developments of the post-war period.

Prior to 1945 the majority of college and university students in the United States favored privately-supported institutions. By 1951 the situation was reversed. In 1958 only 42 per cent of the higher education population was enrolled in the private institutions; 58 per cent in state colleges and universities. Though private endowments were appreciably augmented during this post-war decade, the proportion of the financial burden of higher education borne by government funds increased substantially.

Thus the mid-century was the turning point of higher education in all English-speaking countries, marking its passage from private to public support. Though all British universities are private corporations, they cannot escape the responsibility of public institutions since 70 to 80 per cent of their support comes from treasury grants.

The future of higher education as a public enterprise is unpredictable. It is possible that a decade or two will pass before it will be possible to assess the effects of the change from private to public support. Questions have already been raised and more will be asked. For example, will universities be as free to experiment, to establish new departments, to discard others, to modify purposes and procedures, to determine what shall be taught, who shall be taught and who shall teach? Those who provide support have a reason to be interested in these matters. In case of differences of views between the universities and the government agencies, which will prevail?

In the United States, which has a long history of publicly-supported institutions, difficulties have arisen when governments have sought to invade the traditional domain of universities. In some cases conditions of employment have been prescribed, such as oaths of allegiance; books in the library have been proscribed; and political affiliations have been cited as reasons for removing professors. The Supreme Court ruling on race or color discrimination has resulted in changing admission policies. Non-discrimination clauses have for some years appeared in government contracts with universities for instruction or research. In the more flagrant cases of violation of university autonomy in the United States the universities have usually succeeded in maintaining their integrity, frequently with the help of strong independent institutions. Without their aid in times of crises the outcome of the battles for autonomy might well have been different. In countries where all the universities are dependent upon government funds for survival, maintaining institutional integrity might be more difficult. Canada is the only British Commonwealth country with a system of privately-supported colleges and universities, and these now receive substantial Dominion government support.

The U.G.C. in Britain has served higher education admirably and with great distinction for forty years. It has won the plaudits of educators, and practically the universal approval of the British public. Its procedure has been so generally approved that other countries have followed the example. India in 1953 created such a committee, called a commission, and Australia in 1958 projected a plan for one. As a means of safeguarding university autonomy and of providing against political interference which sometimes accompanies government grants, the Grants Committee arrangement is the most effective device yet conceived.

This does not mean that it has evoked no criticism. The budget bureau has complained that the accounting rendered by the universities leaves much to be desired, that expenditures are not sufficiently scrutinized and supervised and that the sums involved are much too large to be handled without a more accurate definition of the purposes to which they are to be devoted. From time to time members of the teaching and administrative staffs of the universities have expressed concern over the Committee's policies and procedures. Though in the main staff members have agreed that the needs stressed have been in the national interest, they have doubted the wisdom of government prescribing the purposes for which grants shall be used. They would much prefer block grants to the institutions, leaving their expenditures to the discretion of the university authorities. They call attention to the fact that this was the method of operating in the early years of its history.

Toward the close of World War II the Committee made a number of earmarked grants for science, medicine, teacher education, social science and international studies, following recommendations made by committees bearing the names of Barlow, Goodenough, Clapham, McNair and Scarborough, their chairmen. The experience with these grants led to the view that in general grants should not be earmarked. However, in 1957 capital grants announced were chiefly for housing and equipping, science and technology, and additional sums were allotted for operation and maintenance to enable university enrollments to expand 40 per cent. The plans of the U.G.C. assumed "that approximately two thirds of the expansion in the number of students will be in science and technology."

If the "assumption" of government, with respect to the fields of study to be stressed in the admission of students, should be interpreted as a mandate, the question would arise as to whether institutional integrity is involved. Though all may be agreed that science and technology should be the emphasis in 1957–1962, to the extent that the expectation of the treasury is considered binding by the universities, their autonomy is affected. This raises the question whether in the nature of the case universities can be free if dependent upon public funds for their operation. The government obviously has the right to choose the programs it will support, and the institutions are free to accept or reject grants. When government grants constituted only a minor fraction of the university's income the problem was simple. It is when they involve the major portion of operating funds that the delicate question of the relationship of government to the universities becomes crucial.

This is an issue in all the countries concerned in this study. It is as old as the universities themselves, but its particular relevance today stems from the degree of institutional dependence upon government assistance which now prevails. When the taxpayer becomes the chief patron of higher learning he must ultimately be reckoned with. In India in 1957 the matter was freely discussed on the platform and in the press, one leader declaring that invasion of university autonomy "was present in one form or another in all the universities functioning in the country." In Canada the fear of this prevents the universities in the Province of Quebec from accepting support from the Dominion treasury. In the United States it is a live issue in university circles everywhere. A panel discussion of the subject "Issues in State Control of Higher Education" was held in San Francisco on April 10, 1957. At that meeting Mr. Plock, who for twenty years or more had been a member of the Board of Control of the University of Iowa, set forth some of the more subtle ways by which government exercises controls:

Much has been made of the argument that if governmental controls deal with budgetary and financial matters alone they do not affect the integrity of the institution. That argument is pure fantasy. If time permitted, numerous examples could be given of unwarranted controls exercised by state comptrollers, of state personnel directors who have prevented academic promotions by their definitions of educational positions, of state budget directors who have prevented the creation of new academic positions, of state purchasing agents unwilling to or unable to obtain teaching equipment and supplies when needed, or pre-auditors attempting to define institutional policies, of state building authorities and boards of public works either unfamiliar with or unwilling to heed the needs of the educational institutions.[1]

In the light of recent developments the fact that university education, a private enterprise for more than seven centuries, has now become for all practical purposes a public enterprise, that this change could have a fundamental effect upon the status of institutions of higher education, and in view of the widespread dissatisfaction over controls now exercised by governments or government agencies, it is of first importance that high-level consideration be given to a reformulation of the tenets of university autonomy under modern conditions and a reaffirmation of its significance to the stability and progress of higher learning. It may be that some modification of the traditional definition of university integrity is required in the light of the new relationship of governments to universities. If so, these should be defined and the meaning of university autonomy clarified. It is a task for which the universities have the major responsibility and in which they have a great stake.

It may be argued that decisions in so fundamental a matter have to be hammered out on the anvil of experience, that changes will be made gradually through solving specific problems as they arise. On the other hand, there is a chance that by yielding to more and more government pressures the ideal of university integrity might be destroyed by attrition and higher education relegated to the position of a function of government like highways, health or defense. However remote such a possibility, it suggests the wisdom of an earnest consideration of the means of safeguarding the autonomy of universities in the critical period ahead, when the adjustment is being made to the change in the source of support of colleges and universities.

The Arts Faculties—Status and Objectives

In moving from private to public support universities are faced with a variety of considerations which have new significance. More than ever it becomes imperative that goals of instruction be made explicit and efforts to achieve them realistic.

What are the purposes of the Arts Faculties in the Commonwealth countries and the colleges of arts and sciences in the United States? They constituted the central core of university education for centuries. It was not until 1876 that Johns Hopkins, the first modern American university, was founded, with emphasis on graduate and professional work. Since then the role of the college has declined rapidly in importance. In most large American universities it is now a relatively minor segment. More serious still, it is sometimes chiefly a service division for a wide variety of pre-professional courses. In the Commonwealth universities the Arts Faculties enroll usually 40 per cent or less of the students, and even then, as in the United States, much of the work is in the nature of service courses for professional faculties such as commerce, agriculture, architecture, law, engineering, etc.

In the United States the outlook for colleges of arts and science has concerned educational leaders for many years. A variety of efforts to strengthen them characterized the period between the two World Wars. Honors courses, survey courses, major and minor requirements and finally the general education movement were some of the attempts made to revitalize the program. No satisfactory solution of the problem has yet been reached.

The future of the Arts Faculty is also a deep concern in Britain. At the Home Universities Conference in 1956 devoted to the subject "Impact on the Universities of the Government's Policy for the Expansion of Technological Education," Sir Eric Ashby (V.C., Queens University, Belfast) said: "The first problem is the future of the Faculties of Arts. The second problem is the place of humanities in Faculties of Technology. Both of these problems are part and parcel of a bigger problem, namely how to preserve as an integral part of university work those aspects of the humanities which science and technology will never render obsolete."[2]

The conception that liberal education is synonymous with

"culture," and that therefore "culture" is the objective of the arts and science program, has wrought much mischief. If "culture" is its only object the liberal arts college should be abolished; on the other hand, if "culture" is not a by-product it deserves to suffer the same fate. Unless Arts Faculties and their American counterpart, the Arts and Science Colleges, succeed in re-interpreting their functions in the light of modern needs and in re-constituting the curriculum to achieve them, they may well become obsolete before the end of this century if modern trends continue.

Universities without the liberalizing education which the Arts Faculties have traditionally provided become little more than technical, scientific or professional institutes. It is ironical that at a time in the world's history when wisdom and understanding are primary needs, when society is rife with ideologies and beset with conflicting claims, the universities should be stressing more and more technological, scientific and professional education to the neglect of those studies designed to provide an understanding of man and his society. This derives, of course, from the obvious and urgent need for more scientists and technologists and a failure to sense the less obvious but deeper need for the stabilizing influence of wise and understanding leadership. The Arts Faculties have failed to make clear this need, or the role which they can play in providing it. To achieve this is a central mission of the Arts Faculties in these times.

Since Sputnik appeared advancement in science and technology has seemed imperative as a matter of national and international security. But ideas are more powerful than satellites or hydrogen bombs. The ability of the West to prevail, if open conflict with Russia should overtake us, would depend upon the strength of the conviction of Western peoples as well as upon their weapon potential and military skill. Thus ideas and concepts which are basic to convictions become indispensable equipment in the arsenal of those who would defend Western ideals. It is the Arts Faculties that have a responsibility for providing this equipment.

A curriculum focused upon the ideas, concepts and ideals which undergird Western civilization would provide a liberal education which includes an understanding of our society and its motivations. To trace the origin and development of the concepts of human dignity, inalienable rights, freedom of inquiry, truth, goodness, justice, duty, etc. would provide a solid core for understanding our heritage. Whence did they come? When did they appear? What ideas joined together to form them? They obviously did not spring full-blown from the mind of an individual, but were fashioned in the crucible of experience, even though someone with imagination had to crystallize them and express them in understandable terms, just as Newton had to state the laws of gravity before the principle was recognized. What more stimulating task could present itself than to unravel the story of man's quest for concepts and principles by which to order his own life and thought and to regulate his society?

Just as the humanist digs around the roots of great concepts and ideals of society, so the social scientists will be concerned with the social, economic, political and religious institutions which are based upon the concepts of inalienable rights, economic and moral laws, integrity, justice and fair play. This concern would lead the learner back to original sources, to the basic concepts found in the Graeco-Roman and Judeo-Christian history, literature and philosophy. In such an effort he would not only come to understand his society, its currents and countercurrents, but also the basis for his own views and outlook. This approach would have the merit not only of making learning realistic and vital, but of insuring that all important aspects of human thought and experience, including religion, would engage the attention of the learner.

If ideas and concepts are used as criteria for the selection of subject matter it will assist in the unification of knowledge. For instance, the more fundamental concepts underlying economics, sociology and political science are the same. They need not, therefore, be taught separately. The rights, duties and responsibilities of a citizen remain the same whatever the activity in which he is engaged. For example, the rights to equal consideration as a member of society, as a worker in the free enterprise system and as a voter at the polls represent a single concept. The duties and responsibilities likewise represent single concepts applicable alike to social, economic and political man.

Again, if institutions are under consideration, it is clear that whether they be social, economic or political in character they are often founded upon the same basic ideas. Free public schools, free hospital service, free enterprise in business and industry and free elections at all levels derive from the same notion of man's relation to his society. Similarly if honesty, integrity, and the institutions set up to foster them are being considered, they need not be treated separately in the several social science disciplines, for they apply alike to all. Thus, if concepts and ideals be the centers around which subject matter is organized, surprising economies might be effected. The number of courses could be reduced and the effectiveness of learning enhanced. The fragmentation of knowledge would be diminished and the student assisted in the synthesis of subject matter.

A variation of the method suggested for the humanities and social studies is applicable to science as a humane subject. President Conant's well-known plan of teaching science to the non-science major by giving him an understanding of the way in which a scientist works and how he achieves results suggests one approach. In essence he developed a number of case histories of scientists with special reference to important discoveries made by them, considering how they were arrived at and developed, and how they affected subsequent investigation. Instead of beginning with the scientist one might begin with basic scientific concepts familiar to the student and trace their origin and development. In this way he might come to understand even more clearly the nature of science and scientific methods. It would lead him to perceive what the discoverer had to work with, how he reached his conclusion and the relation of that discovery to others that followed. He would begin to realize how laws unite facts and concepts unite laws to form the orderly world of science. Such a method would enable the student to deal with discoveries in both the physical and biological sciences by the choice of the examples to be studied. The instructor's problem would be to select those likely to be of most interest to the student and at the same time the most revealing. The story of the notion of gravity derived from watching an apple fall, the application of this to celestial bodies, how Newton came by it, what it contributed to our conception of order in the universe, its value in interpreting various phenomena such as the structure of the solar system, the cause of the tides or the organizing principle in the celestial world, is an example of the method. Tracing the concepts of species (plants and animals), of the circulation of the blood, of evolution, of matter, mass, weight, energy, etc. could provide an absorbing course of study for the student seeking to understand the nature of science and the scientific method.

Some such approach as that briefly sketched above should make learning a vital, realistic and exciting adventure. Beginning with notions already familiar to the student it launches at once into a search for meaning. The knowledge required would be for a definite purpose, and when acquired the facts would be clustered around ideas in such way as to be retained with least difficulty. Furthermore, understanding would be the goal, and facts just the means to the end. The fact-idea-concept organization of teaching could give new vitality to Faculties of Arts, provide a realistic and balanced program of education, deal with fundamental concepts, avoid the trivial and replace the prevailing chaos with order in the curriculum and in methods of instruction.

Another major contribution which such a program could make is an understanding of the ideals which are central to Western culture. Democratic peoples have been handicapped in the contemporary ideological conflict by the fact that they have not been as well acquainted with the tenets of democracy as their adversaries have been with those of Communism. The educational systems of the West are largely to blame for this weakness. They have taken too much for granted. They have assumed that young people brought up in a democratic society understand the ideas and ideals upon which it rests and hence have not stressed them sufficiently in schools and colleges.

The fear of converting educational institutions into propaganda agencies has also played its part. The cult of *objectivity* in instruction has resulted in the failure of the colleges and universities to engage in legitimate educational efforts to acquaint students with the fundamentals of Western concepts, modes of thought and ideals. Until rival economic and political systems arose, the need for such education was not recognized. Though the past decade has made this need crystal clear, the educational systems have not yet adjusted to it. Ideals worth fighting for are surely worth inculcating. It can be done without violating the principles of sound education.

The curriculum and instructional method briefly sketched above are cited to illustrate one way of giving a new meaning to the arts college program. Some plan for restoring it to a central place in university education is a paramount need. By making its goals clear and realistic, its contribution to the education of youth might be re-established and the prestige of the Arts Faculty reclaimed.

Professional Education—Quality and Tone

In the preceding section the status and role of the arts college has been considered at length. It is the surest index of the quality of the university as a whole. Apart from the few institutions devoted chiefly to science and technology, the greatness of the American university is measured largely by the nature and quality of its Colleges of Arts and Science. Even in the technological institutions the divisions concerned with basic education have been emphasized and expanded in recent years. In addition, the professional schools of universities—medicine, theology, law, architecture, nursing, etc.—have stressed humanistic-social studies. Some medical schools have added social scientists to their faculties, and recent studies of legal, theological, architectural and nursing education in the United States have emphasized the need for basic studies.

In the Commonwealth countries dissatisfaction with the technical and professional education programs is characteristic of university faculties. In Canada engineering schools list courses in philosophy in some cases and religion in others as required subjects.

The Indian universities are seeking to develop a program of *general education*. The chair of social medicine in Britain and the humanities professorship in Adelaide, Australia, are examples of efforts to provide basic studies in professional education.

The matter of breadth in education is not merely the concern of faculties, but of leaders in other areas. For example, in Canada the Royal Commission on National Development in the Arts, Letters and Sciences had much to say on this subject: "There is a persistent illusion that what we call the humanities is mere educational embroidery, perhaps agreeable but certainly irrelevant. It is easy to forget that the liberal arts provide not the decoration but the fabric itself"; further, "Humanistic studies do not belong only to the faculty of liberal arts but should pervade the professional schools as well. They should permeate the entire university."[3] The late President Sidney Smith of Toronto University put the matter somewhat differently. He said: "If every professional school were stripped from the university it would still be essential to our country and civilization, for it enshrines and inculcates liberal education, that is, education for freedom—freedom under the law, the priceless heritage of Western Civilization." [4]

Mr. Menzies, the Prime Minister of Australia, in an address to the House of Representatives (November 1957) urged the importance of humanistic studies. "But I hope," he said,

that we will not, under current pressures or emotions, be tempted to ignore the basic fact that civilization in the true sense requires a close and growing attention not only to science in all its branches, but also to those studies of the mind and spirit of man, of history and literature and language, and mental and moral philosophy; of human relations in society and industry; of international understanding, the relative neglect of which has left a gruesome mark on this century.

Let us have more scientists and more humanists. Let the scientists be touched and informed by the humanities. Let the humanists be touched and informed by science, so that they may not be lost in the abstractions derived from out-dated knowledge or circumstances. That proposition underlies the whole university idea. It warrants and requires a great variety of Faculties and the constant intermingling of those who are engaged in their disciplines. [5]

Sir Eric Ashby pointed out in 1956 that in Russia about one-eighth of the curriculum in the technological institutes is devoted to the humanities and the social sciences and said: "If Russia thinks it worth while to make technological students spend an eighth of their time on literature and history and economics, and to pass examinations on these subjects, we should at least examine the proposition closely." [6] He suggested the development of humane studies which relate directly to the technology. For example, the student of metallurgy might be led to study the history of industry since the seventeenth century and from that to a consideration of the sociology and ethics of industrial societies on the theory that since technology is concerned with the applications of science to the needs of man and society it is inseparable from humanism. Though this is a logical approach, apparently no university has made a serious attempt to devise a curriculum embodying the principle.

Some universities have allowed a free afternoon each week in which plays, musicals, general lectures, etc. are provided with the object of stimulating interest in artistic and humanistic fields. It was suggested that this would supply the cultural needs of science and technology students. To assume that such a program is a worthy substitute for humanistic-social studies is to reveal a wholly unrealistic conception of the purpose of such studies or of student needs.

The lethargy of Faculties of Arts and the traditional reluctance to change in universities are responsible to some extent at least for the lack of a more vital program. It is difficult to develop new courses which would insure that university graduates would comprehend the nature of the contemporary crisis, would have some notion of the economic and social consequences of industrialization and technology, and would have some acquaintance with economic, scientific and industrial history. It would require the historian to reorient his thinking, to explore new fields, to exercise his imagination in the development of new courses. The literary scholar would have to read new books, think new thoughts and adopt new approaches in instruction. The philosopher might need to reinterpret his Aristotle, Descartes, Hegel and Kant in the light of modern developments, including the social and economic changes imposed by scientific and technological advances. The quality of industrial leadership might be strengthened and a renaissance of the Faculties of Arts might be effected by this reconstitution of their programs.

The changes suggested for students of science and technology should be paralleled by comparable reforms in other professional fields. The system which fails to provide instruction designed to give the prospective doctor, lawyer or teacher an understanding of his society is missing one of the chief purposes of university education. The doctor should have a knowledge of the history of medicine, of man's quest for *mens sana in corpore sano,* of the effect of industrialization on the health and welfare of the people, of the nature of modern society as it affects social stability and progress and of the role of the doctor in that society. Likewise the business and industrial leader, the lawyer and the teacher require a basic understanding of their society, its backgrounds, its currents and countercurrents, the place of their occupations, the effects of industrialization on professional progress, etc. Universities cannot afford to ignore their responsibilities for providing some basic understanding of our heritage and of our present social needs and trends. The tone and atmosphere of university life would be greatly improved if such a program were provided in all professional faculties. It would require collaboration between Arts and professional Faculties. The initiative and chief burden of such a development would probably fall to the Arts Faculties, but they could not succeed without the active cooperation of the professional schools.

A central problem in modern society is the lack of a common background of social understanding on the part of leaders in various fields. Specialization has developed to such an extent that specialists in one phase of a discipline can scarcely communicate with those engaged in another. For example, the nuclear physicist may have difficulty understanding the specialist in relativity; the surgeon has little in common with the psychiatrist; or the inorganic chemist with the biochemist. In view of such difficulties the need for some common basis of understanding between scholars and professional leaders in the several fields becomes all the more essential. In the United States the four-year undergraduate program, which is the usual requirement for admission to the professional school, is designed to provide this common background, but the content of the college course for intending physicians is a matter of debate.

The universities in the next decade will be so absorbed in

the task of providing housing, libraries, laboratories and staff to care for mounting enrollments that they may continue to cling to outmoded traditions in curriculum, methods and objectives. The number of teachers will be inadequate, space will be over-crowded, the caliber of the average student will perhaps be lower and his interests will be more varied. These conditions will make it difficult to undertake the basic changes, but university leadership cannot escape the consequences of neglecting to put its house in order. University education is now a public enterprise, and subject to public scrutiny. Danger lies ahead if goals are not realistic, convincing and understood. The traditional university spirit must be protected and strengthened as scientific, technological and professional programs expand. To achieve this, basic changes in curricula, methods and goals will be needed.

This is the challenge of the mid-twentieth century decade to the universities of the Commonwealth and the United States. In most of these institutions faculties are concerned about many aspects of the educational programs. This concern has led to action in too few of them. In the nature of the case some changes cannot be achieved by institutions working independently. For example, those affecting length of term, provision of adequate audio-visual aids, reallocation of services and functions between institutions, and certain types of curriculum change can be accomplished more effectively by concert of effort. Those universities which have a common language and a common background would have the best chance of planning and achieving significant reforms if they should be convinced of the need and were organized to undertake it.

These considerations—the responsibilities of universities as "public" institutions, the need for clarification of goals in the Faculties of Arts and the quality and tone of university education with special reference to preparation for the professions —are scarcely more important than a series of issues relating to student selection and guidance and the variety and confusion in degrees granted. The constitution of the governing bodies and the regulations under which they operate are in the main outmoded; the organization and functioning of the faculties do not meet modern requirements; the selection and guidance of students is haphazard; and the multiplicity of degrees, both undergraduate and postgraduate, is bewildering.

The remnants of history and tradition in evidence in the constitutions of governing boards, and in the statutes and regulations by which they operate, are the chief characteristic of the organization of the older universities. The newer ones in Britain and in the other Commonwealth countries have been influenced largely by the older patterns. In the light of the new demands made upon universities in modern times, the organizational scheme is cumbersome and frequently ineffective.

When appointments to chairs in universities require months, or even a year, because of traditional practices, it is obvious that changes in procedure are overdue. The administrative problems requiring solution when student bodies are small can be handled effectively with the simple *Faculty* organization, but when they are doubled and trebled, a more elaborate structure is required. Postgraduate studies are especially in need of attention. The haphazard informal arrangements found in some British programs leading to the Doctor's degree derive from lack of administrative personnel. With adequate supervision, stimulation and guidance the number of full-time postgraduate students could probably be doubled. On the other hand, in most universities of the United States graduate programs should be overhauled, standards raised and the character of research modified to insure more significant projects.

The lack of attention to educational policy is a common fault of both British and American universities. Neither the governing boards, administrations nor faculties give systematic thought and effort to educational planning. The result is that often changes are effected through outside pressures. Many of the trivial subjects found in colleges and universities, particularly in the United States, have been inserted in response to public demand. The pressures in the years immediately ahead will be more severe than formerly. The larger student bodies will have more varied interests and desires for a wider range of subjects. It will, therefore, be essential that faculties and administrations be alert to these pressures and clear as to the direction of desirable changes in university programs.

The relation of faculties to governing boards in American universities is less satisfactory than in the Commonwealth institutions. The American boards of control, ranging in number from three to one hundred, usually have greater powers and less contact with faculty members. Many American universities do not have faculty senates. Too much power is delegated to the president, who may or may not communicate the wishes of the faculty to the board of control. In most institutions faculty members should have a greater voice in policy-making, especially in academic matters.

Student selection and guidance are other areas in which Commonwealth countries are particularly weak. While in general their universities do a better job of selection than those of the United States, since they exercise more selectivity, they do not make the same effort to attract talented students who fail to apply for admission. The guidance program is less adequate in the British than in the American institutions. The addition of personnel officers, deans of students and counselors, and greater use of aptitude tests might strengthen the expanding Commonwealth universities.

The commercialization of university sports, the bane of American higher education, has been largely avoided in Commonwealth countries. Healthy competition between students in various sports makes for well-rounded development, but when carried to excess through commercialization it becomes a millstone retarding progress. The malpractices occasionally connected with commercialized athletics have from time to time cast a sinister shadow over American higher education.

In both America and Commonwealth countries student organizations need more attention. They are too numerous in many universities, absorb too much of the students' time and frequently they have sprung up with little supervision and expanded without proper guidance. American universities suffer more from excessive student activities, but they are not unknown in the Commonwealth universities. If the English-speaking countries are to compete successfully in education, scientific and technological achievements, it may be necessary to consider whether there is a substantial waste of energy involved in extra-curricular activities.

Speaking of competition also raises the question of the length of university terms. In the countries embraced in this study they vary from twenty-four weeks at Oxford and Cambridge to thirty in the civic universities of Britain and to thirty-six or less in American institutions. In other countries, including Russia, terms exceed forty weeks. Apart from the problem of competition, it is difficult to justify less than maximum use of the vast physical plant and equipment which colleges and universities represent.

Finally, there should be a re-examination of the degrees awarded, with a view to effecting some uniformity of meaning and reduction in number. The table below indicates the number of undergraduate and graduate degrees in the British Commonwealth and the United States.

	American	British[7]
Varieties of Bachelor's degrees	227	312
Varieties of Master's degrees	123	152
Varieties of Doctor's degrees	69	92
	419	556

The lack of uniformity is illustrated by the fact that the M.A. may mean nothing more than the B.A., as at Oxford and

Cambridge, and in some Indian universities; in other cases it may mean one or two years of graduate work; in the Scottish universities it is the first-level degree corresponding to the B.A. in all other institutions; and the honors M.A. requires an additional year in Scotland while it requires the same time as a pass M.A. in Australia.

The B.Sc. is a graduate degree at Oxford, but an under-graduate degree in most other British universities. The new B.Phil. was described as a better "degree" than the D.Phil. Such inconsistencies make for confusion which retards educational progress. A reduction in the number of degrees and uniformity of meaning would advance the cause of higher education in many ways.

Conclusion

Success in the competition prevailing in the modern world will depend upon the quality and scope of educational and scientific programs. The winner in the race for supremacy will be the side which achieves scientific and intellectual superiority. As J. R. Killian, Jr. recently said: "For the first time in history, superiority in scientific stature has become a contest among nations." Success in that contest will depend more upon the effectiveness of the educational system than upon any other single factor. It is, therefore, of primary importance that the universities and colleges of competing countries be operated at maximum efficiency. No effort should be spared to eliminate defects, to strengthen weak links, and to insure that the maximum number of able young people be given training commensurate with their abilities.

It is obvious from the review of higher education in the United States and the Commonwealth that drastic reforms will be required to achieve maximum results by way of educational and scientific advances. The universities are fettered by cumbersome traditional procedures, lack of realistic goals and methods of instruction, ineffective means of identifying, attracting and holding the talented youth, and failure to make use of the tools which science and technology have made available for aiding the learning process. If the danger of being outdistanced in the educational-scientific race is real, as recent developments suggest, can we afford the handicap of inefficiency, of university sessions one-half to two-thirds of the year in length, and of confusion in terminology, degrees, curricula, methods and goals?

These are some of the questions which have arisen constantly in the course of this study, and the corollary: what could be done to solve the problems which they suggest? After many months of study and checking possibilities the following conclusion was reached. A Commonwealth-American Commission on University Education, established on a five- to ten-year basis, for the purpose of delving deep into the needs of higher education and serving as a clearing-house for information on ways and means of meeting them, might provide a partial solution to many kinds of problems. If soundly conceived and composed of top leadership from the several countries involved, it is possible that substantial progress could be made. Such a commission could work with and through the Commonwealth Association and the American Association of Universities in the consideration of plans for the improvement of university education. Such a commission might serve the following purposes.

1. Collect data on problems in the various countries in the several divisions of the universities—undergraduate, professional and postgraduate education and research—and from time to time make recommendations for the improvement of the program of higher education in the several countries.

2. Disseminate information to the various faculties and schools of the universities with respect to experiments in progress, studies being made, problems encountered and solutions attempted.

3. Encourage experiments and studies looking to improvement in university organization, financing, housing and staffing.

4. Promote studies of student counseling and guidance, and experiments designed to improve student organizations and services.

5. Emphasize the need for greater attention to educational policy-making in universities and to the development of the machinery for effecting desirable changes.

6. Stimulate interest in the clarification of objectives, the development of more effective methods and the reduction of curriculum offerings.

7. Foster interchange of faculty members between universities in the various English-speaking countries, thus enabling each country to profit from successful experience in others.

8. Assist in coordinating the work of British and American universities in their collaboration with universities in underdeveloped countries.

9. Promote lectureships in the various disciplines with a view to passing on first-hand information about research, instruction and services.

10. Consider such basic questions as the status of university autonomy, the length of annual university sessions, the university's role in technological research, and the ways and means of promoting emphasis on basic humanistic-social studies.

Anglo-American cooperation in wartime was essential to victory over common foes and later to the solution of common economic problems. If collaboration in military and economic affairs proved helpful, it is not unreasonable to suppose that it would serve a useful purpose in the area of university education. The influence of a high-level commission acquainted with what is taking place in the university world and devoted to a consideration of common problems and needs could serve to encourage workers in the educational vineyard and to inspire public confidence in the future of higher education.

Moreover, such a body could stimulate and assist efforts at improving programs in all the areas involved.

Each country should be able to learn useful lessons from others and to receive assistance in the solution of their problems. In the rapid expansion of university work in science and technology Britain might profit from the longer and wider experience of American universities in this area. The United States colleges and universities could learn much from the successful British efforts in humanistic studies. South Africa might be able to get valuable assistance from such an organization in solving its problem of the relation of the universities to the government. Australia and New Zealand might find value in contacts with American state universities which have had a somewhat longer experience than they in the operation of tax-supported universities. India and Pakistan might profit from the assistance of countries with a broader experience in developing higher education for a democratic state as they seek to provide an adequate and well-rounded university program for their vast populations.

Such a commission might prove useful to foundations in identifying areas of need and of opportunity. It should be able to command the advice and services of the leadership of American and British universities in the consideration of specific questions that might be raised by institutions of higher learning.

Such a commission would have validity only if the leaders in America and Commonwealth countries believed in its possibilities. The nature and variety of the problems of university education would seem to warrant it and the vitality of the concerns over them suggests both professors and administrators might welcome its establishment.

APPENDIX I

Partial List of Those Interviewed in Commonwealth Universities

UNITED KINGDOM

Prof. R. S. Aitken, V.C., University of Birmingham
Sir Edward Appleton, V.C., University of Edinburgh
Prof. J. F. Baker, Dean, Engineering, University of Cambridge
Prof. N. S. Boulton, Chemistry, University of Sheffield
Sir Maurice Bowra, Warden, Wadham, University of Oxford
Prof. A. J. Brown, Economics, University of London
Dr. A. W. Chapman, Registrar, University of Sheffield
Prof. Mansfield Cooper, V.C., University of Manchester
Prof. E. F. Cutcliffe, Registrar, Imperial College, University of London
Prof. B. W. Downs, Master, Christ's College, V.C., University of Cambridge
Sir Lionel Elvin, Institute Education, University of London
Prof. H. W. Fairman, Arts Dean, University of Liverpool
Dr. J. F. Foster, Sec'y, Association of Commonwealth Universities, 36 Gordon Square, London, W.C. 1
Sir Hector Hetherington, Principal, University of Glasgow
Prof. H. A. Jones, Dep. Dir., Extra-Mural Studies, University of Liverpool
Prof. G. P. Jones, Former Dean, Arts, University of Sheffield
Sir David L. Keir, Master, Balliol College, University of Oxford
Prof. V. Knowles, Registrar, University of Manchester
Dr. J. V. Leach, Registrar, University of Leeds
Prof. J. F. Lockwood, V.C., University of London
Prof. A. C. B. Lovell, Jodrell Bank Ext. Sta. Dir., University of Manchester

Provost H. J. McConnell, Trinity College, University of Dublin

Mr. T. J. Morgan, Registrar, University of Wales

Sir Charles R. Morris, V.C., University of Leeds

Sir Philip Morris, V.C., University of Bristol

Sir James Mountford, V.C., University of Liverpool

Sir Keith Murray, Chairman, U.G.C., 38 Belgrave Square, London, S.W. 1

Prof. W. R. Niblett, Dir., Institute Education, University of Leeds

Mr. B. S. Page, Librarian, University of Manchester

Prof. A. M. Parker, Extra-Mural Studies, University of Birmingham

Prof. M. H. L. Pryce, Physics, University of Bristol

Prof. S. G. Raghould, Dir., Extra-Mural Studies, University of Leeds

Sir Sidney Smith, Rector, University of Edinburgh

Mr. M. M. Spencer, Institute Education, University of Oxford

Prof. J. R. Squire, Pathology, University of Birmingham

Prof. G. Templeman, Registrar, University of Birmingham

Prof. N. R. Tempest, Dir., Institute Education, University of Liverpool

Prof. Michael Tierney, Principal, National University College, University of Dublin

Prof. H. J. Trump, Dir., Institute Education, University of Glasgow

Sir Ralph Turner, Dir., School of Oriental and African Studies, University of London

Dr. W. D. Wall, National Fdtn., Ed. Res., London

Prof. J. M. Whittaker, V.C., University of Sheffield

Prof. Charles H. Wilson, V.C., University of Leicester

Prof. J. F. Wolfenden, V.C., University of Reading

AUSTRALIA

Mr. H. B. Basten, Asst. to V.C., University of Adelaide

Prof. Herbert Burton, Principal, Canberra University College

Prof. J. G. Connell, French, University of Adelaide

Mr. J. Connell, Deputy-Registrar, University of Queensland, Brisbane

Prof. J. W. Davidson, Dean, School of Pacific Studies, Australian National University (A.N.U.), Canberra

Prof. A. J. Dunstan, Dean, Arts Faculty, University of Sydney

Prof. J. C. Eccles, School of Medicine, A.N.U., Canberra

Prof. J. R. Elliott, Dean, Arts Faculty, University of Tasmania
Prof. G. G. Firth, Dean, Commerce, University of Tasmania
Prof. A. J. Francis, Dean, Engineering, University of Melbourne
Prof. Reuben Frodin, Fulbright Professor, N.S.W. University of Technology, Sydney
Mr. A. A. Gamble, Public Relations Officer, University of Sydney
Sir Keith Hancock, Dir., School of Social Sciences, A.N.U., Canberra
Prof. D. K. R. Hodgkin, Asst. Registrar, A.N.U., Canberra
Mr. R. A. Hohnen, Registrar, A.N.U., Canberra
Prof. K. S. Isles, V.C., University of Tasmania
Mr. F. H. Johnston, Registrar, University of Melbourne
Prof. W. R. Love, Commerce and Economics, University of Queensland, Brisbane
Prof. J. C. Mahoney, Dean, Arts Faculty, University of Queensland, Brisbane
Prof. B. T. Mayes, Dean, Medical Faculty, University of Queensland, Brisbane
Mr. G. I. McCauley, Registrar, New South Wales University of Technology (N.S.W.U.), Sydney
Sir Leslie Melville, V.C., A.N.U., Canberra
Sir Mark L. Mitchell, Deputy V.C., University of Adelaide
Prof. D. M. Myers, Dean, Engineering, University of Sydney
Prof. M. L. E. Oliphant, Dir., School of Physical Sciences, A.N.U., Canberra
Prof. A. R. Oliver, Engineering, University of Tasmania
Prof. F. J. Olson, Education, University of Queensland, Brisbane
Prof. G. W. Paton, V.C., University of Melbourne
Prof. D. W. Phillips, Engineering, N.S.W.U., Sydney
Prof. S. H. Roberts, V.C., University of Sydney
Prof. Hugh N. Robson, Medical Faculty, University of Adelaide
Dr. J. S. Rogers, Dean, Graduate Studies, University of Melbourne
Prof. F. J. Schonell, Education Faculty, University of Queensland, Brisbane
Mr. Berry Scott, Acting Librarian, University of Queensland, Brisbane
Prof. J. L. Still, Dean, Science Faculty, University of Sydney
Mr. J. D. Story, V.C., University of Queensland, Brisbane
Miss Margaret Telfer, Registrar, University of Sydney

Prof. A. D. Trendall, Master, University House, A.N.U. Canberra
Prof. J. L. J. Wilson, Dir., Extra-Mural Studies, University of Sydney

NEW ZEALAND*

Prof. C. C. Aikman, Law, Victoria University College, Wellington
Prof. E. Beaglehole, Psychology, Victoria University College, Wellington
Prof. H. Belshaw, Economics, Victoria University College, Wellington
Dr. S. G. Culliford, Asst. to Principal, Victoria University College, Wellington
Dr. G. A. Currie, V.C., University of New Zealand, Wellington
Dr. F. J. Llewllyn, Rector, Canterbury University College
Mr. K. J. Maidment, Principal, Auckland University College
Dr. J. Williams, Principal, Victoria University College, Wellington

CANADA

Dr. R. A. Allen, Vice President, University of Western Ontario, London
Dr. Claude T. Bissell, Carleton College, Ottawa (now V.C., University of Toronto)
Dr. G. L. Brodersen, Assistant Dean, A. & S. College, University of Manitoba, Winnipeg
Prof. K. B. Callard, Public Administration, McGill University, Montreal
Rev. G. Caron, Dean, Canon Law, University of Ottawa
Prof. W. R. Coleman, Principal, Huron College, University of Western Ontario, London
Prof. Philip Garigue, Vice Dean, Social Science, University of Montreal
Prof. A. Gauthier, Mathematics, University of Montreal
Prof. P. Gendron, Dean, Science, University of Ottawa
Prof. J. A. Gibson, Dean, A. & S. College, Carleton College, Ottawa
Dr. A. R. Gordon, Dean, Graduate Studies, University of Toronto

* The four University Colleges—Otago, Canterbury, Auckland and Victoria —were changed to Universities after my visit in 1957, and the Principals are now Vice-Chancellors. The University of New Zealand is, however, the only institution there authorized to grant degrees.

Prof. H. C. Gunning, Dean, Engineering, University of British Columbia, Vancouver

Dr. G. E. Hall, President and Vice-Chancellor, University of Western Ontario, London

Dr. C. E. Hendry, Director, School Social Work, University of Toronto

Dr. Cyril James, Principal, McGill University, Montreal

Mr. Marc Jarry, Secretary-General, University of Montreal

Prof. S. A. Jennings, Assistant to the President, University of British Columbia, Vancouver

Prof. A. L. Kuehner, Chemistry, University of Bishop's College, Lennoxville

Rev. R. Lavigne, Dean, Arts College, University of Ottawa

Rev. H. Legare, Dean, Social Sciences, University of Ottawa

Dr. J. J. Lussier, Dean of Medicine, University of Ottawa

Rt. Rev. Mgr. Irenee Lussier, Rector, University of Montreal

Dr. J. A. MacFarlane, Dean, Medical School, University of Toronto

Prof. Albert Mayrand, Secretary, Faculty of Law, University of Montreal

Prof. W. C. J. Meredith, Dean, Faculty of Law, McGill University, Montreal

Rev. R. Normandin, Rector, University of Ottawa

Dr. J. L. Riopelle, Secretary, Faculty of Medicine, University of Montreal

Dr. Murray G. Ross, Vice-President, University of Toronto

Dr. Hugh H. Saunderson, President, University of Manitoba, Winnipeg

Rev. R. Shavenell, Dean, Psychology & Education, University of Ottawa

Prof. G. M. Shrum, Dean, Graduate Faculties, University of British Columbia, Vancouver

Dr. B. E. Smith, Dean, Education, McGill University, Montreal

Dr. M. S. A. Woodside, Dean, Arts Faculty & Acting President, University of Toronto

INDIA

Dr. A. Appadorai, Director, Indian School of International Relations, Delhi

Mr. Bashiruddin, Librarian, Aligarh Muslim University

Dr. S. Bhagavantam, V.C., Osmania University (now at Bangalore Research Institute)

Dr. K. P. Bhatnagar, V.C., Agra University

Dr. A. Bhattacharya, Principal, Hindu College, Delhi

Dr. A. N. Basu, Principal, Central Institute of Education, Delhi

Lt. Col. G. C. Chatterji, V.C., Rajasthan University

Dr. C. D. Deshmukh, Chairman, University Grants Commission, Delhi

Dr. S. R. Dongerkerry, Rector, University of Bombay

Mr. Douglas Ensminger, Ford Foundation, Delhi

Prof. Fisher, Syracuse University, Fulbright Professor, 1956–57

Dr. J. C. Ghosh, President, Planning Commission, Delhi

Dr. A. Das Gupta, Librarian, University of Delhi

Dr. Fowler Harper (Yale), Visiting Professor, University of Lucknow

Mr. Syed Hossain, Registrar, Aligarh Muslim University

Dr. V. S. Jha, V.C., Banaras Hindu University

Mr. Humayun Kabir, Minister, Scientific Research and Cultural Affairs, Delhi

Raj Kumari Amrit Kaur, Minister for Health, Delhi

Dr. A. N. Kholsa, V.C., University of Roorkee

Prof. V. D. Mahajan, East Panjab University, Delhi

Dr. G. S. Mahajani, V.C., University of Delhi

Judge G. G. Malkani, Bombay

Mr. Clifford Manshardt, Deputy Public Affairs Officer, U.S.I.S., Delhi

Mr. Samuel Matthai, Secretary, University Grants Commission, Delhi

Dr. Radha K. Mookerjee, V.C., University of Lucknow

Sir A. L. Mudaliar, V.C., University of Madras

Dr. B. P. Pal, Principal, Indian Agricultural Research Institute, Delhi

Dr. S. Radhakrishnan, Vice President of India, Chancellor, University of Delhi

Prof. K. N. Raj, School of Economics, University of Delhi

Dr. Raja Ram, Principal, St. Stephens College, Delhi

Dr. V. K. R. V. Rao, Delhi School of Economics, University of Delhi

Mr. K. K. Rathpalia, Director, Irrigation Institute, Roorkee

Dr. Saidi, V.C., Aligarh Muslim University

Prof. K. N. Sen, Principal, Asutosh College, University of Calcutta

Dr. J. S. Sharma, Librarian, Banaras Hindu University

Prof. M. C. Shukla, Vice Principal, College of Commerce, University of Delhi

Mr. K. L. Shrimali, Deputy Minister of Education, Delhi

Prof. N. K. Sidhanta, V.C., University of Calcutta

Dr. H. Swift, Principal, Lady Harding Medical School, Delhi

Dr. M. S. Thacker, Director, C.S.I.R., Delhi

Mr. Everett Woodman, Wheat Loan Fund, Delhi

PAKISTAN

Lt. Col. A. B. Ahmad Haleem, V.C., University of Karachi

Mr. M. Ahmad, Educational Adviser to Government of Pakistan, Karachi

Dr. George Gant, Ford Foundation, Karachi

Mr. Horace Hildreth, American Ambassador to Pakistan, Karachi

Prof. Hoffman, University of Pennsylvania, School of Public and Business Administration, Karachi

Mr. Richard Miller, Director, Asia Foundation, Karachi

Dr. M. R. Siddiqi, V.C., University of Peshawar

Mr. H. S. Suhrawardy, Prime Minister, Pakistan, Karachi

UNION OF SOUTH AFRICA

Prof. T. Alty, V.C. and Principal, Rhodes University, Grahamstown

Prof. V. G. Bockeberg, Chemistry, University of Witwatersrand, Johannesburg

Prof. G. R. Bozzoli, Mechanical Engineering, University of Witwatersrand, Johannesburg

Prof. H. E. Brink, Physiology, University of Stellenbosch

Prof. E. M. Brookes, History, University of Natal, Durban

Prof. J. F. Burger, Education, University of Stellenbosch

Prof. F. G. Butler, English, Rhodes University, Grahamstown

Prof. J. C. Coetzee, V.C. and Principal, Potchefstroom University

Prof. D. V. Cowen, Law, University of Cape Town

Prof. E. van Deventer, Economics, Potchefstroom University

Prof. G. A. Elliott, Medicine, University of Witwatersrand, Johannesburg

Prof. J. A. Gledhill, Physics, Rhodes University, Grahamstown

Prof. J. Gordon, Dean, Medicine, University of Natal, Durban

Prof. H. R. Hahlo, Dean, Law, University of Witwatersrand, Johannesburg

Mr. A. J. de V. Herholdt, Registrar, University of Witwatersrand, Johannesburg

Prof. O. S. Heyns, Medicine, University of Witwatersrand, Johannesburg

Prof. D. H. Houghton, Economics, Rhodes University, Grahamstown

Prof. J. M. Hyslop, Mathematics, University of Witwatersrand, Johannesburg

Prof. R. W. James, Acting Principal, University of Cape Town

Prof. J. M. Joubert, Agriculture, University of Stellenbosch

Prof. A. M. Keppel-Jones, History, University of Natal, Durban

Prof. J. F. Kirsten, Philosophy, University of Stellenbosch

Mr. P. J. Koorts, Education Department, Union of South Africa, Pretoria

Prof. D. W. Krueger, History, Potchefstroom University

Prof. E. G. Malherbe, V.C., University of Natal, Durban

Hon. D. Mastert, M.P., Union of South Africa, Capetown

Prof. W. D. Maxwell, Theology, Rhodes University, Grahamstown

Prof. A. B. van der Merwe, Psychology, University of Stellenbosch

Mr. A. J. Pretorius, Registrar, University of Stellenbosch

Prof. C. H. Rautenback, V.C., University of Pretoria

Prof. J. V. L. Rennie, Dean, Arts, Rhodes University, Grahamstown

Prof. C. S. Richards, Dean, Commerce, University of Witwatersrand, Johannesburg

Prof. H. M. Robertson, Economics, University of Cape Town

Prof. D. J. van Roog, Dean, Arts, Potchefstroom University

Prof. C. G. W. Schumann, Economics, University of Stellenbosch

Prof. M. H. Slabber, Agriculture, University of Stellenbosch

Mr. C. Kenneth Snyder, American Embassy, Pretoria

Prof. R. L. Straszacker, Dean, Engineering, University of Stellenbosch

Prof. W. G. Sutton, V.C., University of Witwatersrand, Johannesburg

Prof. I. Glyn Thomas, Vice Principal, University of Witwatersrand, Johannesburg

Prof. C. A. du Toit, Zoology, University of Stellenbosch

Prof. R. Truter, Engineering, University of Stellenbosch
Mr. Ernest Wentzel, National Student Union, Cape Town
Prof. Monica Wilson, Anthropology, University of Cape Town
Prof. L. M. Young, History, University of Natal, Durban

APPENDIX II

Footnotes

Introduction

1. Mr. L. S. St. Laurent, Prime Minister of Canada, in an address on the Universities at the University of Toronto, October 27, 1950.
2. George F. Kneller, *Higher Learning in Britain*, pp. 241–242.

CHAPTER I
The University in Transition

1. John Ruskin, *Crown of Wild Olive*, p. 46.
2. Sir Eric Ashby, *Technology and the Academics*, p. 74: "In the large Universities in particular, there is a kind of intellectual curtain separating faculties of science and faculties of arts."

CHAPTER II
Backgrounds—British Commonwealth

1. Data gathered from the 1957 *Commonwealth Universities Yearbook*.
2. University of London Calendar 1956–57, p. 395.
3. Compiled from 1957 *Commonwealth Universities Yearbook*.
4. Compiled from *Canadian Universities and Colleges*, 1956.
5. Compiled from 1957 *Yearbook* and from reprint of 1958 *Commonwealth Universities Yearbook*.
6. In Article by R. S. Aitken, V.C., University of Birmingham, *Weekly Times Review*, April 24, 1958.

CHAPTER III
Backgrounds—The United States

1. Table on enrollments in graduate schools 1890 to 1954, *American Universities & Colleges*, 7th edition, pp. 52–53.
2. Compiled from data in 7th edition, *American Universities & Colleges*.
3. Table from which ratio of enrollment to population was compiled, *American Universities & Colleges*, p. 32.
4. *American Universities & Colleges*, 7th edition, p. 92.
5. Professor Wayland's "Report to the Corporation of Brown University on changes in Collegiate Education," March 28, 1850, pp. 1–76.
6. Harvard University Committee on the Objectives of General Education in a Free Society, Harvard University Press, Cambridge, Mass.

7. Report of Study Team on General Education, Ministry of Education, 1957, Government of India, p. 13.

CHAPTER IV

Nature and Aims of Higher Education

1. George F. Kneller, *Higher Learning in Britain*, p. 100.
2. ———, *op. cit.*, p. 10.
3. Victoria University at Manchester, courses listed in the University Calendar.
4. *Commonwealth Universities Yearbook*, 1957, p. 1380.
5. Calendar, University of Sydney.
6. *American Universities & Colleges*, 7th edition, p. 1156.
7. President A. Whitney Griswold, *In the University Tradition*, Yale University Press, p. 20.
8. University Grants Committee Report, p. 76.
9. As quoted in George Kneller, *op. cit.*, p. 132.
10. Sir Richard Livingstone, *Some Thoughts on University Education*, p. 23.
11. *Red Brick University*, pp. 78–79.
12. George F. Kneller, *op. cit.*, p. 130.

CHAPTER V

Organization of Higher Education

1. University of Bristol Calendar, *Red Brick University*, p. 82.
2. University of Wales Calendar.
3. University of Glasgow Calendar.
4. *Red Brick University*, pp. 80–81.
5. *Loc. cit.*
6. *Op. cit.*, p. 81.
7. Report of Committee on Australian Universities, Sir Keith Murray, Chairman, 1957, Section 340.

CHAPTER VI

Financing Higher Education

1. Proceedings, National Conference of Canadian Universities Meeting, Ottawa, November 12–14, 1956, p. 222.
2. Statement by Prime Minister Menzies in the House of Representatives, November 28, 1957, Section 17 of P.M.'s statement.
3. Proceedings, National Conference Canadian University Meeting, Ottawa, November 12–14, 1956, pp. 220–221. Figure for United States, 1953–54, *American Universities & Colleges*, 7th edition, p. 57.
4. Table 1, p. 220, table 4, p. 222. Proceedings, National Conference Canadian Universities Meeting, Ottawa, November 12–14, 1956.
5. *Op. cit.*, pp. 220–222.
6. *The Open Universities of South Africa*, Witwatersrand University Press, p. 5.

CHAPTER VII

Student Life, Organizations and Services

1. *Seven Essays on Commonwealth Universities,* p. 82; reprint from *Commonwealth Universities Yearbook,* 1958.
2. *American Universities & Colleges,* 7th edition, p. 38.
3. *Op. cit.,* p. 37.
4. Data compiled from *Commonwealth Universities Yearbook,* 1957.
5. *Commonwealth Universities Yearbook,* 1957, p. 1813.
6. *American Universities & Colleges,* 7th edition, p. 91.

CHAPTER VIII

Women and Higher Education

1. Compiled from *Commonwealth Universities Yearbook,* 1957, and *American Universities & Colleges,* 7th edition.
2. Althea K. Hottel, *How Fare American Women?,* p. 2. A Report of the Commission on the Education of Women of the American Council on Education.

CHAPTER IX

Professional Education—The Learned Professions: Theology, Law, Medicine

1. Proceedings, National Conference Canadian Universities Meeting, Ottawa, November 12–14, 1956, pp. 8–9.
2. Data for table gathered from calendars of the universities named.
3. The unpublished table prepared by Dr. Hugh N. Robson, Professor of Medicine, Adelaide University.
4. Data compiled from *Commonwealth Universities Yearbook,* 1957, sections on India and Pakistan.
5. *American Universities & Colleges,* 7th edition, p. 141.

CHAPTER X

Professional Education—Teaching

1. George F. Kneller, *Higher Learning in Britain,* p. 89.
2. *Encyclopaedia Britannica,* 1958 Edition, Volume 21, p. 864, article on Training of Teachers.
3. "The Contemporary Challenge to American Education," *N.E.A. Journal,* Vol. 47, p. 3, 1958.

CHAPTER XI

Professional Education—Science and Technology

1. *Hearnshaw Centenary History of King's College* (1838), pp. 146 ff.
2. *Bellot University College,* London, 1826–1926, p. 266.

3. As quoted from *Industry and the Technical Colleges*, 1956, p. 25 (Cmd. 9703, para. 73).

4. Table from article by H. J. Brown, reprint from *Journal of the Institution of Engineers*, Australia, September 1949, entitled "Trends in Higher Technological Education and Developments in New South Wales," p. 9.

5. *Op. cit.*, p. 4.

6. *Op. cit.*, p. 5.

7. Presidential address to the British Association, 1948.

8. This is the fifth of a series of resolutions passed by the Federation Conference of British Industries in 1946, all of which dealt with the need of strengthening technical training.

9. This table is from *University Development 1952–57*, p. 75.

10. Compiled from *Commonwealth Universities Yearbook*, 1957. Data on India and Pakistan incomplete, hence not included.

11. Report of Committee on Australian Universities, Sir Keith Murray, Chairman, Section 284.

12. Compiled from *Canadian Universities and Colleges*, 1956.

13. *Engineering Research*, published by C.S.I.R., New Delhi, 1954, p. 9

14. Edward Danforth Eddy, Jr., *Colleges for our Land and Time*, p. 10.

15. Table compiled from the data given in *American Universities & Colleges*, pp. 121–130.

16. Royal Commission on National Development in the Arts, Letters and Science (1951); Chairman, the Hon. Vincent Massey, pp. 135–136.

17. Sir Eric Ashby, *Technology and the Academics* (1958) pp. 85–86.

CHAPTER XII
Extension and Extra-Mural Studies

1. Universities Council for Adult Education, Report 1955–56, p. 28.

2. *Op. cit.*, p. 26.

3. Adult Education at the University of Leeds, 1946–56, p. 19.

4. *Loc. cit.*

5. Universities Council for Adult Education, Report, 1955–56.

6. J. R. Morton, *University Extension in United States*, 1953, p. 21, pp. 12–13.

CHAPTER XIII
Problems and Prospects of Higher Education

1. Seven Essays on Commonwealth Universities, reprint from 1958 edition, *Commonwealth Universities Yearbook*, p. 62.

2. Professor J. E. Harris, Bristol, Home Universities Conference 1956 Report, pp. 26–27.

3. Professor J. M. Coulson, Home University (1956) Report, p. 33.

4. *Loc. cit.*

5. As reported in the *New York Times*, October 12, 1958.

6. Address by Dr. J. C. Ghosh at the Centennial Celebration at the University of Calcutta in January 1957.

CHAPTER XIV

Summary and Conclusions

1. Address by Richard H. Plock, "Issues in State Control of Higher Education," April 10, 1957.

2. Report of Home Universities Conference (1956), p. 70.

3. Report of the Royal Commission on the National Development in the Arts, Letters and Sciences (1951); Chairman, the Hon. Vincent Massey.

4. Report, Canadian Association of University Teachers.

5. Address to House of Representatives, November 28, 1957, in which he announced action of the government on Murray Committee Report on Australian Universities.

6. Report of Home Universities Conference 1956, p. 71.

7. Data compiled from *Commonwealth Universities Yearbook*, 1957, and *American Universities & Colleges*, 7th edition, 1956.

APPENDIX III

Bibliography

AFRICA

Bozzoli, G. R., *Engineering Training and Education*. mim. 1951.

Cape Town, University of, and University of the Witwatersrand, *Conference, The Open Universities in South Africa, 1957*. The Rustica Press. 1957.

Coming of Age, drama, opera, ballet, mime. Little Theatre. Pamphlet. 1952.

Duminy, J. P., *Technical Education and Vocational Training in The Union of South Africa*. Typewritten copy. 1957.

Gordon, Prof. I., *Report of the Government's Intended Action to Remove the Faculty of Medicine from the University of Natal*. Hayne and Gibson, Ltd., Durban. 1957.

Kritzinger, Dr. C. C., *Wool Textile Research in South Africa*. Address given before the Congress of the N.W.G.A. in Bloemfontein, November 29, 1956. mim.

Natal, University of, Non-European Section, *Help Your People*. Pamphlet. n.d.

Commemoration Number, 1949. Printed for University of Natal by Natal Witness Ltd., Pietermaritzburg. 1949.

University of Natal Development Foundation, *The New Durban Medical School Responds to the Challenge of Africa*. Pamphlet. Hayne and Gibson, Durban. 1957.

National Union of South African Students, *Newsletter No. 8*. June 27, 1957.

O'Dowd, Michael C., and others, *The African in the Universities*. 2nd ed., 44 pp. Pub. by National Union of South African Students, 148 St. George's Street, Cape Town. 1954.

Rhodes University, *Vice-Chancellor's Report to Convocation*. March 30, 1957. Grocott and Sherry.

Robertson, Hector Monteith, *South Africa, Economic and Political*

Aspects. Published for the Duke University Commonwealth-Studies Center, Duke University Press, Durham, N.C. 1957.

South African Wool Textile Research Institute, *Report* to the National Wool Growers' Association in Congress at Bloemfontein, November 27–30, 1956.

Stellenbosch, University of, Bureau for Economic Research, *A Survey of Post-War Economic Conditions in the Union of South Africa and Prospects for 1957.* Printed by Cape Times Limited. *Economic Diagnosis and Business Forecasting.* Pub. No. 4. 1954.

Union of South Africa, Department of Education, Arts and Science, *Annual Report for the Calendar Year, 1955.* Government Printer, Pretoria.

Separate University Education Bill, A.B. 58, 1957, G839. State Information Office, *The South African Indian, 1956.* Pamphlet. Voortrekkerpers, Ltd., Johannesburg.

West Africa, Commission on Higher Education, *Report* Cmd. 6655. Chairman: Rt. Hon. Walter Elliot, H.M.S.O. 1945.

Witwatersrand, University of the, Bulletin, Faculty of Commerce, *Part-time University Courses for Accountants' Clerks, 1957.* Horters, Ltd., Johannesburg.

General Information and Regulations for Degrees and Diplomas in the Faculty of Law, 1957. Witwatersrand University Press.

AUSTRALIA

Adelaide, University of, *Summary of Information, 1956.* mim. (Data presented to Murray Committee)

Australia, Commonwealth of, Department of Labour and National Service, Pamphlet No. 40, *Choosing a Career, Civil Engineering.* December 1956.

Australian Humanities Research Council, *Annual Report No. 1,* 1956–57. Adelaide: The Griffin Press. 1957.

Australian National University, *Details of Visits by Research Staff to Other Universities and Institutions During 1956 and January–June, 1957.* 702/1957. mim.

Descriptive Brochure, 1955. Produced by the Australian News and Information Bureau for the Australian National University. Printed in Australia by Waite & Bull, Sydney.

General Description of the University. Melbourne University Press, Carlton N.3, Victoria.

Activities at the Australian National University to Which Representatives of Other Universities and Research Institutions Have Come (January 1956 to September 1957) (For the Murray Committee Inquiry.) September 1957. 698/1957. mim.

Australian National University, *Report of the Council for the Year Ending 31 December, 1956.* F.1405/57. By Authority: A. J. Arthur, Commonwealth Government Printer, Canberra. The Parliament of the Commonwealth of Australia.

Australian Vice-Chancellors' Committee, *Submission to the Committee on Australian Universities,* July 4, 1957. Melbourne University Press, Carlton, N.3, Victoria.

Australian Vice-Chancellors' Committee on Australian Universities, *Submission September, 1957* (Sir Keith Murray Report). Printed by Melbourne University Press, Carlton, N.3, Victoria.

Bok, Bart J., *Brief Outline of Possible Research and Development Plans at Mount Stromlo Observatory.* mim. 1957.

Borrie, W. D., and Ruth M. Dedman, *University Enrolments in Australia, 1955–1970.* Australian National University Social Sciences Monographs, Canberra. 1957.

Brown, H. J., *Trends in Higher Technological Education and Developments in New South Wales.* Reprint from the Journal of the Institution of Engineers, Australia. September 1949.

Buscombe, William, *Research at the Mount Stromlo Observatory.* mim. (Prepared for the Journal of the Royal Astronomical Society of Canada, Vol. 52. 1958.)

Clarke, Donovan, *Drama and Theatre in Tertiary Education in Australia.* mim. n.d.

Clinical Medical Professors from Australian Universities, *Report of Meeting,* May 25, 1957 at Melbourne. mim.

Commonwealth Office of Education, Information Statement No. 11, *Degrees and Diplomas Awarded by Australian Universities.* Revised February 1956.

Commonwealth Scientific and Industrial Research Organization, *Eighth Annual Report* (for year 1955–56), No. 89 (Group F) F.6593/56. Printed and published for the Government of the

Commonwealth of Australia by A. J. Arthur, Commonwealth Government Printer, Canberra.

Education, Department of, Sydney, *Guide to Post-Primary Courses, Examinations and Scholarships, 1957.* A. H. Pettifer, Government Printer. 1957.

Eggen, Olin J. (Lick Observatory), *The Australian Commonwealth Observatory.* Reprinted from SKY AND TELESCOPE, Vol. XV, No. 8. June 1956.

Lojkine, A. K., *The Mount Stromlo Observatory.* Australian National University, Research School of Physical Sciences. July 11, 1957. Canberra, A.C.T. mim.

Melbourne, University of, *Submission to the Committee on Australian Universities, 29 July, 1957.* Melbourne University Press, Carlton, N.3, Victoria.

Menzies, Robert Gordon, Prime Minister of Australia, *Speech to the House of Representatives,* November 28, 1957. (Relative to the Murray-Morris Report.)

Moorhouse, C. E. (University of Melbourne), *Tertiary Technical Education in Australia.* Reprint from COMMONWEALTH ENGINEER for November 1, 1956.

New South Wales University of Technology, *Automation and Australia, Symposium 11th–12th September, 1956.* P. O. Box 1, Kensington, Sydney.

The Water Resources of Australia—Their Control and Development, Symposium, November 29th–30th, 1955. New South Wales University of Technology.

Partridge, P. H., and others, *Symposium on the Place of the Australian University in the Community,* and Post-Graduate Studies in the Australian Universities. Australian Vice-Chancellor's Committee. (Papers delivered August 11 and 12, 1955.) Melbourne University Press.

Queensland, University of, *Faculty of Commerce and Economics, Handbook for 1956–58.* University of Queensland Press, Brisbane. February 6, 1956.

Submission Presented to the Committee on Australian Universities, on behalf of the Senate of the University of Queensland, 1957. Printed at the University Printery, St. Lucia.

Roberts, Stephen H., Emeritus Professor, *Letter to Graduates of*

the University of Sydney from the Vice-Chancellor and Principal.
Pamphlet. April 1957.

Scarrow, Howard A., *The Higher Public Service of the Commonwealth of Australia.* Duke University Commonwealth-Studies Center, Duke University Press, Durham, N.C. 1957.

Schonell, Professor F. J., *Educational Challenge in a Changing World.* mim. (A.B.C. Talk—24/9/57)

Story, J. D., Vice-Chancellor, *The Committee on Australian Universities,* University of Queensland Gazette, No. 38. September 1957.

The University Amendment Act. University of Queensland Gazette, No. 37. May 1957.

Sydney, University of, Department of Tutorial Classes, *Discussion Groups Syllabus, 1957.* Australasian Medical Publishing Company, Ltd., Sydney.

Forty-Third Annual Report of the Sydney University Joint Committee for Tutorial Classes, 1956. Australasian Medical Publishing Co., Ltd., Sydney.

Department of Tutorial Classes, *Kits, A New Way of Learning Through Group Activities.* Holland & Newton, Printers, Leichhardt. Pamphlet. n.d.

Department of Tutorial Classes, *Some Papers in Adult Education.* Conpress Printing Limited, Sydney. November 1955.

Vice-Chancellor and Principal's Report on the Finances of the University of Sydney. Capital Requirements. April 1957. mim.

CANADA

Banff, School of Advanced Management, *Prospectus for Sixth Annual School of Advanced Management.* February 4 to March 16, 1957.

British Columbia, University of, Department of Extension, *The University Serves Your Community.* 1954. *21st Annual Report, 1956–57.*

Canada, Government of, Reference Papers No. 58. April 16, 1951. *Canadian Universities—Historical.*

Canadian Association of University Teachers, *Brief Submitted to the Royal Commission on Canada's Economic Prospects, January, 1956.* mim.

Canadian Labour Congress and Canadian Association for Adult Education, held at Ottawa, December 1956, *Conference Report, Labour-University Cooperation on Education.*

Dominion Bureau of Statistics, Education Division, *List of Institutions of Higher Education in Canada,* Reference Paper No. 48. Pub. by Authority of the Right Hon. C. D. Howe, Minister of Trade and Commerce. Edmund Cloutier, Ottawa. 1954.

Hall, C. Wayne, and others, *A Century of Teacher Education, 1857-1957.* Institute of Education, McGill University. Pamphlet.

Industrial Foundation on Education, *The Case for Corporate Giving to Higher Education.* Report No. 1. December 15, 1957.

Lower, A. R. M., and others, *Evolving Canadian Federalism,* by A. R. M. Lower, F. R. Scott, J. A. Corry, F. H. Soward and Alexander Brady. Published for the Duke University Commonwealth-Studies Center, Duke University Press, Durham, N. C. 1958.

Manitoba, University of, *President's Report, 1956-57.*

McGill University, *Annual Report for the Year 1955-56.* McGill University and Royal Victoria College, *Statutes Enacted November 28, 1939—Amended to May 31, 1957.* mim.

Meredith, W. C. J., *A Four-Year Law Course On Theoretical and Practical Instruction.* Reprinted from THE CANADIAN BAR REVIEW for October 1953.

Montreal, Ecole Polytechnique, *Modifications au Programme d'Etudes.* n.d.

National Research Council, *Review for 1956.* N.R.C. No. 3976. Ottawa.

Ottawa, University of, *A Catalyst for Science at the University of Ottawa.* Pamphlet prepared by Sponsors' Committee. n.d.

Toronto, University of, *Quarterly for January, 1957.*

Western Ontario, University of, *We Meet the Challenge to Education.* Pamphlet prepared by campaign leaders for fund drive. n.d.

COMMONWEALTH

Bauer, P. T., *Economic Analysis and Policy in Underdeveloped Countries.* Published for the Duke University Commonwealth-Studies Center, Duke University Press, Durham, N. C. 1957.

Jennings, Sir Ivor, *Problems of the New Commonwealth.* Published for the Duke University Commonwealth-Studies Center, Duke University Press, Durham, N. C. 1958.

Mansergh, Nicholas, and others, *Commonwealth Perspectives* by Nicholas Mansergh, Robert R. Wilson, Joseph J. Spengler, James L. Godfrey, B. U. Ratchford and Brinley Thomas. Published for the Duke University Commonwealth-Studies Center, Duke University Press, Durham, N. C. 1958.

Oliver, Henry M., Jr., *Economic Opinion and Policy in Ceylon.* Published for the Duke University Commonwealth-Studies Center, Duke University Press, Durham, N. C. 1957.

INDIA

Alagappa Chettiar College of Technology, Journal, *Altech.* University Centenary Number. (University of Madras, 1956–57.)

Aligarh Muslim University, Department of Education, *Extension Services for Teachers.* 1956–57.

Bhatia, B. D., *Behavior Problems in Children at Home and School.* Extension Services Pamphlets No. 2, Dept. of Extension Service, Central Institute of Education, Delhi. Kingsway Press. n.d.

Billig, Dr. K. *Research and Building Construction in India.* Bulletin of the Central Building Research Institute, Roorkee. (Council of Scientific and Industrial Research Institute, New Delhi, April 1953, No. 1, Vol. 1.)

Board of Scientific and Industrial Research, *A Review.* Council of Scientific and Industrial Research, New Delhi. 1954.

Bombay, University of, Centenary Souvenir, *University of Bombay, 1857–1957.* Bombay. 1957.

Cadambe, V., *Engineering Research in India.* Council of Scientific and Industrial Research, New Delhi. 1954.

Central Institute of Education, Delhi, *Annual Report, Foundation 1956,* Albion Press. Delhi.

An Experiment in Teacher Education. Publications Division, Ministry of Information and Broadcasting, Central Institute of Education, Government of India. September 1954.

M.Ed. Students, *Short Reports of Studies in Education and Psychology,* Vol. 1, 1952. University Press.

Chandiramani, G. K., *Technological Education in India.* Publication No. 239. National Printing Works, Delhi. 1956.

Council of Scientific and Industrial Research, *Annual Technical Report for the Year Ended 31 March, 1954*. Also *Report for Year Ended 31 March, 1953*. C.S.I.R., New Delhi.

Dongerkery, S. R., *A History of the University of Bombay, 1857–1957*. Bombay University Press. 1957.

Dutt, Sunitee, *Prognostic Value of Higher Secondary Examination of Delhi*. C.I.E. Studies in Education and Psychology. Pub. No. 7, Central Institute of Education, Delhi. 1956.

Government of India, Central Institute of Education, *Extracts from the Ordinances & Syllabus for the Master of Education Examination*. Delhi University, 1956.

Extracts from the Ordinances & Syllabus for the Bachelor of Education Examination. Delhi University, 1956.

Government of India, Ministry of Education, *Aims and Objectives of University Education in India*. Pub. No. 157. National Printing Works, Delhi. 1954.

Basic and Social Education, 1956. The Model Press, Ltd.

The Concept of Basic Education. Pub. No. 211, 1956. Kapur Printing Press, Delhi.

Education Quarterly, November 1956. Special Unesco Conference Number. Albion Press.

General Education, Report of the Study Team, 1957. Publication No. 261. Hind Union Press.

Progress of Education in India, 1947–1952. Quinquennial Review. 1953.

A National Plan of Physical Education and Recreation, prepared by the Central Advisory Board of Physical Education and Recreation, Ministry of Education, Government of India, 1956. Publication No. 237. Albion Press.

Indian School of International Studies. *Bulletin of Information*, January 1956–57. Delhi Press.

Report on the Working of the Indian School of International Studies, 3rd October, 1955–2nd October, 1956. University Press, Delhi.

Indian Year Book of International Affairs, 1956, Vol. V, University of Madras. Madras-Diocesan Press. 1956–57.

Kabir, Humayun, *An Indian Looks At American Education*. Eastern Economist Pamphlets, New Delhi. November 1, 1956.